TOOLKIT

FOR SMART LIVING

TOOLKIT

FOR SMART LIVING

Marvin Snider, Ph.D.

Mill City Press

Langdon Street Press
212 3rd Avenue North, Suite 570
Minneapolis, MN 55401
1.888.645.5248
www.langdonstreetpress.com

ISBN - 978-0-9799120-6-1
ISBN - 0-9799120-6-7
LCCN - 2007943413

Book sales for North America and international:
Itasca Books, 3501 Highway 100 South, Suite220
Minneapolis, MN 55416
Phone: 952.345.4488 (toll free 1.800.901.3480)
Fax: 952.920.0541; email to orders@itascabooks.com

Typeset by Tiffany Laschinger

Printed in the United States of America

I am grateful for the privilege of having worked with many families of different backgrounds. I dedicate this book to these families, including my own, from whom I learned so much

ACKNOWLEDGMENTS

I want to acknowledge the invaluable contributions made by family, friends, and colleagues in the writing of this book. Larry Bader, Ph.D. spent endless hours in meticulously going over every page. He was particularly helpful in clarifying concepts and how they were implemented. Steven Ward provided critical perspective as a teacher with hands-on experience with students and families. My social worker daughter, Beth Snider Glick, read many drafts and offered insight as a professional and mother of two daughters. Arnold Kerzner, M.D., gave both his professional perspective as a psychiatrist and support as a friend. Deborah Maren, a court reporter, gave me the benefit of her practiced eye for detail and her views as a reader outside of the mental health field. Stacy Glickman, M.S.W. gave me the benefit of her experience as a younger colleague. I am grateful to my circle of close friends - Hy and Sheila Kempler, Beverly Bader, Harriett and Dick Kahn, Pat Rogers, and Sy Mintz who offered unequivocal support for my writing. I am incredibly indebted to my wife, Faye, who gave generous input as a professional clinical social worker. Most importantly I value her emotional support and willingness to manage my frequent preoccupation in the course of writing this book.

Table of Contents

PREFACE

This book is intended as a reference book. It is the outgrowth of forty-plus years of clinical practice as a family therapist. I grew up in the professional climate where insight was the major tool for helping people cope with their problems. I soon learned that while this was important and useful, it often was not sufficient to implement change. I frequently found I was able to be helpful without insight being present. In either case, it became clear that people needed help in how to implement the understanding they gained in my work with them. The rate of success increased when they understood they needed to intentionally apply this new learning until it took hold.

As I wondered how to make better use of my accumulated experience, I happened to be looking for a screw driver in my toolbox amidst a collection of tools, each having its own potential for accomplishing a particular task. I found that understanding the general purpose of the tool often wasn't sufficient in making effective use of it. I had to practice enough times to gain the needed skill.

It occurred to me that the same thing applied to psychological tools. Having insight is like knowing the general purpose for a given tool. This knowledge does not automatically turn into skilled usage. I needed practice and, often times, help in making the most effective use of the tool. As an example, there are different ways to use a hammer. When I used it appropriately, I accomplished what was needed. When I did not, I got a bruised thumb.

From this perspective emerged the idea of developing a psychological toolkit. My wife's creative bent provided the title, Toolkit for Smart Living. This book is organized in two sections. The first section contains six topical areas: tools related to the children, elders, family, health, marriage, and work. The second section describes five sets of tools that may be useful for any subject: communication, effecting change, managing emotions, personal qualities, and managing relationships. The tools in each section have a description and directions in how to apply it. I recognize that many readers may have familiarity with parts of the material. The criteria for including an item was my belief that it would add some new insight or perspective beyond what may already be familiar.

The items range from broad topics as health care to narrow ones as managing TV. They all share in common concerns that caused families to seek help over the years.

How to Use this Book

This not a book intended to be read from cover to cover. It may be read as you would an a dictionary or encyclopedia. It covers a broad range of topics each of which will be of interest to different people depending on their interests, concerns and stage of life. Consult the table of contents for a listing of topics in alphabetical order within each category. Each topic stands on its own and does not depend on any other topic for understanding or application. The male pronoun is used for convenience and should be understood to apply equally to women. I have used the he/she reference for emphasis when needed. The case material presented is based on a composite of different cases in the interest of protecting confidentiality.

One of the questions I had to answer was how much material to include on each topic. Many of the topics are broad in scope. I presented the minimum amount of material needed to get the basic ideas across. References are provided for readers desiring more in depth information.

Section I

TOOLS FOR SPECIFIC SUBJECTS

ADOPTION

Fred and Sally were excited about the prospect of having children. They couldn't wait to start having a family. But it didn't happen! At first they were patient. Even though they knew it might take time, they hoped it wouldn't take too long. Their patience gradually evaporated as the months passed with no sign of pregnancy. This disappointment also impacted their intimacy as it slowly shifted from the pleasure of spontaneity to scheduling for ovulation. When this didn't work they began to look at each other with a jaundiced eye - which one of them was the problem? This anxiety marched them off to the doctor's office.

The romance of having a baby disappeared along the way. Now it was one intrusive test after another. It was a lot more demanding on Sally because there were more things to check: hormone levels, ovulation, menstrual cycles and more. This put pressure on their relationship as they waited for the jury's verdict which validated their dreaded fear that having their own child was not to be.

Sally was shocked by the news that she was not able to conceive. She vacillated between anger and guilt. She felt she lost a part of herself. What was going to happen to their marriage? Would Fred want to divorce her? Should she divorce him so he could find a real woman! Could she go on with the marriage?

There were many questions, a roller coaster of mixed feelings, and no simple answers.

Fred had his own struggles. While he was glad that he wasn't the problem, he hurt for Sally and what her disappoint meant to both of them. He was caught between his sadness and his love for Sally. What was he supposed to do with his sadness at not becoming a father?

They went through a rocky period in working out how this problem would affect their marriage. After much struggle, they decided that they loved each other and didn't want to end their marriage. The next best option for having a family was adoption.

The inability to have a child is a devastating experience for couples like Fred and Sally whose life vision included having a biological family. This becomes even harder when the disappointment creates problems in the marriage. This may be the last stop after the painful revelation of infertility and the added burden on the spouse who carries the biological difficulty, as was the case with Sally. It made her feel less a woman and left her feeling angry and guilty for not being able to do her part in having a child. Sometimes these marriages end in divorce when they cannot overcome their disappointment. Those that can, consider adoption after they come to terms with their sadness. Still others make a life without children.

There are adjustments to be made once the idea of adoption is accepted. Missing will be seeing how the physical inherited characteristics of father and mother are visible in their child. Feelings of interrupting the genetic family heritage may be troubling. There also may be anxiety about whether you will have the ability to love another child in the way you would have loved your biological child. These are but a few of the concerns that you may have. Being able to talk with a counselor about the adjustments you face in adoption can be very helpful in making the transition.

Finding an appropriate child for adoption can seem overwhelming. How does the process work? How long will the process take? What children are available? and others. Having to be evaluated for fitness as parents only may add an unpleasant reminder of infertility.

Any preconceived desired for a particular sex or age is tempered by availability. If your desire for a specific age is not available, there is the alternative of a child from another culture, race and an older child. Consideration of these choices should include evaluation of the unique challenges each one presents. These are most challenging decisions since there are many uncertainties and no easy way to evaluate them. Once made, there is no return policy.

Once a child arrives, by birth or adoption, you do the best job possible you can in raising him/her. You may not be able to control the birth process, but you are on equal footing with biological parents in how you fulfill your parenting responsibility.

You are likely to wonder whether, when, or how to tell your child he is adopted. There is no set time to do this. In general, do this in a manner comfortable for you. Be guided by the child's maturity in understanding what is involved in adoption. Very often natural events occur which provide a useful opening for discussion. It might be learning a friend is adopted, reading about it, or being questioned by other children. Your child may even ask if he is adopted which may be prompted by the awareness he/she notices no apparent similarity to either parent.

In any event, take the time to tell your child he is adopted and how happy you were for the opportunity to choose him/her. Answer any questions he may have in as simple and succinct manner as possible. Don't give any more than the basics unless your child asks questions. Sometimes parental anxiety leads to saying more than is helpful. Give your child some time, perhaps a week or two or more, to let them think about what you told him/her. Answer any questions and do not raise the subject again. Let your child know that you are available for any questions he may have in the future.

Another trial for adoptive parents generally comes when your child is in his teens or early adulthood, when he may become curious about his biological parents. He may express the desire to learn about them and even want to find them. You may feel threatened by competition of another parent and be tempted to view this desire as a reflection on your parenting. Quite to the contrary, his talking to you about this is more an affirmation of your relationship in his willingness to talk to you about a subject he is aware may make you uncomfortable.

Take the opportunity to turn what could be an unhappy time into a positive one by supporting his natural curiosity. This will only help strengthen your relationship with him/her. Finding and even developing a relationship with biological parents cannot take the place of the love bond that you have developed in raising him.

Mastering the adoption process

1. Pay attention to your disappointment at not being able to have your own biological child. Talking to a mental health professional will help with this adjustment. Address any conflicts you may have about not having your own child. This will help your adjustment to being an adoptive parent easier and more rewarding.

2. Work out how you will tell family and friends about your fertility problems and your decision to adopt. This will stop annoying questions about when you are going to become parents.

3. Make a survey of adoption agencies and availability of children.

4. Consider adoption after you feel you have come to terms with not having your own child. Moving too quickly will make it harder on you and your adopted child. Discussion with an adoption agency will help you decide when the time is right and may also help you talk to other couples who have had the same concerns as yours.

5. Decide on what age would be of interest. Survey the range of possibilities for adopting. If it looks too hard or will take too long to get a child, consider children of another race or from another country. The adoption agency will help you decide the merits of each possibility and kind of adoption that will fit for you.

6. Considering adoption of a child of another race should include understanding the issues this child is likely to encounter. Talk to families who have adopted children of a different race to understand what it would be like. Helpful, but may be difficult to accomplish, would be to include families in which this has worked out well as those where it has not.

7. Learn about the culture of your adopted child when it is different from yours. Consider helping your child learn about his culture of origin as age appropriate and is of interest to him/her. This will help strengthen your relationship because it carries a message of caring and respect.

8. At some point it may be useful to be in a group of adoptive parents. These

Marvin Snider, Ph.D.

groups are helpful to parents in being able to support and learn from one another in raising adoptive children. Finding this kind of group may be gained from social service agencies such as Family Service.

References:

Complete Adoption Book: Everything You Need To Know To Adopt a Child, Laura Benvais-Godwin & Raymond Godwin, Adams Media Corporation, 2005, 690 pages

Over the Moon: An Adoption Tale, Karen Katz, Henry Holt & Co. 2001, 32 pages

Attaching in Ad: Practical Tool for Today's Parents, Deborah D. Gray, Perspectives Press, 2002, 391 pages

Adopting Parenting: Creating A Toolbox for Building Connections, Jean Mcleod & Sheena McRae, EMK Press, 2006, 560 pages

Twenty Things Adopted Kids Wish Their Adoptive Parents Knew; Sherrie Eldridge, Delta; Reissue edition, 1999, 240 pages. Paperback

Raising Adopted Children: Practical Reassuring Advice for Every Adoptive Parent, Lois Ruskai Melina, Collins, 1998, 400 pages. Paperback

DEATH OF A CHILD

Bad news ended the comfortable family life of Carol, Jack and their three children, Matt 12, Josh 9, and Sara 7 the day they got the news that Josh had an incurable illness. They were devastated by the thought they were going to lose this bright, imaginative and loving child as they watched him gradually deteriorate. The doctors could not be sure how much time they had with this rapidly developing illness. They struggled with their own grief and worried about how to help Josh and the other children deal with theirs. Meanwhile they all had to make an effort to continue to cope with the daily realities of work, school, and the other necessaries of daily living: shopping, cooking, cleaning, laundry and more. They had to do all of this while trying to cope with the deep pain they all felt. The parents were also concerned about not letting their preoccupation with Josh's illness overshadow the needs of Matt and Sara.

There were times when their differences in how to manage Josh's illness created problems in their relationship. The seriousness of these differences surfaced when they had a major argument that lasted for a week about how to deal with his care. The combined stress of coping with Josh's medical condition and their belief that each knew better than the other led to questioning whether their marriage could survive. Deterioration of his condition brought them to realize this is not what they wanted.

They were all at Josh's bedside when the inevitable happened. They were able to grieve as a family which brought them closer. Carol and Jack felt it was important to involve the children in participating in planning for the funeral to the degree they

wanted to do so. They didn't want them to feel overlooked or neglected. They made a point of encouraging Matt and Sara to openly grieve.

A parent's worst nightmare is the death of a child. Gone are the joys and hopes in mentoring that new life. Coming to terms with this overwhelming and unavoidable loss is filled with dread and darkness. Added pressure comes from helping your other children cope with their feelings of loss. The effort becomes even more difficult when the efforts of well-meaning people are not helpful. This makes it all the harder for Carol and Jack to manage your own grief.

The way in which the death occurs adds further difficulty. Death by accident leaves no time to prepare. You are consumed by the shock and what it means. Death through illness is kinder but no less painful. It gives you a chance to begin preparation for the inevitable. It doesn't hurt less but it gives time to adjust to it. At the same time there is the effort to savor whatever quality of life is possible with the sick child as long as possible.

The stress from differences between you and your spouse in coping with your child's illness and his impending death may put great stress on your marriage. This can add further to your family's trauma if your inability to resolve differences leads to divorce. This can be avoided if you place reaching consensus on major decisions as a priority over prevailing over the other. It will be especially challenging to do this when emotions get to the point of disrupting rational thinking. It is best not to make decisions when under great emotional stress.

Coping with the death from illness

1. Preparation for the impending death begins when hearing the inevitable will happen within an all too soon and undefined time period. This uncertainty only increases the difficulty in coping as it did for Carol and Jack and their family.

2. Allow time to feel the impact of the disastrous news. This should be done both singly and with your spouse and children as it fits your collective comfort. Turn to any source that provides comfort: clergy, extended family and friends. The release of expressing the distraught feelings is necessary to better enable coping. This is best done without judgment about why the death happened or who contributed to it. It is a time be united in grief and to help one another.

3. The need to revisit grief will likely happen periodically, especially when something occurs to remind you of the deceased child. Coping will be easier when expressing grief is kept to times when the pressure builds and needs expression. At other times these feelings need to be held in check to help the other children cope and attend to necessities of daily life. This will take all your psychic energy.

4. As the end gets close, gather your energy for attention to making necessary arrangements and for what follows its immediate aftermath. Don't automatically decide your children are too young to participate. They will benefit from helping in planning and attending the funeral as their age and emotional maturity permit. Being a part of what is happening helps them deal with their grieving for what they are able to handle.

5. Help the surviving children cope with their concept of death, their own mortality, and the loss of a sibling. This includes allowing them to express their feelings when they are moved to think about missing their sibling. Answer questions in as simple form as possible but do not give more than what is requested.

Coping with unexpected death

1. It is helpful to allow the expression of your feelings of shock and overwhelming grief that are the first reactions to your child's death. Avoid the tendency to suppress such expression for the protection of others. Venting these feelings will make it easier for you to cope and will provide a positive model for your children. Decisions that have to be made will best be done when judgment is not unduly clouded by suppressed grief.

2. It is not uncommon to experience anger and guilt feelings that may also be aroused. Both are attempts to cope with the overwhelming grief. These feelings need to be expressed but not allowed to compromise facing the painful events that need attention.

3. Deal with making arrangements of the aftermath of your child's death as outlined in item 4 above. Also help your children deal with their reaction as described in item 5 above.

Coping with impact on the marriage and creating a memorial

1. Pay attention to establishing a joint effort in coping with all matters related to your child's illness and ultimate death. Maintaining a healthy marital relationship is essential to the well being of both of you and your children. Do not hesitate to seek professional help as soon as it becomes apparent you are not able to manage this on your own.

2. At some point you may find it helpful to establish some form of memorial for the deceased child. This is a way to keep the positive memory of him/her alive. This is useful if it does not unduly interfere with the family's attention to their ongoing needs and interests. The memorial may take many forms depending on the family's means and interests. It might involve celebrat-

ing the deceased child's birthday every year, establishing something in the child's name, or volunteering in an organization related to the child's illness. The possibilities are limited only by your imagination and resources.

References:

Beyond Tears: Living After Losing a Child, by Ellen Mitchell Carol Barkin, Audrey Cohen, Lorenza Colletti, Barbara Eisenberg, Barbara Goldstein, Madeline Perri Kasden, Phyllis Levine, Ariella Long, Rita Volpe, St. Martin's Griffin (January 13, 2005) 192 pages, Paperback

Take Your Time, Go Slowly: After the Tragic And Sudden Death of a Child. for the Parents And Siblings With No Time to Say Good-bye. Ronald Snyder, Authorhouse ,2005) paperback: 180 pages

35 Ways to Help a Grieving Child, by Dougy Center for Grieving Children, Dougy Center, 1999, Paperback: 55 pages

Help Your Marriage Survive the Death of a Child, by Paul C. Rosenblatt, Temple University Press, 2000, 184 pages

On Children and Death, Elisabeth Kubler-Ross, Scribner; Reprint edition, 1997, 288 pages. Paperback

DRUGS

Tony, 16, grew up in a middle class neighborhood. He was the second oldest son of three children. He had an older brother Tom, 18, and a younger sister, Joy, 13. He was an average student and a good athlete who was very involved in basketball. He tended toward a group of friends who were a little older than he was.

He had his first encounter with drugs at a party when he was fourteen. His friend's parents were out when they experimented with drinking beer. It was bitter, but none of the four boys were willing to admit it for fear of being seen as weak. They developed a taste for it after a few tries. This started a pattern over the next two years when they had the opportunity. They liked the buzz that came with alcohol.

Tony's experience with alcohol carried over into experimenting with marijuana since he was curious after hearing about it from his brother, Tom. He liked the feeling that it gave him. He got increasingly involved with it to the point it began to interfere with his school work. Meanwhile, Tom had became aware of the downside of drugs and gave them up. He felt responsible for having influenced Tony's foray into marijuana and tried to get him to do the same.

Taking drugs is a choice! Tom was an example of someone who chose against using drugs once he got past the curiosity stage. Many others make a different choice. For these people the choice is to indulge in self nurturing. They go for fleeting fantasy over more responsible choices. People often get into drugs to seek relief from the burdens of life or to be part of the culture that delights in exploring the heights of new emotional experiences or succumbing to peer pressure.

You will have a difficult time, as a parent, making a case against drugs if you indulge in the same behavior. *Do what I say not what I do* does not work. If it is good for the you why isn't it good for your child. Trying to draw the distinction between permissible adult and child behavior doesn't work for very long.

There is a seemingly never ending stream of drugs that vary in their impact and degree of risk. Marijuana is a long standing mainstay which is at the milder end of the continuum. It has been in popular usage since the 60's and is commonly used by many people in spite of being an illegal drug. One of the major dangers in taking drugs is the lack of assurance in knowing what is actually being taken. People all too often trust their lives to what the drug dealer says with disastrous consequences.

Alcohol is the most abused drug of all. Unlike other drugs it is can be deadly not only to the person taking it but to other people who become innocent victims. The news frequently carries the tragedies of victims of drunken drivers. It is amazing how often courts allow drivers who drink to keep repeating their offenses even after multiple accidents that kill and destroy property.

Addictions are a lot harder to break than they are to acquire. Alcoholics Anonymous is a well known effort whose mission is to help its members gain control over their drinking. It's twelve step program has mixed success. Other efforts involve detoxifying programs followed by an educational residential program. They also have mixed success with a significant recidivism rate. Family members often become unintentional enablers in supporting a family member's bout with alcohol. They do this by the example they set, providing easy access to alcohol, inadequate supervision, and too little education about the use of drugs. The vise like grip of addictions does not easily give up its prey.

Coping with Addictions

For the person with an addiction

1. Accept you have an addiction. Denial will only make you more entrenched.

2. You have a choice to live with the addiction or choose to overcome it.

3. Choosing to live with it will likely make your life more difficult and adversely affect those close to you.

4. Choosing to overcome the addiction will not work unless you are committed

to doing what it takes - your active participation. Addictions are difficult to overcome even with you want to give it up.

5. Get into a program to help you overcome your addiction - Alcoholics Anonymous or a drug treatment program.

6. Build learning from your rehabilitation experience to change your life style. Recognize that a rehab program is a start not an end to the effort. You will need to resist the temptation to return to your addiction under stress or disappointment.

7. Take responsibility for any slippage in your recovery. Don't hold others responsible for your behavior. The problem is not whether slippage will occur as long as the focus is on getting back on track.

8. Take advantage of any help you can get. Let those people close to you to know how they may help you. This does not make them responsible for your behavior.

9. Don't get angry at people with good intentions trying to help you. Let them know what is helpful and what is not.

For family members of a person with an addiction.

1. Be alert to signs of an addiction by noticing changes in behavior, mood, or interests.

2. Let the person affected know of your concern. Let them know you will not knowingly do anything to support the addiction.

3. Respect a person's right to engage in an addiction. Let them know how it affects your and other's relationship with him.

4. Be available to help your family member enter a rehab program. Determine if there are any ways you can be helpful in their recovery. Don't impose your values.

5. Anticipate that a person may not always be able to give a positive response for the help they request. If they reject your consistent efforts to respond to their request, let him know you will no longer make the effort. Holding the person accountable for his behavior may be help that is needed.

6. Be aware of the message you give in your own behavior regarding the use and abuse of drugs.

References:

Adolescent Drug & Alcohol Abuse: How to Spot It, Stop It, and Get Help for Your Family, Nikki Babbit , Patient Centered Guides, 2000, 296 pages. Paperback

Ten Talks Parents Must Have Their Children About Drugs & Choices (Ten Talks Series), by Xenia Becher, Dominic Cappello, Hyperion 2001,379 pages, Paperback

Drugs and Your Kid: How to Tell If Your Child Has a Drug/Alcohol Problem & What to Do About It, Peter D., Ph.D. Rogers, Lea Goldstein, New Harbinger Publications, 2002, 180 pages. Paperback

Drug and Alcohol Abuse: The Authoritative Guide for Parents, Teachers, and Counselors, H. Thomas Milhorn, Da Capo, 2001, 416 pages. Paperback

Dirty: A Search for Answers Inside America's Teenage Drug Epidemic, Meredith Maran, HarperSanFrancisco, 2004, 320 pages. Paperback

Teens Under the Influence: The Truth About Kids, Alcohol, and Other Drugs- How to Recognize the Problem and What to Do About It, Katherine Ketcham, Ballantine Books, 2003, 432 pages.

Buzzed: The Straight Facts about the Most Used and Abused Drugs from Alcohol to Ecstasy, Fully Revised and Updated Second Edition (Paperback) by Cynthia Kuhn, Ph.D., Scott Swartzwelder, Ph.D., Wilkie, Wilson, Ph.D., Leigh Heather Wilson, &Jeremy Foster, W. W. Norton & Company, 2003, 320 pages.

FAMILY SIZE

Alan and Betty recently got engaged. They got into a discussion about how many children they would like to have. Alan thought that two sounded about right. Betty wanted a larger family. She thought that four would be ideal. The reason for their difference became clear. Alan's choice was guided by his sense of financial responsibility providing for four children. The uncertainty of what income his hardware business would provide put too much pressure on him. He felt he would do well to provide for two children with all the things he and Betty would want them to have: nice home, college education, vacations and more. He wasn't sure this would be possible with more than two children.

Betty's desire for four children came from being one of four children in her own family. She enjoyed growing up with her siblings and wanted the same for her children. She didn't worry too much about finances. Her family wasn't wealthy and they managed pretty well. She had faith in Alan's ability to earn a decent income. Besides, she will probably want to work when the children were in school.

People usually enter marriage with the prospect they will have children some-

will want to have. Start with some number based on your own experience or some ideal. Whether your ideal comes to pass depends on a number of considerations some based on your choice and others will be out of your control.

Those over which you have control include:

- *Choice of career:* This will impact on whether your income will limit the number of children you will be able to support. It will also affect what time you will have available for raising children. Alan was more realistic than Betty about what they could financially manage.

- *Desired life style:* This involves whether you will have a life style conducive to raising children. This includes where you will live and what range of interests you wish to pursue and how this will affect the priority you set on raising children. Alan and Betty agreed that providing their two children with the quality of life style they wanted for the family may limit having more children.

- *Religion:* Your religious beliefs may affect how many children you have. This will influence your attitude towards abortion and the use of contraceptives. Alan and Betty's shared Congregational background did not impact their view of family size.

- *Division of labor:* The will affect the degree to which you and your spouse are able to negotiate a division of labor in raising children. Betty was comfortable assuming the primary responsibility for child rearing. Alan agreed to help out as much as he could.

- *Priorities:* The priorities you and your spouse set between raising children, having careers, pursing individual and joint interests outside the family will impact your choice. Your priorities at the start of parenting may change over time which will also have impact. Alan and Betty were able to adjust their priorities over time that was satisfactory for both of them.

- *Quality of marriage:* Shaky marriages will likely limit the confidence in having children. Alan and Betty had a strong marriage that did not affect their choice of family size.

- *Experience in raising each child:* The idea of having a family is one thing. The actual experience may be another thing. A positive experience will invite having more children. Your enthusiasm will likely diminish if child rearing becomes a trying experience.

Considerations over which you will not have control include:

- *Infertility:* Sometimes infertility limits the number of children. For others it prevents having any children. Some marriages are not able to survive the disappointment of infertility.

- *Health problems:* A serious chronic illness in any member of your family may impact on having one or more children.

- *Change in finances:* Change in income and change in expenses may change the ability to support another child.

There are ambitious couples who want to have it all: dual careers, children, and the ability to provide them with a proper education and the cultural development experiences-travel, summer camps, lessons of all sorts. Some may manage this financially, but for all, the emotional demands can be daunting. Money cannot buy quality relationships. Children need time that isn't competitive with work, cell-phone, and more. Children tend to get short shrift when parents can't manage competing needs. This results in everybody being unhappy and lays the groundwork for wounded marriages and troubled children.

Nannies, however good, or other loving care givers do not take the place of parents. The situation becomes more tenuous when care givers do not provide the needed care and at worse are abusive. Working parents may need to depend on other care givers. It would be wise to screen the values of these care givers. Otherwise, you may potentially put at risk that your children may be raised in ways counter to your own values.

Managing Family Size

The desire to have children starts before marriage. It helps to enter marriage with compatible views about having and raising children. This consideration should take into account emotional involvement as well as the anticipated financial means you hope to acquire and what you hope to provide them. This will be influenced by whether you intend to be a two career family and what impact this would have on raising children.

1. Develop some idea on the cost of raising a child through age eighteen and the possibility of college.

2. Make an estimate of your income over time and how many children you feel you could support. Take into account that the way you space your children will make a financial difference especially at the time of college. It is combination of these two items that led Alan and Betty to agree on starting with a goal of two children.

3. The needs of raising children may lead to conflict between parenting obligations, career goals and the desired number of children. This is particularly the case when both you and your spouse wish to have a career and there is a desire to continue dual careers after having children. There is likely to be less difficulty when both of you are able to agree on sharing parenting responsibilities.

4. Work out an agreement on a workable division of labor to be followed in raising your children. Start with a preliminary collective understanding on a division of labor. This will periodically need to be revised as circumstances and needs change.

5. It helps to be able to have children by design. It is very satisfying when these expectations are realized. Be prepared when nature doesn't cooperate. Some marriages are not able to survive this possibility when having biological children is a priority.

6. The reality of having children can only come from the experience of having them. Your attitude about having more children may be changed by the experience of each child. A child that is easy to raise will have a different impact on whether to have another one than one that proves to be very challenging.

7. The spacing of children will also affect deciding on the number of children. Having children faster than intended can change your perspective. Too many children in diapers will test the will of even the most optimistic parent.

8. A child that has physical or emotional problems will require more than the usual attention and make unexpected financial, emotional and time demands. This will affect the desired size of family. It will also require keeping the needs of this child in perspective so that you don't unduly deprive other children of their needs. It also requires that you do not let problems in raising your children cause problems in your marital relationship.

9. Your hope for a desired number of children may be painfully undermined by unexpected problems from childbirth, illness, or fertility problems. Don't hesitate to get help in making this adjustment if it becomes difficult.

References:

Just the Right Size. D. Polit & J. Berman, Praeger Publishers, 1984 Inc., 224 pages

Unequal Childhoods: Class, Race, and Family Life, Annette Lareau University of California Press, 2003, 343 pages. Paperback

PARENTING

Brad and Margaret had three children, Charles 14, Carol 12, and Heidi 11. Brad was an electrical engineer and Margaret was an elementary school teacher. They both grew up in families with happy memories and wanted to be sure they provided their children with the same kind of experience. They had their share of difficult times with their parents. Good feelings about their childhood was not only about the positive times but also the ability they had to get over the difficult times in ways that worked pretty well. They agreed there were a number of things they needed to do to provide their children with same kind of good feelings they had growing up.

- *To model a good set of values to guide the way they behaved*
- *To provide a loving and supportive family climate*
- *To feel good about themselves and trust in their own judgment*
- *To make sure they got a good education*
- *To have clear and fair expectations that respects what matters to them*
- *To make sure that discipline is used to teach rather than to punish*
- *To teach them to be accountable for their behavior and to expect the same from other people*
- *To work out disagreements so that everybody felt their needs were respected*
- *To contribute to the family welfare and look after one another*
- *To have fun as family*

They realized this was a tall order to accomplish. They agreed they will need to work together and be available when they are needed to make this happen. It was also of importance to prevent concern for their children crowd out paying adequate attention to their relationship.

In my forty plus years of practice working with families, I found that most parents found the challenge of being a parent daunting. I thought it would be useful to include a synthesis of what I found as the more critical issues parents face in raising a family. Elaboration of the topics discussed hear will be found by consulting references provided at the end of this chapter.

Parenting is a privilege and a responsibility. It is a most demanding job, is expensive to hold, and requires no formal training. You have to be available twenty-four hours a day, seven days a week and for no financial compensation. It comes with the full range of emotions. There are times you will be exasperated, frustrated and angry. At other times you will be filled with joy, pleasure and admiration.

The satisfaction in being a parent occurs even in those families that are faced with adversity. They have children born with illnesses, deformities, or experience accidents that result in permanent injury or incapacity. This is in addition to the usual challenges that face any parent. The management of special needs is both physically and emotionally draining. In spite of these additional responsibilities most of these parents find meaning and satisfaction in helping their children do the best they can.

Your primary job in parenting is to prepare your children for adulthood. There will be times when you feel frustrated and worried because you don't know how to handle a problem and you don't have anybody you can ask in the moment. Just ask yourself, which of the choices available would best help him prepare for adulthood. This will help you learn to trust in your own judgment. Things may not always work out but you will always have the opportunity to learn from experience.

Parents are teachers by what they say and especially in what they do. As parents you set expectations on how your child should behave and to what he should aspire. You try to get this to happen by what you tell them, yet often may overlook the importance of the message and model in your behavior. Children are more likely to follow what parents do more than in what they say when the two do not agree. They also learn from their school experience with their friends, and in religious training. You help your children put together what they learn from the combination of all the things they experience.

Teaching Values

Values are a guide for behavior. Parents are like travel agents. You pick a destination and the travel agent in you shows how to get there and leaves room for any side trips you wish to make. So it is with being a parent. You educate your children to have life goals and show them how to achieve them, leaving room for any modifications they may choose. The values you teach are the guide for their behavior along the way. Brad and Carol learned the importance of teaching values from their own upbringing.

1. Teach your children the values you feel will help them become the kind of person that will help them reach their life goals. These values will be some combination regarding education, religion, work ethic, respect for self, responsibility, manners, social skills and others.

2. Teach them how to how to respect and deal with values differences they encounter outside the family with what you are teaching them.

3. Respect that your children may develop or modify the values you have taught them. This will make it possible to negotiate your differences that will work for both of you. Brad and Carol felt it was important to guide their children not dictate their values.

Teaching your children appropriate behavior

1. Work out an agreement with your spouse on the behavior you expect from your children. Otherwise, they will be caught in the differences between you. This will confuse them and create problems if they are forced to choose between you. This puts your children in trouble no matter what they do. Also helpful is teaching them what you would like them to learn from each of you.

2. Teach your children how to manage differences in expectations from different people: parents, teachers, clergy, friends and others. Help them learn how to handle these challenges in a way respectful of family values and those of their friends.

3. Help them find a way to behave that fits when behavior outside of the home differs from what is expected at home. Standards in your community may change over time that doesn't fit your expectations. Be sensitive to how this affects your child. An example is the use of language which may bother you but is acceptable outside the family.

4. Respect your child having opinions different from yours. This doesn't mean you have to agree with them. You are encouraging him to think for himself. This means he should be able to defend the reason for holding his opinions. Your child will be more able to accept the behavior you expect of him if he feels he is being respected.

Managing Formal Education

Decide whether the available public education will provide your children with what you want them to have. Work with your children's school to make sure they will be properly prepared if you plan on their going to college.

1. Adjust the kind of education you want your children to have that is consistent with their abilities. Make plans for how they will achieve it.

2. Decide on whether the financial means of the family will permit children going to college. The decision will depend on the importance placed on education and its cost, whether your child is needed to help generate family income, or whether their effort will be needed in providing care for younger children or a sick family member.

3. Help your children work out their priorities between school work, sports, hobbies and socializing. It is also a good idea to have unscheduled time to just hang out.

4. Demonstrate to your children that any decision or advice you give them will

take into account what matters to them. This will increase their ability to pay more attention to what you are offering.

5. Don't impose activities on your child you enjoyed or wished you had done unless it matches his interests, abilities and personality. Otherwise, your child may feel that what he wants is less important than what you as parents want for him.

6. Provide your child an atmosphere that helps him develop his natural abilities. He will likely need help in learning to manage his time and help over rough spots.

7. Talk to your child about what he is learning and how he getting along on a regular basis. This will help in the quality of your relationship because of the interest you show in listening to his experiences. Do this with at least the same involvement you have in attending their sports events. This will work well if it is done without judgment or criticism. You will know this is working when your child is able to share his concerns and is able to ask for help when needed.

8. Be careful not to help your child with his home work to the extent he no longer feels it is his. In one situation, a mother didn't understand why her son wasn't pleased with the good grade he got on a report until he told her it wasn't his anymore. It was her grade!

Applying the Power of Discipline

There is a difference between discipline and punishment. Discipline is used to teach. You show your child what he did wrong and what is the right way to behave. Punishment is a get back. Somebody hurts you so you hurt them back. This follows the biblical reference, "An eye for an eye, and a tooth for a tooth." Hitting your child teaches that it is OK to hit when you are angry. Discipline would teach how to express his anger to make things better.

1. Make sure your children know what behavior you expect from them. Being told to be good isn't enough. Their idea of being good may not match yours. Be specific and avoid generalizations. Your expectations should take into account their feelings and abilities.

2. Pay as much attention to letting your children know when you are pleased with their behavior as you do in criticizing them when they misbehave. Unacceptable behavior should be met with what was wrong and direction in how to improve it. Yelling at them for misbehaving shifts the focus from learning to their feeling bad or angry at you for putting them down.

3. Misbehavior that is repeated should have a consequence. Ideally the consequences should be close to the misbehavior and have something to do with it. If your child violates the limit set on watching TV, he should sacrifice future TV time. If he doesn't do his chore at his convenience then he should do it at your convenience.

The Message in Accountability

Accountability is the obligation to follow through on a commitment. It is an essential trait to learn for success in human relationships whether it be work, marriage, family or friendships. Getting your children to honor their commitments will be more successful when they know that they won't like what happens if they don't do so. Children are quick to test to see whether you mean what you say. When you don't follow through with behavior you promise or threaten, it sends the message that what you wanted was not that important. Accountability teaches responsibility and is more readably accomplished when you model the behavior you expect.

1. Leave no doubt about what behavior is expected from your child. Being unclear allows for many possibilities that make it easier for your child to manipulate his way out of doing what he didn't want to do.

2. Make sure your child understands what will happen, good or bad, depending on the way he behaves. Children need help in appreciating the benefits of expected behavior and what will happen if they behave differently. Learning will take place faster when accountability is always applied. Otherwise there is the invitation to find ways to get around being held accountable.

3. Teach your children to expect other people to follow through on what they agree to do. They are likely to need help in how to apply this in ways that work. This ability will help them learn to be stand up for what is important to them in ways that will give them a better chance of getting desired results.

Power of Affirmations

Affirmations tell your children their behavior pleases you. They carry the message your children are loved and valued They are given in different ways: praise, rewards, special time with a parent, special privileges and others. Your affirmations will have more meaning when you give them in ways important to your child for best results. What may be meaningful for one child may not be so for another. Affirmations are one of the most potent tools used in raising children when used properly. They will be less effective when given routinely or insincerely.

1. Learn what kind of affirmations are most meaningful to each of your children.

It will not necessarily be the same for each child. Taking the time to find out what is meaningful is itself nurturing.

2. Give affirmations appropriate to the quality and importance of a given behavior. Doing this shows respect for your child's needs and helps him understand what is important to you. It also shows that you are treating him based on who he is and what matters to him and not just an automatic behavior you do for any of your children. Affirmations that sound routine or rote have much less meaning

3. Give affirmations as close as possible to the event which warranted them. If it is delayed, then the connection to the desired behavior should be made clear.

4. Don't give too many affirmations at the same time. When multiple affirmations are appropriate, space them out over time.

5. Be sensitive to how affirmations given to one child may be heard by siblings. Using this affirmation to be an example for another child will not carry the message you intend. There is a better chance it will carry the opposite message and stir up resentment between the siblings. For example, telling one of your children to follow the example of his brother will not make either child happy. In another example, giving one child a gift for some occasion should not include giving another child a gift to avoid hurt feelings. This is most often done with younger children and is a disservice to both children. It weakens the meaning to the first child and makes the other child feel entitled.

6. Pay as much attention to giving nurturing as to critical behavior. Consistency will help the learning take hold.

Creating a Family Identity

Some families are like boarding houses. Everybody does their own thing. They spend little time together and share little about one another's life. At the other end of the scale are families whose lives are overly intertwined. They know each others affairs. They frequently do things together and often have little time for friendships outside the family. In between, are families who have a strong sense of balance between having a close bond with their family and having a life of their own outside of the family. They are there for one another when needed and are respectful of their independence. These families provide a secure base of belonging and feeling loved that gives them confidence in coping with the outside world.

1. Practice respect one another. This is done by respecting differences of opinion, different interests, sharing feelings without judgment between family members.

2. Take into account what matters to your children in setting the behavior you expect from them. This means you would not press them to behave in ways that pleases you but bothers them. This might be their dress or language that are not pleasing to you but are not out of line for the way children of their age behave.

3. Enforce the guiding principle that every one who benefits from the family helps do all the things that need to be done. Chores are given and rotated to balance doing easy or more desirable chores with those that are unpleasant. Family members are held accountable for doing their chores on time and doing them to a reasonable standard.

4. Hold family meetings on a regular basis to work out scheduling and solving problems that affect the family. These meetings should pay as much attention to affirmations as to problems. Also included should be time for fun: songs, jokes and friendly chatter. This makes these meetings more balanced and less of a burden. It also carries the unspoken message that work and play go together.

5. Help children work out a balance between times when they can do their own thing and times when working together is the priority. During these times the benefit of what works for the family as a whole is a higher priority than what individuals need. As an example, your child is expected to go to a family celebration when he would rather be with his friends.

6. Place a high priority on having as many meals together as possible. In practice, this usually means dinners. These meals should be a time for sharing experiences, thoughts and humor. It should not be a time for dealing with problems. View this as a time to share the comfort and support of one another.

7. Encourage friendly competition to permit the opportunity to talk and argue about different ideas. This may be about sports, TV programs, news and more. This will give you the chance to talk about things that you want your children to understand about the world around them. This will help develop their interest in the outside world and feel good about being together. The learning gained in these discussions will help build the children's confidence in holding their own in the outside world.

8. Set clear lines between parents and children. Don't try to be your children's friends. Be friendly, love them. They need to understand the difference between being a parent and a child. Always being popular is not in the job description of being a parent. They need to have the security that you will protect them even if you don't like what they do.

9. Make time for open discussions and debate on their merit. There are also time when you, as parents, have the responsibility for making decisions that

underlying frustration, anger and vulnerability. A better outcome is accomplished if you are able to restrain your natural inclination to react in kind. Your adolescent is more in need of soothing his hurt than criticism. Ignore what he is saying and focus on acknowledging his upset. Express interest in what is upsetting to him. Things will quiet down quickly if he is able to accept your interest. The situation will get better even if he rejects your offer. Your response will avoid escalating the problem because your adolescent will not have to deal with the guilt over your anger at his bad behavior.

References:

Parenting With Love And Logic, Foster W. Cline, Pinon Press 2006,16 pages

Parenting Teenagers, Revised Edition, Don Dinkmeyer & Joyce McKay, Random House, Inc., 1998, 154 pages. Paperback

Early Adolescence: Understanding the 10 to 15 Year Old, Gail A. Caissy, Da Capo, 2005, 284 pages. Paperback

Blackwell Handbook of Adolescence, by Andrea Bastiani Archibald, David Bard, Bruce Bayley, and Michael Berzonsky, Blackwell Publishing Limited, 2005, 680 pages. Paperback

The End of Adolescence, Philip Graham, Oxford University Press, 2004, 276 pages Paperback

Don't Take It Personally: A Parent's Guide to Surviving Adolescence. John, A Davis LCSW, Break Inn Books, 2004, 164 pages

SEXUAL BEHAVIOR

Frank and Linda, parents of two adolescents, Gail 17 and Roger l5, were uncertain on how to help their children understand and manage their sexual feelings. This became relevant when she began to show interest in relating to boys. They didn't want to overstate their interest, but wanted to be sure she understood how to cope with her sexuality. They knew they would have to deal with the issue on birth control at some point. They struggled with this because they didn't want to be giving her implicit permission to have sexual relations. On the other hand they didn't want her to risk pregnancy. This led to discussions about the place of sex in relationships.

Roger overheard the discussions and had some questions of his own. This resulted in talking to him about sexual behavior from a male point of view. They had the same conversation with him about managing his sexuality in a relationship. They tried to be clear that birth control was not a license to engage in sexual relationships.

They wanted to be sure in their discussions with both children that they understood the emotional challenges and risks of disease that went with sexual relations.

I'm sure many parents wish that their children's hormones didn't kick in until they were adults. But that isn't going to happen. Adolescent sexual behavior is a trying concern for parents and their adolescents. This has always been a concern, but it is all the more so with the devastating advent of aids and other sexually transmitted diseases. Parents face the challenge of how to raise their children in an age of sexual freedom and high vulnerability to diseases.

In earlier times parents had a hard time engaging in a forthright discussion of sexual behavior with their children. It was common place for children to learn the facts of life from outside the home from friends and other sources of information. The accessibility of sexual material on the internet, movies, videos and open discussion makes it all the more imperative that parents take a more proactive stance in educating their children about how to relate to their sexuality. Societal debate about who should be responsible for sex educations whether in schools, under the guidance of religion, or at home does not help in addressing the concern. The primary responsibility is with parents.

This requires coming to terms with your own attitudes and comfort level in discussing sexuality. If this is not possible make sure your children get educated from a reliable source. Keep in mind the behavior you model in matters related to sex will have a major influence on your children. This behavior involves your attitudes and behavior regarding issues of sexuality

Parents like Fred and Linda often face the dilemma of whether to provide birth control for their daughters. They were caught in the fear that providing birth control carries the implicit permission to engage in sexual behavior. This has to be weighed against the risk of pregnancy and sexuality transmitted disease if it is not provided. This is not necessarily a reflection on an adolescent's maturity but a recognition that situations can get out of control. Ultimately it becomes a judgment call between the parents and their daughters based on their maturity and their perceived ability to control their behavior.

The education about sexual behavior is not limited to the physical act. Too often lacking is education regarding the responsibility that goes with it. This regards tempering the call of raging hormones with social responsibility. This involves attention to the consequences of sexual behavior both physical and emotional. Adolescents need help in coping with various situations.

- Adolescent boys not taking advantage of girls. This generally applies to males but could also apply to females.

- Being sensitive to the impact of gossip. This happens with bragging about sexual conquests which is made worse when names are used. Also to have awareness of potential damage to reputations. Keeping in mind that reputations are much easier to tarnish and harder to regain.

- Learning how to channel sexual energy in other than impulsive behavior. Educate your children to understand that control of sexual impulses has the best chance of success when it is interrupted well before it gets to the point of getting out of control.

- Understanding the consequences of a pregnancy on all concerned, the involved individuals and their families. To guard against vulnerability to peer pressure or desire to go with the crowd that contradicts held values.

Addressing sexual behavior

1. Decide, as parents, your comfort level in educating your children regarding their sexual understanding and behavior.

2. Work out an agreement with your spouse on the standards and guidelines for educating and monitoring your children's sexual education and behavior.

3. Determine whether you are able to provide the necessary education. If you are not, develop a constructive alternative to provide this education. Do not indulge in self recrimination if you are not able to provide it yourself. Keep in mind that the first priority is that they get the needed information, not whether it comes from you.

4. Discuss with your children their attitudes towards sexual behavior. Provide an atmosphere for their being able to ask questions. Answer these questions in a direct manner without judgment. Let your children know your value system and the basis for it. Assure your availability for any questions that may come up about their sexual behavior.

5. Discuss the pros and cons of birth control with your spouse and make a joint decision about whether to provide it.

6. Periodically update your children's' attitudes toward sexual behavior.

7. Be alert to any changes in personality or behavior. This may be a sign of a problem brewing in sexual and/or drug behavior. Discuss your concerns when this is noted. Do this in a supportive and non-confrontive manner. To do otherwise will only make the situation worse.

8. Build and maintain trust with your adolescent to ensure a continuing constructive relationship.

References:

Puberty, Sexuality and the Self: Girls and Boys at Adolescence, Karin Martin, Routledge, 1996, 176 pages, Paperback

Talking Sexuality: Parent-Adolescent Communication: New Directions for Child and Adolescent Development, S. Shirley Feldman, & Doreen A. Rosenthal (Editors), Jossey-Bass, 2002, 117 pages.

Adolescent Development: The Essential Readings, Gerald Adams (Editor), Blackwell Publishing Limited, 2000, 360 pages. Paperback

Adolescent Sexuality in Social Context, Susan Moore, Routledge, 1993, 256 pages.

Adolescent Sexuality in a Changing American Society: Social and Psychological Perspectives for the Human Services Professions, Catherine S. Chilman, John Wiley & Sons, 1983, 334 pages.

SIBLING RIVALRY

Michael, 13, and Sumner, 11 are brothers. Michael is an honor student and a good athlete. He is of average height and build for his age with brown eyes and dark brown hair. Sumner is a good student with modest athletic ability. He is two inches shorter than his brother and tries to stretch to his full height when with Michael so he will feel as tall as he is. Sumner also has brown eyes and a slender build. They go through periods of being very close and for reasons unclear they shift to being at each other's throats. Sumner often gets frustrated when he can't do as well as his brother And he keeps expecting to do so. He has a hard time remembering that his brother has a two and a half year head start over him. They often tease one another that frequently ends in a battle. They get physical when their tolerance for one another's barbs go too far. This usually leads to a period of ignoring one another. After awhile they gradually find their way back to being friends and the cycle repeats itself. Sumner gets competitive and angry at his parents when he feels they pay too much attention to Michael's athletic achievements and not enough to his achievements.

Siblings learn to love and to fight from one another. These relationships become the proving ground for friendships outside the family. They also learn how to work together and support one another, especially with outsiders. They can be at each other's throats one minute and the best of friends the next. They compete for their parent's attention, affection, and for getting what they things they want. What one has or gets soon becomes a must have for the other. They can also become co-conspirators as they attempt to outwit their parents. Age difference feeds their rivalry as the younger sibling wants to have and do what the older one has or can do as was the case with Michael and Sumner. Being close in age makes the competition even stronger. More pressure is added when one child has more talents than the other in looks, intelligence, or more. This is hard on the sibling who both admires and is jealous of the sibling who has more going for him/her. One child being a problem for parents can encourage the other one to become the "good child". This becomes one more way for each child to

Living with sibling rivalry

1. Take into account that no two children grow up in the same family. Each child comes into a different family- the first born, the first of a given sex, and being the youngest. Also having impact is the number of siblings and age differences between siblings. Each of these characteristics provides a different family environment for a new child.

   The same applies to the social and financial climate. It is not uncommon for the first child to arrive when parents have modest means and are treading the path to make their mark. A child arriving a few years later may come into a family that is better off and a happier family. Parents get wiser with experience and treat younger children differently than their first children.

2. Plan on younger children wanting to be like their older siblings. They can have a harder time if you let them do things that are out of reach for their physical or emotional maturity.

3. Do not take sides when children come to complain about the bad things a sibling did. Hold them both responsible for what happened without your personal observation. This will discourage their doing this again to get their way or get back at one another. This may be harder to do when the less confident child is the one complaining. But if you don't do this you may be saying it is OK to manipulate to get your way. The other child will be angry at your taking sides and find ways to get back at the one who complained. Everybody loses.

4. Do not hold one child responsible for the behavior of another. Each child has to learn to be responsible for his behavior.

5. Do not get involved too quickly when siblings are arguing. They should be given a chance to find their own solutions. Get involved when you are concerned about safety or when they have gone as far as they can in working things out. It would be helpful to have them look at what happened and how each one could have handled it differently. This should be done when their emotions have cooled down enough so they can learn from what you are trying to t each them. Involving them in problem solving will help them find better ways to get along.

6. Do not fall into the trap of assuming that each child is entitled to have what another child has.

7. Educate children that each child is treated separately according to need

and ability to use what is received. This will shift focus from competition to appropriate need. It also gets away from the notion that what one child has the other should also have it.

8. Teach children to be respectful and to help each other. Let them know you are pleased not only with school performance or what they do in their sports but also for the way they support and respect one another. This would also mean times they put the other's needs first.

9. Put as much importance on letting your children know when they have be-haved well than when they do things wrong. Don't do this with anger and yelling because that will get in the way of their paying attention to what you are trying to teach them. You will get more accomplished by telling them in a quiet voice what they did wrong and what they should have done. This makes doing things right a lot more attractive and keeps any angry feelings from getting in their way. Even more will be accomplished when siblings learn this from one another and see who can demonstrate appropriate behavior.

References:

Siblings Without Rivalry: How to Help Your Children Live Together So You Can Live Too, Adele Faber & Elaine Mazlish, Collins, 2004, 272 pages. Paperback

Understanding Sibling Rivalry: The Brazelton Way, T. Berry Brazelton & Joshua D. Sparrow, Da Capo Press, 2005, 61 pages. Paperback

Keep the Siblings, Lose the Rivalry, Todd Cartmell, Zondervan, 2003, 240 pages. Paperback

The Baffled Parent's Guide to Sibling Rivalry, Marian Edelman Borden, McGraw-Hill, 2003, 176 pages. Paperback

Loving Each One Best: A Caring and Practical Approach to Raising Siblings, Nancy Samalin, & Catherine Whitney, Bantam Press, 1997, 224 pages. Paperback

Preventing Sibling Rivalry: Six Strategies to Build a Jealousy-Free Home, Sybil Hart, Free Press, 2001, 224 pages.

SINGLE PARENT

Debra, 35, is divorced after eight years of marriage. She has a five year old blond and blue-eyed daughter, Allison. Her marriage to Tom, an architect, went well for about three years after which they began to have problems they weren't able to resolve. Separation occurred after three years of struggle and divorced followed a year later.

Debra is a real estate broker who does well enough to provide basic support for herself and her daughter. Tom's alimony helps but it isn't always reliable.

Allison has been an easy child to raise for the most part. Debra enjoys Allison's warmth and creativity. She has a good time with her which is enhanced by her easy going manner. She loves coloring and playing with her dolls.

Allison wasn't too affected by the divorce because her father was not around very often because of his preoccupation with his start-up business. She has a friendly relationship with him but not a close one. The continuing pressures of his work make spending time together irregular. She gets along with him when they are together and has learned not to expect too much from him.

Debra has some difficulty juggling her work schedule with that of Allison's because seeing clients often comes at awkward hours. It's been hard to develop reliable backup. Tom has not been able to be of much help because of his schedule and his lack of comfort in parenting. Sometimes she is able to get some help from her sister Helen or from some neighbors. The pressures of work, parenting and keeping up a home do not leave much time for herself or a social life. The joy Debra gets in raising Allison and seeing her blossom is what sustains her.

Being a single parent can be lonely and often overwhelming but it doesn't have to be. Being both mother and father is a daunting challenge under the best of circumstances. This is offset by the many satisfactions in guiding your child through to adulthood. Dealing with the absence of physical, emotional support from a spouse and too little money can be difficult and feel overwhelming when it happens. Life is much easier when you have a cooperative and supportive ex-spouse. Debra's case falls somewhere in between. Life gets easier as your child's needs for your attention diminish with age.

It is a good idea to guard against parentifying a child, that is treating your child as you would turn to another adult to complain about adult problems, asking them to understand beyond their experience or take on responsibilities not appropriate for their age and maturity. This can arouse a child's feeling guilty and responsible for the parent's difficulties while helpless to do anything about it. These expectations will complicate his following a normal developmental path.

Single parenthood can leave too little time or energy for your own personal and social needs as Debra found. Dating arouses concern about how it will affect the children, especially when there may be different people over time. Your children may go between wondering whether the new person may become another parent or fear loss of parental attention. You also may have concern about whether your having a child will make it harder to find a new relationship. This becomes much less of an issue or even an asset when your child and the new person are comfortable with one another.

The single parent's ex-spouse, when available, can lighten the load by both physical, financial, and emotional support or be a source of added problems. Things get much more difficult when the non-custodial parent doesn't honor commitments of time and money, demeans or criticizes child rearing, or is unreliable with visitations. A troubled marriage that ends in a hostile divorce leaves many scars that can become an ongoing struggle for all concerned. The prospect of repeated court appearances over issues of money, custody, and visitation are a constant threat .

Being a single parent doesn't mean having to sacrifice your own needs. It is desirable for both you and your child to make room for your having a life separate from being a parent. Your child will benefit from the renewed energy that comes from taking care of your own needs.

The way you become a single parent makes a difference in how you adjust to it. The trauma and grief will be especially difficult when the death of your spouse was unexpected. Death from illness provides time to anticipate and prepare for the change. Commitment to a spouse does not necessarily end with death. For some people, thoughts about the lost loved one can affect how he/she thinks and behaves for years.

Becoming a single parent from divorce has its own traumatic impact when it results from a troubled marriage, especially over a long period of time. Oftentimes, the struggle continues after divorce over child related issues. On the other side, a divorce can be a relief from all the stress and struggle. With it comes a renewed sense of freedom.

Managing single parenthood

1. The possibility of divorce should start you thinking about how to prepare for it. Begin to think about possibilities for childcare coverage among family and friends, or other sources of support.

2. Ideally both parents should jointly discuss with their children the impending divorce. This should include: making clear that the divorce is not because of their behavior. Let them know they will have the emotional and physical commitment of both parents, who they will live with, and how they will visit with the other parent. The reason for the divorce should be given as parents growing apart without blame or criticism.

3. When the divorce is too hostile, each parent will have to discuss the items in 2 above separately. Both parents should not involve their children in their struggles with one another. Violations will hurt all concerned.

4. Place a high priority on finding a way to have a life separate from being a custodial parent This includes time for exercise, social life and other interests as are needed. This needs to be done as much for your children as for yourself. Your having some semblance of a balanced life will help you be a more loving and satisfied parent.

5. You and your children will benefit from taking part in community activities. This will make it easier when you are doing interesting things with people outside the family.

6. Have your children help with household chores as they become able to perform them. This is helpful to you and also helps prepare your children for adulthood. This assumes that children are only given responsibilities that fit their abilities and maturity.

7. Have weekly family meetings to discuss planning, scheduling and family problems that will help build security and family spirit. These meetings should also include doing some fun things like telling jokes, singing or games.

8. Don't use a child as a sounding board for complaints about their other parent. It is important for your well being to be able to express these concerns. Do this with family, friends, or a therapist who are able to be helpful sounding boards.

9. Make sure you pay as much attention to giving your children affirmation when they do things you appreciate as you give criticism when they misbehave.

10. Don't let your emotions build up to the point you lose control. One of the problems of being a single parent is that you don't have another parent to help out when you get too upset. You can manage this by paying attention to when you begin to feel the buildup of emotions. Back away when this happens until you are able to regain more control over your emotions.

As an example, when you begin to feel exasperated by your child, say something like; "I can't deal with this now, I'll take this up later when I'm not so angry." This not only prevents you from doing something you will regret, and it also provides a model for your children to follow.

References:

The Single Mother's Survival Guide, Patrice Karst, Crossing Press, 2000, 112 pages. Paperback

The Single Parent Resource: An A to Z Guide for the Challenges of Single Parenting, Brook Noel & Art Klein, Champion Press, 2005, 354 pages Paperback

Going It Alone: Meeting the Challenges of Being a Single Mom, Michele Howe, Hendrickson Publishers, 1999, 144 pages. Paperback

Successful Single Parenting, Gary Richmond, Harvest House Publishers, 1998, 264 pages, Paperback

Chicken Soup for the Single Parent's Soul: Stories of Hope, Healing and Humor, HCI, 2005, 400 pages. Paperback

A SPECIAL NEEDS CHILD

Marvin Snider, Ph.D.

Johnny, 11, is a bright child for whom school work is a real struggle. He has trouble with details and focusing his attention. He also has difficulty sitting still in school. His need to constantly be moving is an ongoing concern to his mother, Janet. He has been diagnosed with a hyperactive/attention deficit disorder. These difficulties get in his way in relationships with other children which only heightens his symptoms. He is an imaginative and engaging child when his behavior doesn't get him in difficulty.

Johnny's father, Russell, and his mother got into struggles over how to best work with John. He felt that Janet's micro-managing him was contributing to John's problem. This became an ongoing issue when they were not able to work out a plan acceptable for both of them. They recognized that professional help was necessary to provide their child with the help he needed. Johnny showed marked progress once this was accomplished.

John is one example of children who have needs that require special help. Having a child with these needs is both a challenge and an opportunity These children have a harder time feeling good about themselves which makes it harder to have friendships or do things other children can do. Being teased for their difficulty is one more problem to overcome. A child with special needs may require help in feeling good about himself and staying that way in spite of his problems.

Special needs encompasses several conditions: physical disabilities, speech control, receptive or expressive problems, emotional disabilities, need for continuous movement, and learning disorders. People are often uncomfortable in not knowing how to respond to a child with these needs. They often wind up making the special needs person feel badly even though they didn't mean to do so. There was nothing subtle about John's problem. His difficulty sitting still was quite apparent.

Help your other children learn how to pay attention to their sibling's unique needs and to their own needs. This becomes harder as the needs become more severe. Siblings should be encouraged to be helpful as they are able. This will help them feel valued and reduce naturally felt resentments at how their sibling's disability affects them. They will need your help to talk about their feelings without feeling disloyal to you or their sibling. It is also helpful for there to be times when their needs become a priority. This will help them be more accepting of the times when this is not possible.

Guard against letting your collective frustrations in coping with your child's needs become a problem in your marriage. Russell and Janet's difficulty reaching agreement on managing John's problem added a problem they didn't need. This can happen when one of you gets involved in the child's care at the expense of paying attention to the rest of the family. The situation gets worse when the distracted parent is challenged by other family members for their felt neglect.

Coping with the child's unique needs can also be made difficult if one of you felt responsible in some way for your child's problem. This might be an inherited problem, an accident during pregnancy, or the result of an accident. Understand that your life will become only more complicated if you cater to guilt about something you can't change. The only constructive approach is to focus on doing the best you can in the present and future. This gets difficult to do when your best isn't enough. Managing what a special needs child requires can also have a positive effect when it results in family closeness that comes out of shared coping of difficult times. This works best when it is done as a family and not the responsibility of one or two people.

How to help a child with special needs

1. It is not helpful for you to harbor guilt for anything either of you (parents) feels was done that caused their child have a special need. Feeling guilty only makes dealing with the problem harder. Once there are special needs for any reason, the best thing for the family to do is concentrate on doing the best they can and not on blame.

2. Learn what you can do to meet your child's unique needs.

3. Help your child understand his limitation and help learn how to manage it.

4. Encourage your child to be open about his limitations and not pretend he doesn't need help. Doing all he can will help build self confidence. Getting help he doesn't need will get in the way of doing this.

5. Help your child enjoy the things that he can do and highlight his strengths.

6. Help your other children learn about their siblings unique needs and how to adjust to them in a way that is good for both the special needs child and them.

7. Explore whether there are support groups for children with special needs. Also helpful would be a group for siblings of these children.

8. Do not allow your child to use his problems to manipulate the family.

9. Help siblings be respectful of whatever limitations your child's unique needs places on family activities. Encourage the special needs child to be a contributing member in helping out consistent with his abilities.

10. Siblings may need help in how they manage their feelings about the disability and the resulting difficulties that affects them without feeling guilty. They should understand that they don't control what they feel, but they do have responsibility with what they do with what they feel. For example when they get frustrated, they don't take it out on their special needs sibling but know they can talk to a parent about it and not be put down for it.

11. Make an effort for there to be times, whenever possible, when the needs of other children in the family come first. This will help them be better able to cope with less resentment when having to defer to the needs of their sibling's problem.

References:

The Child With Special Needs: Encouraging Intellectual and Emotional Growth, Stanley I. Greenspan, Serena Wieder, & Robin Simons, Perseus Books, 1998, 496 pages.

From the Heart: On Being the Mother of a Child With Special Needs, Jayne D. B. Marsh, Woodbine House, 1995, 149 pages. Paperback

Including the Special Needs Child: Activities to Help All Students Grow and Learn, Grace Bickert, Incentive Publications, 2002, 95 pages. Paperback

Breakthrough Parenting for Children with Special Needs: Raising the Bar of Expectations, Judy Winter, Jossey-Bass, 2006, 288 pages.

Building a Joyful Life With Your Child Who Has Special Needs, Nancy J. Whiteman, Linda Roan-Yage, Jessica Kingsley Publishers, 2007, 208 pages. Paperback

Stepping Out: Using Games and Activities to Help Your Child with Special Needs, Sarah Newman, & Jeanie Mellers, Jessica Kingsley Publishers, 2004, 240 pages. Paperback

MANAGING TV

Harold and Kathryn are parents of Ethan, 8, and Jane 6. They are both charming and delightful children who demand a lot of attention. Both parents have demanding jobs, Harold as an attorney and Kathryn as a real estate broker. Harold works long hours and often is late in coming home for dinner. Kathryn is always struggling to juggle her work schedule which often requires attention at inconvenient times that interferes with her motherly obligations. She often uses TV to occupy the children so that she can prepare meals, do the laundry, or other necessary chores. Harold is sympathetic and feels guilty that his work gets in the way of his being more helpful. They both recognize that they have a tendency to use TV as a baby sitter too often. They feel bad about it but find that sometimes it is the only way they can get things done.

The use of TV is also a problem at dinner. Harold likes to watch the news during meals which interferes with Kathryn's desire to have pleasant conversations. Harold tries to accommodate to her wishes by trying to do both which makes dinner time more stressful and unpleasant. Eventually he recognized the futility in this effort and deferred to Kathryn's view which he acknowledged was more appropriate.

It is too easy to let TV watching become a habit. TV is used in different ways: to entertain, to provide company, to avoid what you don't want to do, used as a baby sitter and more. It also gets in the way of people talking to one another. Some families find it easier to watch TV over dinner than to talk to each other. For other people it is their constant companion. TV can be a powerful tool for education and entertainment or it become an addiction. Watching by appointment makes the best use of TV and avoids the downside. Watching TV because it is handy gets in the way of enjoying relationships and activities in creative self expression in art, music, writing or other ways.

1. Decide whether you are satisfied with your TV watching habits. Check out how much you watch because you like a program or just to see whatever is on. Also give some thought to what you would do that you would enjoy if you didn't have TV. Keep in mind that TV watching without purpose undermines feeling good about yourself.

2. Do the same with your children's TV watching. Have them work out a balance between TV and other active interests. Set limits on the amount and kind of TV they watch. Pursuing other active interests will help them feel good about themselves and help their relationships with other children. This might be in sports, music lessons, hobbies or artistic pursuits. Encourage your children to broaden their interests.

3. Set time limits for watching TV for entertainment. This time may be separate from educational TV. Limited TV time will help them learn to set priorities on how they use this time. Don't let yourself be manipulated into changing the rules otherwise you will be in a constant struggle.

5. Recreational TV may be useful as a reward for doing what is expected as homework and chores when they have a good balance with doing other kinds of activities.

6. Engage your children as part of the solution in TV management. Have a family meeting to work out a plan for TV watching that is acceptable for everyone. You will get better cooperation when they have been involved is setting limits. It is essential for you to consistently hold them to their commitments for this to be successful.

7. Keep in mind your TV habits become a model for your children to follow. You will likely have problem if you have a double standard for watching TV, one for you and one for them.

References:

Early Childhood TV Viewing and Adolescent Behavior, Daniel R. Anderson, Kelly Schmitt, Deborah Linebarger, & John C. Wright, Blackwell Publishing Limited, 2001, 180 pages. Paperback

Don't Be Afraid To Discipline: The Commonsense Program for Low-Stress Parenting That *Improves Kids' Behavior in a Matter of Days *Stops Naggling and Hassling … Relationship *Creates Lasting Results, Ruth Peter, Golden Guides from St. Martin's Press, 1999, 224 pages. Paperback

Changing Children's Behavior by Changing the People, Places and Activities in Their

Lives, Changing Children's Behavior by Changing the People, Places and Activities in Their Lives, Richard L. Munger, Boys Town Press, 2005, 250 pages. Paperback

Harvesting Minds: How TV Commercials Control Kids, Roy F. Fox, Praeger Paperback, 2000, 32 pages. Paperback

Mommy, I'm Scared": How TV and Movies Frighten Children and What We Can Do to Protect Them, by Ph.D., Joanne Cantor, Harvest Books, 1998 255 pages. Paperback

Change Your Child's Behavior by Changing Yours: 13 New Tricks to Get Kids to Co-operate, Barbara Chernofsky, Three Rivers Press, 1996, 208 pages. Paperback

WHETHER TO HAVE CHILDREN

Heather and Mark had been married for five years when the subject of having children came up. It seemed curious to them it hadn't come up earlier. They thought this was due to Mark's absorption in getting his business degree and Heather's preoccupation with Law School and passing the bar. They married right after they both graduated college at the same time and then got caught up in Graduate School and Law School. They were now at a point when they settled into an established life style.

The reminder of hearing colleagues talk about their children brought to their attention that they hadn't seriously considered whether they wanted to have children. They were undecided for two reasons. They were both heavily involved in their careers and weren't sure how having children would affect them. This was particularly the case for Heather, since it would have more impact on her.

They both had some concern about how children would change their relationship. Their uncertainty was reinforced because both of them grew up in troubled families. They had concern about their ability to be good parents given they had such poor role models for parents. There was also the question of how they would deal with parenting. Heather didn't want to sacrifice her career to be a mother and she wasn't sure how much she would be able to count on Mark to share parenting.

There were other concerns with which to contend. They were getting a lot of pressure from their families about when they were going to have children. They also had some questions about life style. They liked living in the city but felt this wouldn't the place to raise children. The prospect of living in the suburbs and having to commute wasn't very appealing. On the other hand, the idea of growing old without having children wasn't too appealing either. They had a lot of questions and too few answers. Their decision got made for them when Heather got unexpectedly pregnant.

People usually enter marriage with the prospect they will have children somewhere along the way. Whether this happens depends on many considerations. Some of them are by choice and others are out of their control.

Deciding to have a child is one of the most important commitments you will make. It is a financial, physical and, more importantly, an emotional commitment. It is more than creating a human life. It is the opportunity to have a major influence on the kind of human being your child becomes. The chances of successful outcome are much greater when you make room in your life for this commitment. This differs from being an add-on to your other interests and obligations. It is too easy to have children fueled by the idea and fantasy of having a child without giving enough thought to what this will involve. Everybody suffers when this happens: the child, the parents, and society when a child's under-nourished upbringing leads to problems at home, in school and worse in the community or with the police.

Considerations in whether to have children

1. Make a realistic assessment of what is involved in having children by talking with parents who have different numbers of children, particularly having one child, two children, three children, four children or more. Having children of the same sex and both sexes offers different challenges.

2. Compare the pros and cons of having children and make a preliminary decision on what will fit for you. This is not something you decide quickly. It is something that you think about periodically. The answer for you will evolve over time as the priorities in your life become clearer.

3. Get information on how the cost of raising a child through high school and possibly college if that would be a goal. Consider how this will impact the life style you wish to pursue.

4. Consider how the demands of having children would impact on your having a career and other interests you wish to pursue. How willing would you be to make sacrifices in raising your children that might interfere with your career or these other interests? These are the issues with which Mark and Heather struggled.

5. Having children requires agreement between you and your spouse if it to be a satisfying experience. This agreement will be meaningful only if you both agree on having a flexible division of labor in raising your children that adapts to the changing needs of both you and your children. This should include how this will impact the division of labor in the event you become a two career couple.

6. Consider whether your having impact on shaping the life of a child is something that would be meaningful to you after you take into account the emotional, psychological, financial demands that go with it.

7. Consider how important it is to you to continue your family blood line.

8. Consider the impact on your senior years with and without children. Give thought to how you would feel missing the experience of being a grandparent and in not having family to look after you in your golden years. The thought of growing old without having children became increasingly important to Heather and added to her concern about whether she could manage motherhood and a career.

9. Be aware that the decision whether to have children is not necessarily a one time decision. Each couple's situation is unique, but it often works best the earlier the better. That is when you will have the most energy and patience but it also is a time when your career is likely to be most demanding.

10. Weigh the above considerations. Make your decision and don't look back. Focus on making the most of what is possible at each stage of your life.

References:

Beyond Motherhood: Choosing a Life Without Children, Safer Pocket, 2002. 208 pages Paperback

Oh No, We Forgot to Have Children: How Declining Birth Rates Are Reshaping Our Society, Deirdre Macken, Allen & Unwin, 2006, 232 pages. Paperback

Childfree and Loving It!, Nicki Defago, Vision, 2005, 256 pages. Paperback

Cheerfully Childless: The Humor Book for Those Who Hesitate to Procreate, Ellen Metter & Loretta Gomez, Browser Pr, 2001, 76 pages. Paperback

Childless by Choice: A Feminist Anthology, Irene Reti, HerBooks, 1992. 87 pages, Paperback

ELDERLY

AGING

Rebecca's sixtieth birthday broke through her resistance to thinking of herself as older. She was living an active and productive life as a wife, mother, grandmother, and teacher as someone who always had an active and curious mind. She recognized that little could be done about her aging body but something could be done about keeping her mind young.

Her husband, Angus was of a like mind. He was retired and kept busy with various volunteer activities. He kept his mind active by being a member of the local university's life long learning program. They traveled some but not as much as they did in the past. The stress of traveling was getting to be too much for them.

Keeping in contact with people of all ages was a way to avoid being overly focused on the challenges that aging presented. Rebecca avoided people of her age range who isolated themselves and were preoccupied with their health issues. Rebecca focused on having a good diet, exercise and good medical care in service of graceful aging.

She also kept involved in politics to stay informed about current issues. She worked with high school students to keep up to date on what was going on with the younger generation. spending time with her grandchildren was always enjoyable as it gave her an opportunity to be with them without having to be responsible for them.

Aging is not a choice! The way you deal with your physical and emotional health is a choice. You take care of your physical aging by having a good diet, regular exercise, annual physical exams and following the directions of your physician.

Psychological aging is more complex. It is separate from physical aging though affected by it. A person of twenty can have the outlook of someone eighty. Likewise, an eighty year-old can have the mind set of a much younger person. Psychological aging has been defined in many ways. I particularly like the view that psychological old age occurs when a person's energies are focused more on the past than the present or the future. In contrast, a young age is characterized by paying more attention to the present and especially on the future than on the past.

In a young psychological age you focus on hope and plans for the future, creativity and visions of what is possible. This gives you the energy to express yourself in business interests, education, artistic pursuits, or in community activities or whatever is of interest to you.

An old oriented psychological age focuses on memories of what was. Positive memories carry the pleasure of reliving meaningful moments and the satisfactions that went with it or reliving negative memories with regrets and criticisms of self or others. This arouses sadness, sometimes anger and feelings of helplessness in not being able to change the past. These thoughts add a burden to physical aging.

Productivity is another way to measure psychological aging. Being productive provides satisfaction that comes from something accomplished. It doesn't matter what form it takes or that it is pleasing to anyone else. It could be something artistic, building something, a beautiful garden, volunteering, a hobby, or having a job. You do things because you enjoy them rather than having to do them. It is most important to keep an active mind and be actively involved in the world around you.

Aging brings a greater chance of illness in spite of your best efforts to live a healthy life. It is hard to adjust to being less able to do things that were taken for granted: not hearing or seeing as well, less energy, more aches and pains, and more trips to doctors. It is tempting to slip into a psychologically old view of focusing on the loss of what one used to be able to do. A psychologically young orientation will focus on how to make the most out of what you are able to do. Getting a hearing aid will help with hearing problems. Visual aids will help with diminished vision. Satisfaction comes from gaining mastery over whatever limitations you may have.

Ways to pay attention to aging

1. Plan to take good care of yourself by having a good diet, regular exercise, annual physical exams, good sleep habits, and more.

2. Try to spend time around people of all ages. Avoid people of your own age who only want to talk about their physical problems or memories. Being around young people can be a benefit to both of you. Young people are stimulating and challenging. They gain from the wisdom that comes from your years of experience.

3. Do things that you enjoy and are mentally challenging. Get involved in activities that give you a sense of accomplishment. This may include: : hobbies, gardening, volunteer work, work, organizational work and community activities. Also include activities like movies, concerts, sports, museums and more.

4. Keep up to date with what is going on in the world around you through newspapers, TV, lectures and discussion on topics of interest with friends. Get involved in community activities or organizations. Keeping an active mind is good protection against psychological aging.

5 Plan things you want to do in the future on projects or traveling.

6. Limit your TV watching to programs that you want to see. Avoid watching TV when you are bored or turn it on to watch whatever is on. Aimless TV time leads to depressed feelings and lacking a sense of purpose.

7. Consult your physician for symptoms that don't go away after two or three weeks.

8. Carefully follow directions for taking medications. Do not stop taking them without talking to your doctor.

9. Make the most out of what you are able to do when aging begins to limit what you can do.

References:

The Art of Aging: A Doctor's Prescription for Well-Being, Sherwin B. Nuland, Publisher: Random House, 2007, 320 pages.

The Denial of Aging: Perpetual Youth, Eternal Life, and Other Dangerous Fantasies, Muriel R. Gillick, Harvard University Press, 2006, 352 pages.

Aging Well: Surprising Guideposts to a Happier Life from the Landmark Harvard Study, George E. Vaillant, Little, Brown and Company, 2003, 384 pages.

Healthy Aging: A Lifelong Guide to Your Well-Being, Andrew Weil, Anchor, 384 pages. Paperback

How to Care for Aging Parents, Virginia Morris & Robert M. Butler, Workman Publishing Company, 2004, 656 pages. Paperback

Breaking the Rules of Aging, David A. Lipschitz, LifeLine Press, 2002, 336 pages

GRANDPARENTHOOD

Tony and Judy had led satisfying work lives. Tony was a successful lawyer and Judy was a unit manager in a computer company that required occasional travel. They also enjoyed raising their three children and were delighted when they became grandparents. However, they soon found the fact of being grandparents was more complicated then anticipated. They got increasingly involved with their grandchildren as they got older. This left them with a dilemma. They were at the apex of their careers and yet they felt drawn to being with their children and grandchildren. This put them in a different place with some of their friends who were happy to be grandparents from a distance.

They recognized a review of their priorities was needed. Their careers were satisfying but they also enjoyed being with family, getting to know their grandchildren and hopefully playing a part in helping them grow up. Choices would have to be made if this was going to happen.

They were out of practice as parents and realized times were different and that they would have to learn how to get to know their grandchildren in a way that fit for everybody. This required their learning to respect their children's way of raising their children even though it made them uncomfortable at times. There was also the awareness that it was not a good idea to give suggestions unless asked.

Harold and Alice are in their sixties. They have three children and eight grand-children. They are busy enjoying their senior years. Harold does volunteer work consulting in non-profit organizations, plays tennis when he can and enjoys his hobby as a photographer. Alice is very involved in gardening, and volunteers at the local hospital. They both enjoy traveling on their occasional trips. They love their children and grand-children but have less patience than they used to have for being around small children. They enjoy seeing them for brief periods of time. This in part is due to some disapproval of how their grandchildren are being raised. They feel the children are too indulged, raised to feel entitled and are undisciplined in some bothersome ways. The children do not show enough respect to their elders, and they are given too much freedom.

These are two examples of different approaches to being grandparents. Grand-parenting isn't for everybody. It isn't about whether a senior has grandchildren. It is about whether there is a desire to behave as an observing or a participating grandparents. Harold and Alice are grandparents who prefer to have limited contact with their grandchildren. They may love them no less but have different priorities in how they wish to spend their time and energy They feel they did their time in parenting and see grand parenting as more of the same. Besides, they don't feel they have the energy and patience to do what is needed. Others, like Tony and Judy, viewed it differently. They wanted to enjoy their grand children and were happy to spend time with them. They viewed being a grandparent as an opportunity to enjoy their offspring without having the responsibility for them, savoring they can back away when they need to do so.

The desire to be actively involved in grandparent activities will in part depend on the historical and ongoing relationship with your children. A history of comfortable relationships will welcome grandparent participation and be a win-win for all concerned. Also of consideration is the comfort level in being with these children. Comfort levels will vary with the grand children's personality and interests. Tony had a close relationship with his grandson, Todd, because they shared an interest in football.

Satisfaction in spending time with grandchildren will also depend on whether you expect your grandchildren to cater to your interests or whether you are willing to get invested in their interests. The latter will likely result in a more satisfying relationship.

For some grandparents, close relationships with children and grandchildren can be both satisfying and have good feelings about creating continuity over generations. Giving your family a sense of the family history that preceded them is a gift to them. It may expand their sense of self and purpose by giving them a tradition to follow. It is common to find family legacies that get passed on. Some families define it in by occupation, whether it be a long history of firemen, policeman, lawyers, doctors, and more. Others may define it in the arts or public service.

Managing grand parenthood

1. Consider the pros and cons of being actively involved with grandchildren. This includes baby-sitting time and participating in activities with them.

For some people baby-sitting is not a chore but an opportunity to enjoy grand children without the watchful eye of parents and even to enjoy spoiling them a little.

2. Define your priorities for how to behave as a grandparent. Consider how active you want to be in the lives of your grandchildren. Negotiate with their parents for the kind of involvement that fits for both you and them.

3. Be aware that your comfort level in being with grandchildren may in part depend on their your respective ages and interests. Some grandparents are more comfortable with infants and very young children, while others do better with older children.

4. Avoid the temptation to tell your children how to manage their children. Your good intentions are likely to come across as criticism. A good maxim to follow is not to give advise unless it is requested. Harold and Alice found that their well-intended recommendations about their grandchildren's behavior was often not welcome. This made it harder to enjoy being a grandparent

5. Get involved in your grandchildren's interests. This will help build a bond with them. Once this is done you will be able to enjoy helping them expand their interests in other areas. It will also give you activities of common interest. This might be exposing them to music, art, sports, or hobbies.

6. Don't have your satisfaction in spending time with grandchildren depend on whether you expect them to cater to your interests. Recognize that your willingness to get invested in their interests will more likely result in a more satisfying relationship. Be open to new ideas and different ways of doing things. This will help you keep young in spirit and have good relationships with your children and grandchildren. Avoid any attempt to suggest that the way things were done in the past was superior to what is happening in the present. This may make you feel better but it will alienate you from your family.

7. You can expand your grandchild's interests in other directions once you establish a good relationship with them. This will not only add to the child's interest and new experiences but is likely to also enhance the quality of the relationship for both you.

8. For some grandparents, close relationships with children and grandchildren can be both satisfying and result in good feelings about creating continuity over generations.

9. To accomplish this will require flexibility in blending the interest and values of all three generations. A grandparent who demands primacy of interests and values will wind up in a lonely retirement.

References:

The Grandparent Guide: The Definitive Guide to Coping with the Challenges of Modern Grand parenting, Arthur Kornhaber, McGraw-Hill, 2002, 400 pages. Paperback

Grand parenting From a Distance: An Activities Handbook for Strengthening Long Distance Relationships, The National Institute for Building Long Distance Relationships, A & E Family Publishers, 2000, 20 pages. Paperback

Grand parenting With Love & Logic: Practical Solutions to Today's Grand parenting Challenges, Jim Fay, Love & Logic Press, 288 pages. Paperback

Grand parenting Redefined: Guidance for Today's Changing Family, Rne M. Endicott, Aglow Publications, 1992, 213 pages. Paperback

Creative Grand parenting Across the Miles: Ideas for Sharing Love, Faith, and Family Traditions, Patricia L. Fry, Liguori Publications, 1997, 80 pages. Paperback

The New Face of Grand parenting… Why Parents Need Their Own Parents, Don Schmitz, Grandkidsandme, 2003, 196 pages. Paperback

The Grandparent Guide: The Definitive Guide to Coping with the Challenges of Modern Grand parenting, by Arthur Kornhaber, McGraw-Hill, 2002, 400 pages. Paperback

Grand parenting With Love & Logic: Practical Solutions to Today's parenting Challenges, Jim Fay, Love & Logic Press, 1998, 288 pages. Paperback

So You're Expecting to be a Grandparent!: More than 50 Things You Should Know About Grand parenting, by Mary Ellen Pinkham, Focus on the Family Publishing 2001, 265 pages. Paperback

The 12 Rules of Grand parenting: A New Look at Traditional Roles and How to Break Them, Susan M. Kettmann, Facts on File, 1999, 206 pages

RETIREMENT

Alvin focused on the good things that were yet to come in the early part of his life. Things began to change when he reached forty. He began to think about what would the second half of his life be like. He didn't do much about this till he reached fifty. He decided it was time to think seriously about retirement.

He consulted a financial planner who helped him and his wife, Alma, think through what kind of life style they wanted in retirement. With his guidance they worked out a conservative financial plan. They realized this was not a one time decision but one that would need to be reviewed every few years to see if any changes needed to be made. The same applied to keeping an up-to-date review of their will.

They also needed to decide when to retire and what retirement meant. Did it mean just not working? What would they do with their time? This led them to realize they both enjoyed the work they were doing. It didn't seem to make sense to stop working at some arbitrary age. It made more sense to work as long as it was fulfilling unless they were no longer able to work. Besides they had no pressing things they wanted to do instead. However, they did think it would be a good idea to begin to try out things they might like to do when they retired. There was agreement on the importance of making sure they had continued health care coverage, since they knew they were going to have more health problems in the future than they had in the past. They got long term insurance to cover their future medical needs. Their financial planner told them this was a good idea to protect their assets if they needed to go into a nursing home.

There would be a time when keeping up their big house would be too much for them. They would do it as long as they could because it would make it possible for their two children and their grandchildren to all visit at the same time.

This raised the question of what options they would have when they had to give up the family home. Getting a smaller house would help but it would still require taking care of a house. The idea of a retirement community sounded appealing. It was something they would need to explore. The challenge would be to find something that fit their needs that would also permit them to stay in close contact with their children's families.

It is never too soon to start planning for retirement which is the time to stop working and enjoy the fruits of your labors. There was a time which meant you were less able to work. Like so many out of date ideas, it is not that simple. It may apply to physical labor. Not so with intellectual ability as was the case with Alvin and Alma. For many people intellectual capacity only mellows with experience until death.

Another old idea is that work is a burden that should be traded for a life of leisure and earned rest. This does not apply to the many people who enjoy and thrive in their work. For others it is a relief from the burden and responsibility of supporting a family.

Retirement requires an accumulation of savings to provide for an unknown number of years. This was not possible for a great many people with too little income for old age. Prior to the Social Security Act of 1935, old age meant depending on one's children or charity for many people. Passage of this act gave a minimal guaranteed income and a sense of dignity. In addition, continuing working gave added income.

Retirement does not necessarily take into account the positive benefits from working: a sense of achievement, feeling productive, feeling valued, social relationships, and more. Social Security deals with the financial part of retirement. People are on their own with the psychological and social adjustment to retirement. Planning for retirement needs to include both.

Planning for retirement

1. A good time to start planning for retirement is when you become established in a career with some idea of your potential income over time.

2. Make a first approximation of anticipated family responsibilities. Update this evaluation every few years.

3. Consult a financial planner for developing a framework for retirement as did Alvin and Alma. One can be found from one's lawyer, accountant, friends or by referral from a professional organization of financial planners.

4. Interview two or three possibilities. Credentials should be checked out. Also important is a feeling of good chemistry with the consultant. This includes technical competence, having a sense of trust and a genuine felt interest in your situation. They get paid by one of three methods. One is by commission from the investments that are made. Another is by a percentage of total investment value, and an hourly rate. The last is the only one in which the financial planner would not have vested interest in which investments are made. Each option has its own pros and cons. Selection should be made on the method that best fits your comfort level.

When to Retire

There is no set time to retire which is the way Alvin and Alma felt. Social convention has set retirement age at 65. People who develop the appropriate financial means can retire as early as in their forties. Many people move to semi-retirement in their late sixties and early seventies. Others don't fully retire as long as they are able to do what they enjoy doing. Sadly, there are those who for financial need have to keep working as long as possible.

The time to retire is also influenced when the requirements of your job become too demanding. In some occupations retirement becomes mandatory at a specified age. For many it is 65 and for others it is 70. Mandatory retirement has the benefit or disadvantage, as the case may be, of having the decision made for you.

Preparing for retirement

1. Set a desired time frame for retirement that would be financially possible.

2. Have a plan for what you would like to be doing after retirement. If possible, start to implement your plan gradually before you retire. This will make the transition into retirement easier.

3. Update this goal every few years to adjust for changing interests and circumstances.

Goals for Retirement

Planning goals for retirement will make adjustment to it more satisfying. This includes the life style one desires, family obligations you expect to have, and whether you expect to keep producing income after retiring. Any continued work is done at your discretion with no long term commitment.

1. Consider possibilities for how you would like to spend your time in retirement.

2. Consult relevant family members for their input and how your plans would affect them.

3. Update these plans every few years.

Managing Health Care

Attention needs to given to long term health care issues. This includes Medicare and supplemental insurance not covered by Medicare. You also have to consider the unpleasant prospect that increasing age is likely to bring significant health issues and how to manage it financially. Long term medical insurance is safest way. This should cover nursing care both in a nursing home and home care. This is offered by many companies with a variety of options. These should be evaluated for the benefits that best suit your needs. Without this insurance you are vulnerable to catastrophic cost that can readily exhaust your assets. Long term insurance will also protect Medicare from placing a lien on your assets if you have to enter a nursing home. Consultation with a financial planner will help avoid this occurrence. Look for a financial planner who has a particular interest in working with seniors.

You should anticipate the possibility of diminished physical and emotional capacity. This happens in two ways. There is the normal wear and tear with diminished physical abilities, diminished hearing that may require a hearing aid, poorer eyesight, decrease in stamina and energy level. These are discomforting to experience. The best approach is to focus on how to make the most of whatever capacity you have rather than on what was lost. To do otherwise is to only make the adjustment more difficult.

The other possibility involves major illnesses that require ongoing medical care that significantly limits physical and emotional capacities. These may leave too little time for other more attractive interests. As before, the best one can do is to focus on making the most out of what is possible. Doing so provides satisfaction and self esteem that you have done all that you can do.

1. Get regular physicals.

2. Add supplemental health insurance to Medicare.

3. Get long term insurance.

4. Consult your physician for symptoms that persist.

5. Take medication as prescribed. Do not discontinue medication without consulting the prescribing physician.

6. Eat a balanced diet.

7. Exercise regularly consistent with your physical condition and physician's approval.

8. Get adequate rest.

9. Anticipate the likelihood of diminished capacities. Focus on how to make the most out of what is possible.

Time with Grandchildren

Retirement provides the opportunity to spend time with children and grand-children in a way that was not possible before. This requires a different kind of adjustment. It means negotiating a mutually acceptable relationship with children. Balancing the needs of grandparents, grandchildren, and the rest of the family takes time to explore what works for all concerned.

The desire to be close to your children and grandchildren will impact your choice of where you will live. This was of much concern to Alvin and Alva. Being too far away will limit contact. Too close may invite over dependence. Grandparents will also face having to integrate their value system with that of their children. Negotiations have to be made in defining what you need from one another.

A related concern occurs when children live great distances from their parents. How to maintain meaningful contact under these conditions is a challenge. The exchange of visits works until there are small grandchildren. The problem becomes greater with the number of children. At these times it becomes easier for the grand-parents to do the traveling assuming finances and physical ability are not a problem.

Distance should not be a deterrent from developing a meaningful relationship with grandchildren. Frequent telephone calls, photos, videos, and emails which convey interest in what the grandchildren are doing can help develop satisfying relationships. This is enhanced when grandparents spend meaningful face to face contact with them when they visit one another.

1. Consider the kind of relationship desired with children and grandchildren.

2. Negotiate with them a relationship satisfactory to you and them.

3. Consider the way to manage pursuit of individual interests with relationships to children and grandchildren. This will require setting priorities when there is a conflict.

4. Negotiate a mutually comfortable way to manage disagreements from both points of view.

5. Do not give advice or criticism unless it is requested.

6. Balance time together that pays attention to everyone's needs. Otherwise, one or the other of you will lose interest.

Where to Live

Deciding where to live in retirement can be a complex process. Giving up the familiarity of a home lived in through much of a couple's' married life can be difficult. The burden of too much upkeep and too little energy can become compelling enough to require a move. The question becomes one of how to down-size. One possibility is to get a smaller house, preferably on one floor. But owning a house still has the responsibility of upkeep all-be-it on a smaller scale.

One alternative is a retirement community. It has important advantages: private space, minimal upkeep, a community of peers, availability of many activities, and medical services as your need for medical care increases. It has the disadvantage of having too little exposure to people of all ages and may involve being too far from access to your children.

1. Evaluate down sizing by comparing the pros and cons of having a smaller house with all its attendant responsibilities with that of a retirement community and the amenities they provide.

2. Consider the importance of closeness to children and grandchildren in the decision of where to live.

Pursuing New and Old Interests

Retirement presents an opportunity to spend more time pursuing established interests or the pursuit of new ones not possible during the working years or the exploration of new ones. Pursuit of these activities provides the excitement and stimulation that fosters and active mind and the satisfaction that comes with it. Alvin hadn't had much time to devote to activities outside of work and didn't think it would change in the near future. However, he did look forward to playing golf when the had more time. He had enjoyed it the few times when he had played.

1. Evaluate whether current interests will provide adequate expression for your energy and creativity.

2. Review whether there are interests that were not possible to pursue during work like that may be currently possible.

3. Explore activities that hadn't been considered of interest before which may be viewed differently.

4.   Periodically review whether to continue as is or whether a change is warranted due to changing health, finances or living conditions.

References:

Your Complete Retirement Planning Road Map: The Leave-Nothing-to-Chance, Worry-Free, All-Systems-Go Guide, Ed Slott, Ballantine Books, 2006, 384 pages. The New Retirement: The Ultimate Guide to the Rest of Your Life, Jan Cullinane Cathy Fitzgerald, Rodale Books, 2004, 486 pages. Paperback

How to Retire Happy: The 12 Most Important Decisions You Must Make Before You Retire, Stan Hinden, McGraw-Hill, 2005, 224 pages. Paperback

101 Secrets for a Great Retirement : Practical, Inspirational, & Fun Ideas for the Best Years of Your Life!, Mary Helen, Shuford Smith, McGraw-Hill, 2000, 160 pages. Paperback

How to Love Your Retirement: Advice from Hundreds of Retirees by Hundreds Of Heads, Barbara Waxman (Editor), Bob Mendelson, Hundreds of Heads Books, 2006, 208 pages. Paperback

Your Retirement, Your Way: Why It Takes More Than Money to Live Your Dream, Alan Bernstein, John Trauth, McGraw-Hill, 2006, 224 pages. Paperback

The Top 13 Warnings Signs That It's Time to Retire, Jim Grant, Betty Hollas & Donna Whyte Char Forsten, Crystal Springs Books, 2006, 16 pages. Paperback

WILLS AND TRUSTS

Howard devoted his career building as large an estate as possible. He wanted his children to have a comfortable life style and not have to struggle the way he had. This was necessary because two of his three children were in careers that would only provide limited incomes. One daughter Sally was a teacher, Sam was an artist, and Jane was a lawyer. He felt more comfortable about her financial future.

Howard considered naming Jane as executor of his estate because she would be the most capable in managing money. There was concern that doing so would cause conflict between the children. Instead he picked a younger member of his law firm to be executor. Trust funds were set up to protect Sally and Sam from their inexperience in managing significant sums of money.

He decided to minimize any problems in understanding his will by reviewing it with them. This would give them the chance to ask questions and perhaps lead to his making some changes. It would also help to minimize any concerns they had about his intentions.

You spend a life time collecting things important to you: money, property, art, and many more. You also care what happens to them after your death given you can't take with you. This becomes your estate. Wills and trusts are instructions on what should happen to your estate. The beneficiaries of the estate can be anyone, but are often family members. The range of beneficiaries generally grows with the size of the estate. Commonly this includes charities and other people who have been important to you. Your will tells an executor how to distribute your assets. It will have to go through Probate court before he can do anything. This makes it possible for anyone who feels he has a complaint to contest the terms of the will.

Oftentimes probating a will and carrying out what it says are routine. At other times it gets complicated. This occurs for various reasons.

- Someone complains that the executor is the wrong person because he is a member of the family and fears he may be biased in his favor. There may also be the added complaint that he doesn't have the necessary skills to do what is required.

- The belief that the will was written under pressure from a family member. An adult beneficiary may not like the idea he has to wait for some time until he gets his money. Usually this is done to wait until the beneficiary has reached an age when he would be better able to handle the money. He may argue that the requirement is outdated.

The terms of a will sometimes trigger family arguments about how the will was written that lead to never ending arguments and permanently change family relationships. It may be helpful to avoid your heirs having conflicts about the provisions of your will by making the terms of the will be known by you. Be prepared to handle whatever entitlements your prospective heirs may expect. You can also reinforce this potential problem by making clear in your will what you are doing and why you choose to do it. This presumes you will be comfortable managing the emotions your heirs may have if they don't like what they hear which is usually not the case. It easier to let your will or trust speak for itself and not take responsibility for how your heirs manage their feelings.

Making a will

1. Make a will as soon as you begin to acquire assets in any form: cash, investments, life insurance policy, stock options, real estate or any other kind of asset.

2. Prepare for the visit to a lawyer with some idea of who will be executor and to whom assets are to be left: family members, friends, or charity.

3. An executor should be a person whom you trust, is mature, has experience in managing finances and ideally has no vested interest in the estate.

4. If having a family member be executor is preferred, getting acceptance by other heirs will help reduce but not eliminate the potential for problems. Your choice should be someone who has the maturity and sensitivity in managing any conflicts that may arise.

5. Decide whether the people to whom you want to leave assets will be able to handle it or whether they will need some help in the form of a trust.

Trusts

There are many different kinds of trusts. There are two types that are most common: revocable and irrevocable. A revocable trust is one that can be changed by the person setting up the trust, called a trustor, after it is created. Trusts are used to avoid federal estate taxes and are often drafted to be irrevocable, the person setting up the trust can't change it. Trusts are also used to avoid Probate Court. Trusts are a way to give away possessions under controlled conditions.

Setting up trusts

1. Consult a lawyer to decide whether having a trust is appropriate.

2. Sometimes trusts are used to be temporary until the beneficiary reaches sufficient maturity to be trusted with full control of what is in the trust. The grantor, the person setting up the trust, needs to decide how long to wait before the person gets control of what is in the trust.

3. Periodically review revocable trusts to see if they continue to be needed or whether the terms of the trust should be changed.

4. A person who sets up an irrevocable trust needs to understand that it depends on the assumption that its terms will continue to be make sense over time or the benefits gained by the trust outweigh any anticipated problems.

References:

Suze Orman Will & Trust Kit, Suze Orman, Hay House, 2005, CD-ROM

The Complete Idiot's Guide to Wills and Estates, Third Edition, Stephen Maple, Alpha, 2005, 384 pages. Paperback

The Complete Book of Wills, Estates & Trusts: Third Edition, Alexander A. Bove, Owl Books, 2005, 384 pages Paperback

The American Bar Association Guide to Wills and Estates, Second Edition: Everything You Need to Know About Wills, Estates, Trusts, and Taxes, American Bar Association, Random House, 2004, 384 pages. Paperback

erations there was little room for this questioning. Times have changed. The pressures on economic survival, mobility, and two career families have eroded that connection for many families. Greater interest in going to college led to greater mobility and independence with children frequently leaving home after college. This often happened when their jobs took them to live in other parts of the country. The result was a shift from family connection to the pursuit of personal interests and less dependence on family. Robert and Elena learned the hard way to be more mindful about the attention they paid to what their elders had to say.

Changes in family financial status has also contributed to erosion of the family connection. Social Security retirement programs help elders be more financially independent. Medicare health insurance and long term care insurance have added to elder's independence. Poor families who do not have these opportunities become dependent on welfare and Medicaid. Elders are often involved in post-retirement activities as volunteering and educational programs that reduce the emotional dependence on their children or other family members.

Emotional connection between the generations is something else. Neither the younger members or the elders can accomplish this alone. The quality of emotional connection will depend on how well the generations are able to manage differences in what they expect from one another.

Everybody benefits when there is mutual respect for different ways of looking at things between the generations. Both groups should resist the temptation to criticize what doesn't fit their views. Elders may criticize young people because they live too much in the moment Young people may criticize older people because they are too slow to accept change. In both cases criticism shuts down taking seriously what the other group has to say. Both groups would be better off paying attention to what they can learn from each other than harping on their differences

Elders will be less upset when they understand that what worked for them may not work for the younger generation because they are living in different circumstances than was their experience. The same applies to young people in reverse. They will have an easier time when they understand that their elders may have a hard time appreciating their ideas and behavior because they didn't live under the conditions in which they live.

Instead both groups would do well to put a priority on finding common ground on their differing views. There will be times when common ground cannot be found. In those cases attention should be given in how to live respectfully with their differences.

Both generations have much to benefit from one another. The older generation can benefit from the energy, optimism, and stimulation from different points of view. The younger generations can benefit from the wisdom and experience of their elders. They can provide caring and support for helping this generation as they become established as adults. This involvement and openness will invite interest and emotional connections. This is all possible as long as both are respectful of one another without judgment and attempts to impose their respective views on one another. :

How to enhance relationships between generations

1. Recognize that there will be differences between the generations because they have had different life experiences. Robert and Elena learned that the differences may not always be as great as they seem.

2. Respect differences instead of judging them. Neither generation should try to impose what they believe important on the other one. Instead, differences are an opportunity to learn from one another.

3. Manage differences through discussion in which both generations explain how they feel. Sometimes one side can get the other to agree to its way of thinking. When this doesn't happen direct efforts at finding common ground acceptable to both generations.

4. Focus on how to respectfully live with these differences when common ground cannot be found.

5. Make time to share enjoyable experiences that include: anniversaries, birthdays, weddings, graduations, picnics, holidays, and just sharing day-to-day happenings. The good will that comes from these times will add incentive to working out differences.

6. Make an effort to help the other generation when needed. It might be the older generation giving encouragement, money, or advice when asked. For the younger generation it might be helping the older generation do things they are no longer able to do, take them to doctor appointments, and helping them learn how to use computers among others. These considerations help to build emotional connections.

7. Make the time for the generations to jointly step back every so often and consider how your relationships are doing in general. This is useful because annoyances happen that for one reason or another don't get talked about. This conversation can help clear the air. Otherwise these annoyances become resentments and can leak out in ways that cause problems that don't have to happen and become harder to solve when they do.

References:

The Sandwich Generation: Caught Between Growing Children and Aging Parents, H. Michael Zal, Da Capo, 2001, 272 pages. Paperback

Love, Power and Money: Family Business Between Generations, Dean R. Fowler, Glengrove Publishers, 2002, 161 pages. Paperback

Keep the Family Baggage Out of the Family Business: Avoiding the Seven Deadly Sins That Destroy Family Businesses, Quentin J Fleming, Fireside, 2000, 336 pages. Paperback

Boomers, Xers, and Other Strangers: Understanding the Generational Differences That Divide Us, Kathy Hicks, Ph.D. Focus on the Family Publishing, 1999, 384 pages. Paperback

Between Generations: Family Models, Myths, and Memories, Paul Thompson (Editor), Daniel Bertaux (Editor),Transaction Publishers, 2005,189 pages. Paperback

Americans at Midlife: Caught between Generations, Rosalie G. Genovese, Bergin & Garvey, 1997, 152 pages.

BLENDED FAMILIES

Francine and Edgar remarried to form a blended family composed of two of his children and three of hers from prior marriages. Francine's children lived with them. His children came frequently on weekends, some week nights and on some vacations.

Francine and Edgar got into frequent struggles when one or the other of their children got into trouble and the involved parent showed bias in favor of his/her child. This made for a chronic tenuous emotional climate and also stressed their marriage. Their struggle was picked up by their children and reflected in mistrust in the step parent and tension between their children. Eventually they recognized that thinking of their children as mine or yours was going to be destructive for everyone.

They decided that they would have to treat all of the children as though they came from the same parents. This was a challenge for all to manage. The parents had to resist the temptation to favor his/her children. This included being able to accept the other parent disciplining one of his/her children without being defensive or intervening. The children had to accept what the step parent said as though it was coming from his/her biological parent. It took some time to make the shift but once they did the emotional climate was much improved.

It took some time and struggle to work out relationships with ex-spouses. Francine's ex-husband had a hard time accepting another man parenting his children. He worried that their attachment to him would undermine the relationship with his children. Edgar was sensitive to this because he was in the same boat with regard to his children.

The other problem concerned getting the grandparents to make the same adjustment to treating all of the children as their own. At first each set of grandparents tended to favor their own grandchildren which created resentment and competition. They were able to make the transition with the consistent effort on the part of Francine and Edgar. Eventually, they were able to see that favoritism created problems for everybody that would have negative impact on their relationship to their grandchildren.

Yours, mine and hopefully ours is what blended families hope to accomplish. Every family has a personality, a characteristic way of behaving, in the same way we think of a person having a personality. One family may be, fun loving, easy going, committed to public service, while another one may be serious, and value the importance of following rules, work before play, and more.

When two families come together to live as one family they are faced with putting their "family personalities" together to form a new family personality that fits for all concerned. It takes time and patience to work out how all the different individual characteristics and different ways of doing things can work together.

It is often difficult to give up the familiar and find comfortable new ways of doing things. This happens because it is easier to stay with what you know than trying something with an uncertain outcome. This often leads to a competition in which each family tries to stay with what is familiar to them.

The best chance for making the transition occurs when the parents of the two families are committed to treating all of their children as though they were their biological children Both of you will need to develop a way to deal with your tendency to favor your own and to have a way of managing it if it doesn't happen. Plan on your children testing your resolve to see if you mean what you say. Francine and Edgar eventually got to this place after a period of trial and error.

An added complication to constructive blending occurs when relationships with ex-spouses are difficult. This may be a challenge, if not impossible, when a divorce has been acrimonious. Concerns of ex-spouses get hard to manage when their issues get expressed around how their child is being raised in the blended family. It can be difficult to sort out legitimate concerns from replaying old grievances. In either case it is for the benefit of all to find a way to overshadow past struggles with focus on coping in the present. Otherwise, the tensions will simmer and be expressed by the children to the detriment of everybody. Francine and Edgar were fortunate in being able to work out their relationship with ex-spouses without creating any significant problems.

Ways to achieve blended families

1. Have a prospective new spouse meet your children to see how they get along under a variety of circumstances. It is helpful when this includes potentially stressful as well as enjoyable times.

2. Bring the families together and see how things work out as a group. Again this should be done under different conditions. People are likely to behave differently when they are unhappy than when things are going well.

3. Check to see if there are likely to be problems in a combined family that might not be resolvable. This might be a clash of personalities, very different interests, or difficulty in being able to get along. This includes the couple's ability to avoid showing favoritism for his/her own children.

4. Discuss the possibility of marriage and get their feedback as not everyone expresses feelings easily about this happening. All questions should be encouraged and answered. The purpose is not to get their permission but to hear their concerns and decide whether there is anything they said that would argue against the marriage. Being a little frightened by the idea is to be expected. Children will have an easier time of it if they feel that their feelings are being considered.

5. Hold joint family meetings to talk about where you will live and how you will make decisions that affect them. All the children should be encouraged to state their needs and opinions. The understanding should be that both parents will try to pay attention to their respective concerns as much as possible. When this isn't possible they will at least know why things can't happen the way they would like.

6. Involve both sets of children in planning for the wedding and the part they will each play. Joint activities help build the blending. Special attention should be paid to making sure both families are being treated equally with respect to their age and ability to be involved.

7. Anticipate that an added consideration will be needed if either family had children of only one sex and the combined families will include both sexes. This may also apply if there is a wide discrepancy in age between the children.

8. The combined families should have regular family meeting to work out day-to-day concerns about scheduling, chores, doctors appointments and more. It is also a time to work out any problems. These meetings will work out better if they also include time to relax together with jokes, music, games after the business aspect is over.

9. Give careful thought to how you will work out relationships with ex-spouses. Anticipate what problems may occur and develop a strategy for how to deal with them. Avoid making judgments about ex-spouse motives. Assume positive intent when questions are raised until you have clear evidence to the contrary. Deal with any conflicts that may arise by keeping focused on the concerned behaviors and avoid making judgments about personality and especially generalizations. Making these judgments will only invite problems.

10. The blending will be happier for all when emphasis is put on "our family" rather your children or mine as much as possible.

11. Encourage extended family members not to make distinctions between your children based on whether they are related by blood.

References:

Becoming Family: How to Build a Stepfamily That Really Works, Robert H. Lauer, & Jeanette C. Lauer, Augsburg Fortress Publishers, 1999, 192 pages. Paperback

Yours, Mine, and Ours: How Families Change When Remarried Parents Have a Child Together, Anne C. Bernstein, 1990, 337 pages. Paperback

Blended Families: Creating Harmony as You Build a New Home Life, Maxine Marsolini, Moody Publishers, 2000, 272 pages. Paperback

Stepcoupling: Creating and Sustaining a Strong Marriage in Today's Blended Family, Susan Wisdom & Jennifer Green, Three Rivers Press, 2002, 272 pages. Paperback

Blending Families, Elaine Fantle Shimberg, Berkley Trade, 1999, 240 pages. Paperback

The Blended Family Sourcebook: A Guide to Negotiating Change, David S. Chedekel, & Karen O'Connell, McGraw-Hill, 2002, 176 pages. Paperback

CULTS AND THE FAMILY

Sara was a happy young lady as she prepared to go off to college. Her first two years were uneventful. She did well and enjoyed the experience. Things began to change in her senior year. Her parents began to get a sense of her distancing. At first they assumed this was part of growing up. Then the tone of her letters began to change. She seemed artificially happy. This was accompanied by reference to finding new enlightenment that was followed by the shocking revelation of having discovered Jesus. Her parents were dumbfounded to hear this from their Jewish daughter who had only a casual interest in religion.

It didn't take long for her parents to recognize that she was in a religious cult. The tension heightened when after a few months she announced an engagement to a dairy farmer whose background was totally alien to hers. This mobilized the parents to find some way to extricate her before they lost her. After an abortive effort they were able to engage an exit counselor who helped arrange an intervention to break the cult's hold on her. This did not go easily since the cult does not take kindly to the risk of losing a member. The intervention had to be conducted in clandestine fashion because it was expected they would come looking for her. It took place in a remote cabin in Maine with family members and an exit counselor. A week of educating Sara in the ways of the cult broke the cult's grip on her. This had to be followed by two weeks in a rehab center to help her make the transition.

Once the cult realized what was happening they came looking for her after filing kidnaping charges against her parents in three states. It took a year for group to stop pursuing her. Sara eventually returned to where she left off. She went to graduate school,

Having a family member in a cult is a devastating experience. This is especially the case when the personality that used to be has vanished. The person looks the same, but the personality is very different. This was the case with Sara.

A cult becomes destructive when the group has a charismatic leader and they use extreme and unethical techniques of manipulation to exploit it members for the benefits of its leadership. Cults are classified in six categories: Religious, Political, Therapy/Self-Awareness, Commerical, New Age, Satanic/Ritual Abuse

There are three major defining characteristics of cults.

- They have a charismatic leader who becomes increasingly the object of worship and abandoning of previous commitments. The organizing focus of the group is to some person, idea or thing. Unquestioned submission to the leader is required. This is necessary to gain the promised rewards of the group. The leader may be to a self appointed representative of God, a proponent of self actualization, self improvement, saving the hungry, or many others.

- The group uses thought reform or coercive persuasion to recruit and hold members

- The majority of families seeking help are normal and are concerned because they detect real and alarming changes in the cult-involved family member. The majority of cult members are psychologically normal. They do not become aware of the goals of the program until late in the process, if ever. This is accomplished through group efforts to recruit, assimilate members, control members' thoughts, feelings, and behavior by a complex pattern of rewards and intimidation. These techniques deprive indi-viduals of their ability to make a free choice and any sense of their own individuality.

- They exploit their members using idealism, financial and psychological manipulation. Members are expected to give or earn as much money for the group as possible. They use a variety of methods to heighten suggestability, subservience, and suspension of individual and critical judgement. They promote total dependency on the group. They attempt to instill fear of leaving the group by the threat that terrible things will happen to them or their families if they do so. The crisis in coping with having a family member be in a cult can often create other problems in the family. Cut-offs from family by a members who is in a cult can affect other family relationships in different ways:

Differences among family members in how to cope with the cut-off of a family member may create conflict between family members or amplify already existing tensions. They also may get involved in blaming one another for the cult membership. The occurrence of any of these conflicts are very disruptive to mobilizing family resources necessary for exiting the family member from the cult.

Coping When a Family Member is in a Cult

Be alert to characteristics that may give indication of a cult presence. It becomes evident in the behavior change in the family member who is in a cult. These behaviors range from subtle to very obvious. They include:

- *Secret behavior:* There is a noticeable change in the family member's effort at behaving as though they had something to hide. Attempts to discuss this are met with denial and some apparent discomfort.

  Change in vocabulary or speech pattern: A change in speech pattern and introduction of some new language. This may include reference to religion in new ways.

- *Emotional changes:* An open friendly manner becomes flat and removed. This was the first indication that something had changed with Sara.

- *Shift in friends and activities:* A noticeable shift is observed to new friends that are not brought home who seem quite different. Old friends are cast aside. Any question about this is dismissed, often with irritation.

- *Dubious financial activities:* There may be shift in spending patterns. Any comment about this is rejected.

- *Disturbing sexual attitudes:* A shift in attitudes towards sexual behavior in a disturbing direction.

- *Abrupt marital decisions:* A precipitous decision is made about the person's marriage. There appears to be a shift of investment from the marriage to some other interest which may or may not be defined.

- *Shifts in religious, philosophical, or political views:* There is a noticeable shift in these views with a categorical and critical quality in favor of a more constricted more platitudinal direction.

- *Extreme commitments:* Commitments are made to do things in a more extreme form. This may include being involved in activities that require a high degree of emotional and physical commitment.

- *Unconventional life style:* There is a shift to interest and practice in an unconventional life style.

- *Changes in appearance:* There is a noticeable change in appearance. This may include dress, demeanor, hair style and way of walking.

- *Vocational turnabouts:* There may be radical shift in vocational interest from what may have been a long standing interest. The explanation for the shift is likely to be vague and intense.

- *Indications of psychological stress:* There is a noticeable shift in stress level which may result from the conflict of dealing with the shift from pre-existing attitudes to new ones which are only partially adopted.

- *Diminished academic performance:* There is a noticeable shift in interest and academic performance. This may be expressed as viewing academics as too limited in service to a more idealistic and vague commitment.

Keep in contact with the cult member by observing the following:

- Maintain contact with the cult member in whatever form is possible no matter how rejecting he may be. Breaking contact out of anger or sense of futility supports the groups propaganda.

- Avoid direct criticism of the cult. To do reinforces the cult view anything outside group is bad, the work of the devil. Non-religious cults have their own unique way of conveying the same message.

- Focus on at being friendly, sharing news of family, missing his/her presence.

- Show interest in understanding the group. This is a way to keep contact.

- Being confused is helpful in getting the cult member to think critically without being directly critical.

- Maintaining contact is helpful in gaining the cult member's cooperation in exiting group.

Contact the International Cultic Studies Association for any information about cults. They can also help you in identifying whether a group may be a cult.

International Cultic Studies Association (ISCA)
P.O. Box 2265
Bonita Springs, FL 34133
 email: mail@icsamail.com
web page: http://www.iscahome.com
Telephone (239) 514-3031

References:

Cults in Our Midst: The Continuing Fight Against Their Hidden Menace, Margaret Thaler Singer, Jossey-Bass, 2003, 400 pages. Paperback

Combatting Cult Mind Control: Guide to Protection, Rescue, and Recovery from Destructive Cults, Steven Hassan, Park Street Press, 1990, 256 pages. Paperback

Recovery from Cults: Help for Victims of Psychological and Spiritual Abuse, by Michael D. Langone (Editor), W. W. Norton & Company, 1995, 432 pages. Paperback

Take Back Your Life: Recovering from Cults and Abusive Relationships, Janja Lalich, Bay Tree Publishing, 2006, 376 pages. Paperback

Malignant Pied Pipers of Our Time: A Psychological Study of Destructive Cult Leaders from Rev. Jim Jones to Osama bin Laden, Peter A. Olsson M.D., Publish America, 2005, 205 pages.

Bounded Choice: True Believers and Charismatic Cults, Janja A. Lalich, University of California, 2004, 353 pages. Paperback

Thought Reform and the Psychology of Totalism: A Study of Brainwashing in China, Robert Jay Lifton, University of N. Carolina Press, 1989, 528 pages.

DUAL CAREER COUPLES

Ethan and Ellen were engrossed in their careers. When they got married Ethan was just out of law school and Ellen was in her senior year. They started out with the usual expectation that Ellen would work until they started a family. After graduation, Ellen got an unexpected opportunity for a great job from an Ad Agency in marketing. She was talented and in charge of an important account within a couple of years . She became invested in having a career which stressed their relationship since it meant that Ethan would have to share more responsibility for running their household than he intended.

Ethan could buy the idea of sharing responsibilities but it was much harder for him to put this in practice. He grew up in a family where women did all of the household chores. He faced the double problem of doing things he hadn't expected to do in addition to having little skill in doing them. At the beginning of their marriage he didn't even know how to turn on the washing machine.

Adding to their struggle was working out priorities when the demands of their respective careers conflicted. Eventually, they agreed to treat each of their careers as equally important. Once this was done they were able to adjust the demands of their careers so there were minimal struggles. Adjusting to the arrival of children was made much easier because they had settled the career issue and how to work out a division of labor once Ellen resumed her career.

Life was much simpler in earlier times when family life was neatly defined. The man earned the money to support the family. He worked his eight or ten hour day on a regular basis. His wife ran the home and took care of the children. Their were clear expectations on what they each did.

Since then life has become more complicated. Women can get educated and be as competent as men and aspire to have their own careers. Both you and your spouse may work long hours and often have work related travel. Ethan and Ellen learned that marriage becomes more complicated when dual careers press for redefining models of managing a family. This was particularly difficult for Ethan and took awhile to make the needed adjustment.

As a couple, you face the challenge of effecting a division of labor that requires frequent readjustment as your careers and needs of your children change. The pressures of daily life and full schedules for both of you and your children leave little time for individual needs and comfortable family time. It was a struggle for Ethan to give Ellen's career equal status.

Managing a dual career couple

1. Respect that both of you have careers you desire to pursue.
2. Decide on whether they are of equal importance of if one is to be subordinate to the other.
3. Decide on the life style acceptable to both of you and define the needed division of labor between you to make it happen.
4. Anticipate how crises in your careers or with your children might be managed to meet ongoing needs of family.
5. Resolve problems as they occur. Procrastination will only make them harder to solve. Satisfactory resolution requires finding solutions acceptable to all concerned.
6. Periodically take the time to step back and assess how well current arrangements are working. Use this time to express any concerns that attention of day-to-day demands did not permit. This will avoid the build up of tensions that may leak out in undesirable ways.

References:

Work Won't Love You Back: The Dual Career Couple's Survival Guide, Stevan E. Hobfoll & Ivonne H. Hobfoll, W.H. Freeman & Company, 1994, 277 pages.

Careers of Couple s in Contemporary Society: From Male Breadwinner to Dual-Earner Families, Hans-Peter Blossfeld, (Editor), Sonja Drobnivc, Oxford

Coupled Careers, Wim Bernasco, Purdue University Press, 2003, 217 pages. Paperback

It's About Time: Couples and Careers, Phyllis Moen, ILR Press Books, 2003, 436 pages. Paperback

Being Together, Working Apart: Dual- Career Families and the Work-Life Balance, Barbara Schneider, (Editor), Linda J. Waite, Cambridge University Press, 2005, 578 pages.

The Second Shift, Arlie Hochschild, Anne Machung, Penguin, 2003, 352 pages. Paperback

The Time Bind: When Work Becomes Home and Home Becomes Work, Arlie Russell Hochschild, Owl Books, 2001, 336 pages. Paperback

FAMILY MANAGER

Irene and Calvin were parents of Rudy, 14 and Clara,11. Irene grew up in a family where everybody worked together to maintain a home. They worked well together for the most part in that family. She gained a sense of responsibility and competence from that experience. Her family also shared many good times together.

Calvin grew up in quite a different environment. He was an only indulged child. He had minimal responsibilities for contributing to the welfare of the family and often reneged on them with minimal objections or consequences from his parents.

Irene and Calvin had struggle working out a division of labor in managing their household when they got married. Calvin agreed in principal that he should share household responsibilities, but it was hard for him to overcome the impact of his childhood to behave in a more responsible way. After some struggle and Irene's persistence they worked out an acceptable relationship.

This battle had to be fought again when their children were old enough to perform household duties. Calvin would be inconsistent. He would vacillate between being too demanding and too lenient. Irene's efforts eventually paid off as the family managed to find a way to work together in getting all the needed chores done.

Being a manager is making sure that your children know how to do what is assked of them and the assignment gets finished in a timely way. This happens in business and in the family. Managing is also about partnership which requires people work together to get needed chores done. This usually includes agreement on what each person will do to make it happen.

Parents are managers in their families. It is your joint responsibility as parents' to see that the family gets what it needs for their welfare, education, and safety. You train their children in how to be good family members and prepare them for becoming a responsible adults and parents if they choose to have their own family.

Being an effective manager

1. Decide what tasks need to be done.

2. Decide what information and skill is needed to complete each job

3. Decide on the importance of each job so that the most important things get done first in case it is not possible to get done all that is needed.

4. Make sure each person knows how to do his assigned job

5. Teach children they are expected to help out in family chores as best they can because they are a member of the family.

6. Define expectations in behavioral terms so there is no doubt about what is expected.

7. Parents make sure each member of the family does what they say they will do.

8. Adjust expectations to age, experience and maturity.

9. Have weekly family meetings to make sure things are getting done the way as need, solve any problems, and let people known when they have done a good job.

10. Liberal use of humor is a useful tool that makes it easier to do jobs, especially when they are boring.

11. Pay as much attention to giving affirmations as you do criticism.

12. Teach your children basic survival skills: how to cook, sew, do laundry, manage minor repairs, and how to manage their time and money wisely.

References:

The Family Manager Takes Charge: Getting on the Fast Track to a Happy, Organized Home, Kathy Peel, Perigee Trade, 2003, 384 pages. Paperback

The Organized Parent : 365 Simple Solutions to Managing Your Home, Your Time, and Your Family's Life, Christina Baglivi Tinglof, McGraw-Hill, 2002, 256 pages. Paperback

The emerging role of the work-family manager, Arlene A Johnson, Conference Board, 1992, 30 pages.

Family Manager's Guide for Working Moms, Kathy Peel, Ballantine Books, 1997, 224 pages. Paperback

FAMILY MEETINGS

Jacob and Grace had three children Kyle 15, Carol 13, and Wendy 11. Jacob had a demanding job as a buyer for a supermarket company. Grace worked full time selling woman's clothing. They had been indulgent parents, both having grown up in

poor families. They wanted their children to have things better than they did. Having a good education for their children was very important to them. This resulted in Grace having to do most of the work in managing the home. Everybody agreed in principal to helping out but it took Grace acting as a drill sergeant to get anything done. This did not sit well with her. It didn't suit her personality or her skills.

One day it got to her! She felt burned out from work and family responsibilities and abused by her family. She blew up at them all and was particularly angry at Jacob. She sat the whole family down and told them how she felt and blamed herself for letting it go so long. She was on strike! Things had to change. She decided that they would have weekly meetings to assign chores and work out schedules. Having to do homework was no longer an excuse for not doing chores!

Family meetings serve the same purpose for families that staff meetings serve in business: a time to share information and work together in accomplishing a common goal of having a good outcome for everybody's benefit . The need for these meetings in business is taken for granted. Not so in families who often find it hard to get everybody together given busy schedules. This gets even harder when meetings become unpleasant.

These meetings play an important part in helping develop and maintain a sense of connection as a family. There are two types of family meetings which may or may not be combined depending on a family's ability to manage them.

The first type of family meeting is a logistical one; Who is doing what chores. Working out schedules for doctor's appointments, sports events, or any other activity that requires family members to be somewhere at a particular date and time. This can usually be done in a short period of time.

The second type is more challenging. The focus in these meetings is on problem solving. It usually involves problem behavior. This may be parents concern about a child's behavior or difficulties between siblings. Grace could have saved herself aggravation if she called a family meeting when she first began to feel beleaguered.

Family meetings will be easier to come by when they also include time for humor and pleasant exchanges. Having this balance helps to make dealing with the less pleasant issues easier to manage.

Conducting family meetings

1. Establish a regular time for family meetings that everyone accepts as a priority.

2. Have an agenda for each meeting. Have a procedure for each family member being able to add to the agenda.

3. It is helpful to have parents alternate responsibility for preparing the agenda for this meeting. This shares the responsibility and also provides a good role model for the children. Children should also be included in the responsibility of preparing the agenda as their maturity permits. This will also help them

to be more invested in the meetings and help develop skills they will find useful in other efforts.

4. Determine whether family meetings can combine organizational matters with problem management ones.

5. In general, it is useful to have all members present for problem management meetings even when a child is not involved in the problem. Doing this may benefit the non-involved child by learning from a sibling's experience. However, there may be times when private meetings with a child are appropriate.

6. End each meeting with some positive interchange with songs, jokes, games or any other mutually enjoyable interchange.

7. Family meetings help to avoid the build up of tensions that weren't settled that would likely erupt into conflicts that are much harder to resolve. It also provides children with the security that issues of concern have a place to be addressed. This avoids the difficulty that sometimes happens when a child feels his stated concern gets acknowledged but never gets the time to be addressed.

References:

Our Family Meeting Book: Fun and Easy Ways to Manage Time, Build Communication, and Share Responsibility Week by Week, Elaine Hightower & Betsy Riley, Free Spirit Publishing, 2002, 136 pages. Paperback

Raising Kids Who Can: Using Family Meetings to Nurture Responsible, Cooperative, Caring and Happy Children, Betty Lou Bettner, 1st HarperPerennial edition, 1992, 160 pages.Paperback

Raising Kids Who Can: Become Responsible, Self-Reliant, Resilient, Contributing Adults and How to Use Family Meetings to Make It Happen, Amy Lew & Betty Lou Bettner, Connexions Press, 2005. Paperback

Family Table Time Kit: A Weekly Family Meeting Kit That's Simple, Practical and Fun, Kimball Family, Family Communications Institute, 2002, 24 pages. Paperback

Family Meeting Handbook: Achieving Family Harmony Happily, Robert Slagle , Family Relations Foundation, 1985, 161 pages. Paperback

HOMOSEXUALITY IN THE FAMILY

Burton and Rose looked forward to visiting their son, Josh, at Harvard. They were proud of him for how well he was doing. Their joy quickly turned into shock

and shame when Josh informed them that he was gay. They were a very traditional couple for whom homosexuality was something 'out there' that was totally foreign in their environment of family and friends. They were caught between their love for their child and their hurt and anger that he could do this to them. They knew very little about homosexuality except that it was seen as something perverse and alien in their environment.

They got a referral from their doctor in Detroit to me in Boston. The three of them came to see me for help in how to adjust to this crisis. Their was no question of their loyalty to their son whom they loved dearly. They needed to understand how this could happen. They needed to come to terms with all of the implications. What will they tell their friends and family? How will they deal with the shame? What will they say at weddings and other occasions when asked about asked about the grandchildren they won't have? They were too flooded to give any consideration for what all of this meant to Josh.

Homosexuality makes a lot of people very uncomfortable. They see it critically as perverse, against God, an attack on marriage, unnatural, a deviant choice, caused by the wrong upbringing, and others. Orthodox religions take a dim view of homosexuality.

Lack of understanding about the source of homosexuality leads to making assumptions and catering to biases. Many people feel homosexuality is a bad choice caused by the wrong environment. Emotions block realization that a person may be born with an inclination towards homosexuality. Supporting this view is the sheer number of homosexuals at all levels of society. In addition many people are threatened by the life style and concern it will somehow undermine the family. Fear blocks reason.

Families with a homosexual member have to come to terms with their own anxieties as well as the reactions of people outside of the family. Parents struggle with guilt about what part they may have played this occurring. This has diminished as the hysteria about homosexuality diminishes and more attention is paid to the possibility of genetic influence. Nevertheless, the struggle continues. Parents, like Burton and Rose, are concerned about how this will impact their child's life. At the same time they begin to mourn the loss of grandchildren that would occur under normal circumstances. The homosexual child gains freedom from having to pretend his sexual preference at the expense of having to deal with the prejudice that goes with it. A family with a homosexual member requires major adjustments by everyone.

Family Adjustment to Homosexuality

For the homosexual member:

1. Declare your homosexual preference if you haven't already come out. Don't apologize for it.

2. Respect that this maybe upsetting to your family. Give them time to cope

with their feelings. They may say hurtful things that should be heard as an expression of their discomfort. This will be hard to do, but is in the best interest of all of you making the necessary adjustment. They are having to make a complex adjustment at many levels. Treat any angry comments as a statement about their anxiety and not to be taken literally.

3. Once the initial reaction has diminished, start what will likely be an ongoing dialogue about how you and your family will adjust to your new situation. This will not be a quick fix. It will take time for all of you to sort out how each of you will deal this change.

4. Eventually you will likely find a partner. You will need to negotiate with your family how they will relate to this person.

For family members:

1. Accept that homosexuality is not a matter of choice.

2. Accept what you feel without judgment.

3. Make the opportunity to express your feelings both individually and jointly

4. Discuss what kind of issues need to be addressed and how they will be managed. This will include helping the homosexual member with his/her own adjustment and how this will affect relationships to the other family members.

5. Talk to other families facing the same situation and learn from their experience.

6. Adjustment to this new situation will take time.

References:

When Homosexuality Hits Home: What to Do When a Loved One Says They're Gay, Joe Dallas, Harvest House Publishers, 2004, 192 pages. Paperback

Now That You Know: What Every Parent Should Know About Homosexuality, Betty Fairchild & Nancy Hayward, Harcourt, 1989, 276 pages. Paperback

Beyond Acceptance: Parents of Lesbians & Gays Talk About Their Experiences, Carolyn W. Griffin & Marian J. Wirth St. Martin's Griffin, 1997, 256 pages. Paperback

Homosexuality and Family Relations, Frederick W. Bozett (Editor), Marvin B. Sussman, Haworth Press, 1990, 52 pages.

Modern Homosexualities: Fragments of Lesbian and Gay Experience, Ken Plummer, Routledge, 1992, 304 pages. Paperback

Marvin Snider, Ph.D.

Kelly and Carl were happy in their three year marriage until they began to experience in-law problems. Kelly feels her mother-in-law resented her because she interrupted the close relationship she had with Carl. This causes a problem in their marriage because Carl lets himself be manipulated by his mother's frequent calls for him to come help her with one problem or another. Carl gets caught between guilt putting his mother off and Kelly's anger if lets it happen too often.

Carl loves his mother but he gets annoyed with her when she becomes intrusive in their lives. Her well intended advice and judgment about how they run their house often gets annoying. Kelly's difficulty in setting limits on her mother in-law adds to the problem. His mother gets offended when they are less than appreciative of her efforts to be helpful.

Contrary to popular view, marriage usually involves more than two people. It involves the marital couple and the relationship to their families. Each spouse has a relationship with the family of his/her spouse. The quality of both of these relationships can have a major impact on of the life of the marital couple. Ideally, there is the possibility of creating a happy community composed of the marital couple and both of their extended families including all the aunts, uncles and cousins.

But this will not happen if either family tries to intrude on how the couple manage their relationship as Kelly soon learned. It also happens if either family objects to the marriage and if the two families do not get along. Objecting to a child's choice of marital partner is one thing. What you do with your feelings is something else. You face the choice of taking your feelings out on the marital couple which will eventually create problems in the marriage or encourage the couple to distance from you to protect their relationship. This approach will also affect the access and quality of relationship you will have with grandchildren. Most families fall in between the extremes of blissful happiness and those who don't get along. These are families that don't find too much in common but find a way to get along for the times they are together.

A more promising approach is to accept your child's choice of spouse and focus your efforts on how to develop a welcoming relationship to this new member of your family. This will involve negotiating whatever concerns you may have that is acceptable to both you and your son-in-law or daughter in-law. This works well when he/she is able to feel accepted and treated as member of the family and not as an unwelcome guest that has to be tolerated.

The same applies to the way the couple's respective families get along. They need to build on their common interests and not focus on judging their differences. This gets more difficult but still possible when there are major differences in social class, religion, race, and ethnic background or life style. It comes down to the choice of making the most of what is possible or catering to your prejudices. At stake is the quality of relationship you want to have with your child and especially with your grandchildren.

The marrying couple also share responsibility for making the in-law relationship work. This was hard for Carl to manage. It will be easier for you, as a spouse to accept responsibility for your part in whether you are acceptable to your spouse-to-be's family. But even so when this isn't the case, make a good faith effort to at least have a civil relationship. You can do this by being sensitive to what is important to them. When differences occur on significant issues, negotiate resolutions that are acceptable to both of you. Consensus will pay off far better than trying to win your point.

Women tend to have more difficulty with in-law relationships with their mother-in-laws. There are multiple reasons for this including a mothers fear of a diminished connection when sons marry and felt competition in matters of maintaining a home and raising children.

The marital couple can play a major role in helping their respective families get along. Avoid complaining to your family about any felt complaints of your spouse's family. Ensure that both families get equal attention. This will be more challenging when your interests coincide more with one family than the other. Let your family know about the good things of your spouse's family in a way that doesn't invite competition.

Working on in-law relationships for parents

1. Focus on the positive qualities of your son-in-law or daughter in-law. Don't harbor resentments of your child's spouse. Let him/her know when you are bothered by a particular behavior in a respectful way you would do with a peer. The goal is work out something acceptable to both of you.

2. Treat him/her with the same regard as you do your own child. This will likely invite the same kind of behavior in return.

3. Don't ask your child's spouse to be accountable for the behavior of his/her family. It is a good idea to avoid asking him/her to act in your behalf with his/her family. It is best to take up any concerns directly with the person involved when possible.

4. Make an effort to get to know your child's spouse by spending one-to-one time with him/her.

5. Don't use your child's spouse as a sounding board for complaints about your spouse or other family members. This puts him/her in an awkward spot.

Working on in-law relationships for marital couple

1. Recognize that you are probably changing the relationship between your spouse and his/her parents. Mothers often feel a diminished relationship when a son marries. This will be the case when he has had a close relationship with his parents and especially with his mother. This was part of Carl's mother's concern. Attending to her needs affirmed his continuing love for her.

2. Behave in ways that demonstrate that any concerns your in-laws had about you as an unacceptable spouse for their child were unfounded.

3. Don't defend your family's behavior. You are not accountable for what they do.

4. Be respectful when your in-laws give you criticism or suggestions you don't want. Let them know that you appreciate their concern but you have other ways or ideas that work for you.

5. Try to be as fair as you can in being sure both families feel they are treated equally.

6. Keep in mind that family relations will be happier when the priority is on finding agreement rather than winning your point of view when you have disagreements.

7. Be respectful of both family's values and participate in major family events often enough to convey respect for what is important to them.

References:

The In-Law Survival Manual, A Guide to Cultivating Healthy In-Law Relationships, Gloria Call Horsley, Wiley, 2001, 288 pages. Paperback

Toxic In-Laws: Loving Strategies for Protecting Your Marriage, Susan Forward, Harper Paperbacks, 2002, 304 pages. Paperback

When Difficult Relatives Happen to Good People: Surviving Your Family and Keeping Your Sanity, Leonard Felder, Rodale Books, 2005, 304 pages. Paperback

Mothers-in-Law and Daughters-in-Law: Love, Hate, Rivalry and Reconciliation, Susan Shapiro Barash, New Horizon Press, 2001, 224 pages. Paperback

The Daughter-In-Law's Survival Guide: Everything You Need to Know About Relating to Your Mother-In-Law, Eden Unger Bowditch and Aviva Samet, New Harbinger Publications, 2002, 166 pages.

MANAGING MONEY

Ellen grew up in a family where her parents had a traditional division of labor: her father managed the money and her mother managed the home. She grew up with little awareness or expectation in how to manage money. This did not present a problem until she left home to be on her own. Initially, she was overwhelmed when faced with having to learn about budgets, banking, saving and giving thought to her financial future. She wished she had been better prepared.

Her father managed the family's finances which worked well until tragedy struck when he had a massive heart attack and died. Once her mother, Joyce, got past adjusting to the traumatic loss of her husband of forty years, she was faced with another trauma. She knew nothing about their finances! She didn't know what money or other assets they had or where to find them. She hadn't paid a bill in years. They had been comfortable financially so she never had to think much about budgets. She knew things would have to be different now. With the help of family, her attorney and accountant she gradually got her financial life in order. She urged her children to learn from her experience to not depend on someone else to manage their finances without their knowing how to do it themselves.

Careful money management provides financial security for the family. This works best when both parents are able to work together on how money is managed. This is desirable even though one spouse manages day-to-day expenses and other financial matters. Making joint decisions on management of money helps to build a commitment to shared responsibility and thereby avoid a common source of conflict in couples.

In past generations, it was common for men to worry about managing money and for women to manage the home. This is no longer the case. Two income families have changed this. Now days, there is more sharing of all aspects of running a home by parents: earning income, managing money, cooking, laundry, cleaning and everything else.

There is another important reason why both spouses should work together. When women weren't involved in managing money, they would find themselves in a desperate place if something unexpected happened to their husband. They were lost in knowing enough about what money or other assets they had or little idea about how to manage them. Joyce learned this the hard way.

The need for this awareness is even more important in the present time with two income families when managing money is more complicated. Both spouses should know what assets they have and where they are. It is also a useful idea to have bank accounts in both names so both spouses have immediate access to them if something happened to one spouse. This will be a little uncomfortable if the marriage is in a rocky place and there is a trust problem between spouses.

You also have an obligation to teach your children how to manage money. This is a very necessary part of their education they can learn from you. Ellen's adult life would have been less difficult when she first started out on her own had she been better prepared. She would have benefitted by better preparation from her parents. This would have been accomplished by regularly observing her parents on a day-to-day basis. It would also have been helpful to be able to ask questions and be guided in the use of money as she was growing up. . Children benefit from listening to how parents discuss money and make decisions in its use.

It is natural for you to want to provide your children with what they want.

This is especially the case for parents who want their children to have what they didn't have growing up or what they just want them to have. Do this in a way that doesn't encourage a sense of entitlement that would contradict any teaching of money management. Requiring children to have jobs helps them learn what is involved in earning money. Requiring them to earn money for things they want is also instructive. Families who live beyond their means create false expectations and lead to conflicts that arise from accumulating debt that will threaten family stability.

Families with less means often have an easier time teaching the management of money. Limited income forces everybody to be more aware of how they spend their money and to be sensitive to one another's needs. It also encourages more respect for the things that money can buy. Children are encouraged to work and gain respect for any contributions they are able to make for the welfare of the family.

Ways to manage finances

1. Hold monthly meetings to review current expenses, agree on the payment of bills, monitor expenses, and discuss any matters relating to balancing income with expenses.

2. Hold periodic meetings with children when they are old enough. This provides an opportunity for educating them about money management, setting priorities for expenses, need for savings, and more. They should be held accountable for how they manage money.

3. Hold quarterly meetings with your spouse to discuss long term finances as investments, retirement, college expenses, weddings, and other special occasions.

4. Both spouses should be fully informed about all aspects of family assets and how to manage them. Spouses who leave financial matters to their other spouse find themselves very vulnerable and overwhelmed when something happens to their spouse and they have little knowledge of existing assets and how to manage them.

5. Strike a balance between current expenses and saving for the future. This includes enjoying their assets versus building an estate for your children.

6. Teach children in your behavior how to manage money.

7. Encourage your children to have jobs appropriate for their age to help them learn respect for what it takes to earn money. This will also serve to have them pay for things they want that you don't think you should provide. You may feel this is a good idea even for things you can provide but feel it would be in your child's interest to pay for it himself.

8. Teach children to balance short term spending and saving for the future.

Having a savings account will help do this. It is also helpful to require some part of earnings be put into savings.

9. Limit the amount of money your children have available for their spending. Having too much money available can be a handicap in learning how to manage money in a responsible way. Have them put any excess in savings.

10. Teach your children the proper use of credit cards. They are very useful and convenient when used responsibly. It gets easy to treat them like cash while forgetting that they are a loan. A good rule of thumb is not to charge anything that you can't pay off in full each month. If this is not possible, a commitment should be made for when it will be paid off and to limit any further credit card spending.

References:

Worry-Free Family Finances: Three Steps to Building and Maintaining Your Family's Financial Well-Being, Bill Staton (Author), Mary Staton, McGraw-Hill, 2003, 246 pages. Paperback

Family Finance: The Essential Guide for Pa rents, Ann Douglas &, Elizabeth Lewin, Dearborn Trade, 2001, 251 pages. Paperback

J.K. Lasser's Managing Your Family Finances, J.K. Lasser, Simon & Schuster, 1976.

Managing family finances with an irregular income, Diane Marie Fiedler, Agricultural Extension Service, University of Wyoming 1983

Yes You Can… Afford To Raise A Family, Sam Goller, Andrews McMeel, Publishing, 2004, 256 pages.

PRESENT FUTURE BALANCE

Janet and Arthur were in a discussion at a recent dinner party that got them thinking about their future. They were in their mid-thirties and married for eight years. They had been so busy in the day-to-day business of family and career that they hadn't had much time to think about the future.

One couple talked about the importance of living frugally so they could plan for their future. The other couples questioned their sacrificing their present live style for an unknown future. They were concerned about the unexpected events that can come up with illness, economic hard times, and the steady increase of college tuition. The discussion turned to how to strike a balance between present and future concerns.

This got Jane and Arthur talking about their situation. The discussion led them

Marvin Snider, Ph.D.

to consider whether they were satisfied with the balance they had between their current life style and how they planned for the future. They concluded they have been a little zealous in planning for their children's education and retirement at the expense of how they lived in the present. They agreed they should pay more attention to their current life style. There was room to do more of the traveling that they enjoyed and pay more attention to replacing some of their old furniture. They thought it would be helpful to consult with a financial planner to check out the feasibility of the revised plans.

How much do you want to sacrifice in your current life style to provide for whatever future you hope to have? This is a much harder question for a married person than if you are single. Both married and single people have to provide for old age, medical care, and how they would like to spend their retirement. Both have to worry about how they will support whatever life style they want to have and what it will take to get it.

A married person has more uncertain questions to consider. He has to take these same questions into account for the members of his family. Having children presses parents to provide a home, food and shelter for their family. They also need to make room in providing for their children's education and planning for retirement. How much attention should be given to building an estate? Attending to these concerns will help you decide how divide your attention between living in the present and the future.

People who don't ask this question set themselves up for an uncertain and probably disappointing future. This happens when you get too busy living in the present while assuming that the future will take care of itself. You are likely to find yourself in a very difficult place if you are unexpectedly faced with medical or financial problems you can't handle. Jane and Arthur did not want to take this risk.

To avoid getting in this kind of predicament requires time and attention to working out some form of plan. Getting help from a financial planner can be helpful in deciding how to strike a reasonable balance for your financial situation.

Achieving a present-future balance

1. Consider present-future balance both for an individual and for the family as a whole. This includes quality of relationships, work, leisure activities, community involvement and others. Pay attention on how to work out these interests that don't cause problems for one another.

2. These present-future balance views are not static and will need to be reviewed on an ongoing basis as needs and circumstances change.

3. Whenever possible children should be consulted for their views. This will improve the probability of finding conclusions that create the least amount of friction. On the positive side, they will improve the quality of relationships.

4. Keep in mind that conclusions may be less important than how you arrive

at them. Being consulted about things that affect you will get a lot better hearing when this is not so. This happens even when the conclusions are not to your liking

References:

Creating Your Future: Personal Strategic Planning for Professionals, George L. Morrisey, Berrett-Koehler Publishers, 1992, 196 pages. Paperback

Person-centered planning: Finding directions for change using personal futures planning : a sourcebook of values, ideals, and methods to encourage person-centered development, Beth Mount, Capacity Works, 2000, 80 pages.

Personal analysis and future planning, Allene B Hassell, Hunter Pub, 1956, 414 pages.

The Parent's Crash Course in Career Planning, M. Harris, McGraw-Hill, 192 pages, 1997, 192 pages. Paperback

HEALTH

Marvin Snider, Ph.D.

DEALING WITH LOSS

Lucy and Kurt were enjoying a close marital relationship for forty-three years when Kurt died of a sudden heart attack as he was standing at the pharmacy counter. Lucy was devastated. It was as though part of her died with him. Her first reaction was disbelief! Maybe it was a bad dream. Once she overcame the initial shock she questioned whether he really died. This was followed by anger at Kurt for deserting her. Once the funeral and the formal mourning period were over, she dwelt on reliving the highlights of all those good years together. These memories were both warming and depressing. Also helpful was the caring and support from the children as they cloaked her with loving attention. She appreciated all they did but it didn't do much to lessen the feelings of loss. She was nagged by wondering whether she could have done anything that would have made a difference.

Eventually she realized the need to think about how to spend the rest of her life. Attention had to be given to whether living alone was desirable and what to do with her time. She knew needed to be busy or face more depression and illness. Lucy missed Kurt but wasn't ready to join him.

She decided to do volunteer work and spend more time helping out with her grandchildren. It was enjoyable to watch them grow up and had missed not spending more time with them.

Losing something important hurts. Most difficult is losing a loved one or close friend. This may also apply to a career, pets, prized possessions or anything else that has had great meaning. Pay attention to your feelings as you cope with your loss and the meaning it has for you. Your reaction is even more challenging when the loss is unexpected as was the case with Kurt's heart attack. It also happens in the case of a fatal accident.

Dr. Kubler-Ross has described the stages that one usually experiences when this happens: shock, denial, anger, guilt, bargaining, depression, and acceptance which is easier when replacement of the loss seems possible.

A person in shock needs time and support to vent his feelings without judgment. It is not helpful for anyone to discourage or shorten the time needed for this expression.

Getting mad at a person who died may seem odd to an onlooker. It isn't logic but heartfelt feeling at what is causing pain from loss. An onlooker can be helpful by focusing on supporting the expression of feelings rather than the logic of what is being said. The same would apply to all other types of losses.

The anger often gives way to guilt. This may happen if a person feels some responsibility for what happened because of what he did or didn't do. Initially, you might be sympathetic to hearing the feelings. This should be gradually followed by comments that help manage the guilt. Back off if the bereaved person isn't able to pay attention to what you are saying. Try again when the person seems more able to talk about his guilt.

Sometimes people try to bargain with God as a way to deal with the the loss. Once the emotion is vented the futility of the effort gives way to depression and a sense of helplessness. During this time you gradually come to terms with the reality of what has happened. A bystander can be helpful by being a patient witness to the expression of feelings. Making comforting comments may also be useful. Do not take offense if the bereaved does not offer acknowledgment of these efforts. In some situations you may be the recipient of some of the anger that is vented at the death. This should not be taken personally as the bereaved is not behaving out of logic but venting feelings at any available target.

Losses gradually becomes accepted. This happens slowly. The time frame can be from the time of the loss to months or even years. In some extreme situations it may never happen. People close to the bereaved can help by keeping in contact and encouraging the mourner to engage in activities that help the person redefine his life situation without the lost loved one. This was a very difficult transition for Lucy. Finding replacements for the her loss of Kurt helped her move on with her life. A person who seems unable to make the adjustment should be encouraged to seek professional help.

Coming to grips with a loss is less complicated when the loss is a temporary one. This may be a job, a lost opportunity, a pet or a prized possession. The acceptance and availability of replacement makes coping with the loss easier. Adjustment to a loss is also made easier when it can be anticipated as it gives time to prepare for its impact and planning for how to adjust to it and consider replacement possibilities.

Coping is harder when replacement of the relationship is not considered an option. He/she will have to find a life without a partner.

Adjusting to a loss

1. A loss you can anticipate gives an opportunity to prepare for it happening. This occurs in the case of terminal illness or the occurrence of some other major event. It could also happen in a marriage that has failed or a close friend who is moving to some distant place.

2. There often is a tendency to focus on prayer and hope when someone is seriously ill. This can be helpful but should not be the only thing to do. One should also consider preparing for the loss. Being supportive to an ill person is both a help to that person and is satisfying to the person giving help. Another possibility is to guess what it will be like to miss the ill person and begin give to prepare for it happening and how to cope with it.

3. A person should give himself time, and space to do the grieving when the loss occurs. This is the time to vent whatever feelings are present in a safe place both alone and with others as comfort and circumstances permit. This is not a time to 'keep a stiff upper lip".

4. There is no set time for mourning. Each person needs to follow his own needs. It is not a good idea to hide your own mourning to protect someone else. Those who are grieving need to find a way to manage grieving that works for all concerned.

5. Developing some form of memorial for the lost relationship is a way to bring closure to the loss and to keep his memory alive.

6. The loss of a marriage can approach the same impact that loss of a loved one. This is especially the case in a long standing marriage for the partner that didn't want the divorce. The challenge is to avoid focusing on blame which will only add the pain of the loss. It is better to deal with the mourning by focusing on what was right about the marriage, what can be learned from it that can help future relationships have a good outcome.

7. People who have been devoted to their pets may experience a similar mourning experience as the loss of a person.

References:

When There Are No Words: Finding Your Way to Cope With Loss and Grief, Charlie Walton, Pathfinder Publishing, 1996, 112 pages. Paperback

I Wasn't Ready to Say Goodbye: Surviving, Coping and Healing After the Death of a Loved One, Brook Noel & Pamela D Blair, Ave Maria Press, Champion Press, 2000, 304 pages, Paperback

Finding Your Way After Your Spouse Dies, Marta Felber, Ave Maria Press, 2000, 160 pages. Paperback

Facing the Ultimate Loss: Coping with the Death of a Child, Robert J. Marx & Susan Wengerhoff, Sheldon Press, 2006, 218 pages. Paperback

Living With Loss And Grief: Letting Go, Moving on, (Overcoming Common Problems), Julia Tugendhat, Sheldon Press, 128 pages. Paperback

Loss and Bereavement: Managing Change, Ros Weston, Terry Martin, & Yvonne Anderson, Blackwell Science, 1998, 268 pages.

DEPRESSION

David was the sales manager in an automobile agency. He was married with two children and life was generally OK. Things began to change with a major down turn in the automobile business. Tension increased at work with more pressure to improve sales. Salesmen became more competitive and testy with one another. David carried his work frustration home which led to more tension there. Their children were having difficult times at school which added to his feeling very discouraged. It seemed that one problem tended to invite another. He had these kind of feelings in the past. They had been temporary and lifted once the problems got resolved.

Things were different this time. His depressed feeling didn't change even when things got better. Business picked up, the children's problems showed some improvement. He felt irritable, sad, and wasn't too interested in talking about what bothered him. This angered his wife. They both got concerned when he lost his usual interest in food and had increased trouble in sleeping. He felt helpless and hopeless. This went on for seven or eight months before he was willing to go get medical help at the insistence of his wife. His doctor prescribed medication for his depression. Things began to improve after two or three weeks when he began to feel more like himself.

Depression is used both as a medical term and in general conversation to describe feeling down, unhappy, or sad. Clinical depression refers to difficulty concentrating, insomnia, loss of appetite, feelings of extreme sadness, guilt, helplessness and hopelessness, and thoughts of death. Daily life has its ups and downs and rarely seems to run smoothly. When the downs persists for more than a short period, you are likely to describe yourself as depressed. You should pay attention to addressing these feelings to avoid their getting worse. David made his situation difficult when he procrastinated getting help.

Ways to cope with depression

1. Try to identify what happened that triggered depressed feelings.

2. Make an attempt to gain control over the situation that caused these feelings. If the situation seems overwhelming, try to break it up into parts each of which may seem more controllable. Suppose a person is feeling depressed about his relationship with his boss over a period of time. He may feel helpless in knowing what to do about it. One option is to discuss his feeling with his boss to see if he feels the same way. Doing this can begin to make the person feel better just because he was doing something active to feel better. He may even find out that he misread the situation which would be a relief and lead to feeling better. Another possibility would be to review the various things that have happened that bothered him. Evaluate each of the times things went wrong and give thought to how to improve them. Dealing with these situations one by one can give a better sense of control and reduce the depressed feeling.

3. There may be times when you are not able change the circumstances that triggered the depressing feelings. Do anything that will give a feeling of having accomplished something. Being able to control something will help deal with the depressed feelings. It will be a reminder that while some things are not in one's control other things are controllable.

4. If none of the efforts seem to help, consult a doctor to see whether medication can make a difference. Sometimes depression can be helped with medication separately or in addition to talking therapy.

5. Being around people who are feeling depressed can affect you when you are in a bad place. Any effort you make to help someone else may not work. You should not understand this as a reflection on your efforts. Take satisfaction in having tried. Separate feeling good about your efforts from whether your efforts were successful.

6. Medical consultation should be sought when depression persists over a period of weeks or at most a few months without times of feeling better.

References:

Undoing Depression, Richard O'Connor, Berkley Trade, 1999, 368 pages. Paperback

Self-Coaching: The Powerful Program to Beat Anxiety and Depression, 2nd Edition, Joseph J. Luciani, Wiley, 2006. Paperback

Undoing Perpetual Stress: The Missing Connection Between Depression, Anxiety and 21st Century Illness, Richard O'Connor, New Harbinger Publications, 2004, 183 pages.

Depression in Context: Strategies for Guided Action, Christopher R. Martell & Michael E. Addis, W. W. Norton & Company, 2001, 224 pages.

Getting Your Life Back: The Complete Guide to Recovery from Depression, Jesse Wright, & Monica Ramirez Basco, Free Press, 2002, 400 pages. Paperback

HEALTH: PHYSICAL AND RELATIONSHIP

Frank ran a successful furniture business. It was getting too much for him. The stress and long hours were taking their toll on his health. He decided he needed a partner. A family friend introduced him to Kyle, as a possible candidate for him. Kyle recently sold his upholstery business and was looking for new prospects.

They met over a drink to explore possible mutual interests. Their first impressions of one another were unremarkable except that Kyle noticed Frank's being on the hefty side. Frank was forty-eight, with a broad build, dark hair, moderate height and

considerably overweight. Kyle was blond, a little taller than Frank, thirty-five, and slender. Frank was dressed casually, while Kyle had on a three piece business suit. This made Frank wonder whether he was going to be dealing with a stuffed shirt. It didn't take long to find out he was wrong.

They briefly exchanged personal histories and their business backgrounds. Frank wondered how transferable Kyle's business experience would be in the furniture business. Kyle was concerned that Frank didn't know much about marketing. Kyle had some concern about Frank's laid back manner. They met a few more times to further explore their respective views on business. They found differences but were able reach agreement on important issues. One sticking point for Kyle was Frank's weight. He didn't want to get into a partnership and have his partner drop dead on him. Frank assured him that he was in good health and in a weight control program.

They also discussed how their partnership might work. After further negotiations over the next two months they decided that they knew each other well both on a personal and business level to consider becoming partners. The partnership ran pretty smoothly for about two years when they developed some strong differences of opinion about how to manage the business which included whether to open more stores. Things got pretty strained for a few months as each one fortified his position. They finally recognized that neither one was going to change his mind and both were aware they had too much invested in the business to end the partnership. Eventually they reached a compromise. There was agreement to expand but at a slower rate than was first proposed.

Good health depends on paying attention to both your state of mind and you're your body. People tend to be more aware of their physical health than they do of the their mental health. This is in part the case because there is no ambiguity about what is required to have good health: good nutrition, exercise, proper rest and more. Less clear is how to take care of emotional health. Maintaining meaningful relationships is an important part of emotional health. Both need attention on an ongoing basis.

Keeping your physical health

1. Do not take your health for granted. It deserves the same attention as you would give to a piece of equipment you care about. You have your car serviced to make sure it will be there when you need it. The same applies to maintaining physical and emotional health.

2. Physical and emotional health affect each other. You need a reasonably healthy body to be able to pay attention to your emotional health.

3. Don't be casual about attention to health. It is too easy to be distracted especially when you are feeling good physically and feel happy. Waiting for symptoms to develop is an unnecessary risk. The best way to maintain health is a good program of prevention. This is accomplished by: regular physicals, nutritious diet, adequate rest, and prompt attention to development of any

physical symptoms or lingering emotional distress. It took Frank a long time to come to the realization that he had taken his health for granted.

4. Demands of modern living result in exposure to chronic physical and emotional stress. Track athletes provide an interesting model. An athlete quickly learns that he can't run the mile like he runs the one hundred yard dash. If he tried, he would never finish. The mile runner has to pace himself to have the energy to finish the mile. People need to think like the mile runner in how they organize their lives. Burnout occurs when people behave like they are running the hundred yard dash instead of realizing they are running the mile.

5. Managing stress can be helped over long periods of time when it is balanced with the down time of relaxation and enjoyable activities.

6. Health is also affected by the people with whom you spend time. You can develop unhealthy habits when you spend a lot of time with people who do not practice healthy behavior. Being around people who regularly have poor eating habits can make it hard to get or keep on a healthy diet. Being around smokers for long periods of time can lead to developing the same problems that smokers get.

7. Maintaining emotional health is enhanced by pursuing enjoyable interests: playing an instrument, listening to music, reading, and gardening that helps you relax and give you a sense of accomplishment. Engaging in these interest is most useful when there is no time pressure or specific thing you need to get done. It is also helpful when you are able to do an activity for as long as enjoy it and can stop whenever you feel like it without missing it.

Healthy Relationships

A relationship starts when two people come together out of a common interest. This applies in family, friendships, work, and even in casual acquaintances. Relationships should not be taken for granted. They need ongoing attention to be sure that they stay 'healthy' for all concerned.

Relationships differ in degree of importance, commitment and length of involvement. The underlying process is the same for forming any relationship. People meet, and see if they have a common interest. If they do, they decide how to conduct the relationship in three ways: behavior that is a must for the relationship to continue, behavior that is acceptable and behavior that rules out having a relationship. Examples of 'must' behavior include acceptable appearance, speaking in a respectful manner, having common interest, appropriate language, and more. Examples of unacceptable behavior include: offensive language, hostility, sarcasm, domineering manner and others. All other behaviors may move to either the required or unacceptable category as either party finds necessary. Inability to agree on significant change will lead to an end to the relationship

A relationship is not static. It changes over time as the relationship deepens and as needs and interests of both people change. The survival of a relationship depends on both people putting their joint priority more on paying attention to what works for both of them than on trying to dominate one another.

Developing a relationship

1. The first step in a new relationship is to surface compatibility: appearance, manners, manner and quality of speech. Check out your comfort level with each other's personality style and way of speaking

2. See if you have enough values and interest in common.

3. Negotiate what is acceptable and unacceptable ways to communicate with one another. This happens gradually over a period of time.

4. There are disagreements in every relationship, even in the best of them. See if you are able to settle your differences in a way that feels OK for both of you. Frank and Kyle's ability to settle their differences about expansion made it possible to continue their successful partnership.

5. See if you are comfortable with the way you both give and receive affirmation and criticism.

6. Relationships are like cars. Every so often they need a tuneup. It is helpful to talk about how you both feel the relationship is going every so often. This gives you a chance to clear up any problems haven't been given enough attention. This should include reminding yourselves of the good things as well as any problems.

7. Respect other people's opinions without judging them. Work out disagreements in a way that makes sense to both of you.

8. If you need to criticize somebody, do it a way that is respectful and without judgment. Don't say, "You are wrong, when you disagree. Instead say, "I disagree with you." The difference is that you don't set yourself up as the judge of what is right and wrong. In doing this you are showing as much respect for the other person having an opinion as you do for yourself.

9. Pay as much attention to saying nice things or giving compliments as you talk about things that bother you.

10. It is a good idea to periodically review your joint overall satisfaction in relationship with the other person. This gives you both a chance to talk about things that bothered you that you didn't have a chance to work out. It also helps to be reminded of the good things in the relationship.

11. Be a good listener.

Marvin Snider, Ph.D.

References:

The "Go Ask Alice" Book of Answers: A Guide to Good Physical, Sexual, and Emotional Health, Columbia University's Health Education Program, Owl Books, 1998, 68 pages. Paperback

Keep Your Brain Young: The Complete Guide to Physical and Emotional Health and Longevity, Guy M. McKhann & Marilyn Albert, Wiley, 2002, 304 pages.

Natural Mental Health: How to Take Control of Your Own Emotional Well-Being, Carla Wills-Brandon, Hay House, 2000, 305 pages. Paperback

Aging Well: The Complete Guide to Physical and Emotional Health, Jeanne Wei & Sue Levkoff, Wiley, 2001, 384 pages. Paperback

Living Longer for Dummies, Walter M. Bortz & Rich Tennant, For Dummies, 2001, 214 pages. Paperback

ILLNESS

Louise, 59, was in a comfortable marriage with two grown children who had their own families. Her husband, Amos, 62, was a carpenter who was beginning to think about retirement. Louise had a checkered medical history. She had asthma since childhood and recently developed diabetes. She had two bouts of pneumonia in the past twenty years. She was well practiced in managing illnesses both in herself and in other members of the family.

All of this was overshadowed by the recent discovery that she had breast cancer. This aroused great concern and support from family and friends. Louise knew from past experience that having a positive attitude was important in coping with her illness. She learned the importance of being as actively involved as possible in managing her treatment. This meant getting at least two opinions before starting any treatment program. She checked out her options and consulted with her doctor and family to decide the best course of action. She also recognized that a serious illness is not just her problem but one that affects the whole family. They would need to support and help one another in coping with her illness.

Healthy is feeling physically and emotionally fit. Illness is not an on or off experience. It ranges from feeling great, a little under the weather, feeling ill, to feeling very sick with a diagnosable illness. There are two parts to illness: physical and emotional. A person may feel good in one and sick in the other or feel the same in both.

Managing illness presents quite different approaches when it is chronic than when it is acute. A chronic illness is one that continues over time, while an acute illness lasts for a short period of time. A chronic illness may require a life style change

health is had by practicing good preventive care. This includes good nutrition, regular exercise, adequate sleep, and regular medical checkups. Symptoms that do not go away after two or three weeks should receive medical attention.

Selection of Care Givers

Selecting care givers outside the family is, at best, a process of trial and error. There are various approaches: word of mouth, referral from one care giver to another, internet search, referral from a professional organizations and the state board of licensing and registration.

1. Interview two or better three potential primary care physicians. The comparison will help you find the best fit. The same should apply in selecting other care givers.

2. Technical competence is not the only criteria. Also important is the chemistry between patient and care giver. Chemistry involves comfort with the care giver's personality, feeling heard, respected, patience and being spoken to in an understandable language.

3. Selection of care givers involves the negotiating expectations of one another. This includes fees, availability, receptivity to questions, phone calls, communication via email and any other concern.

4 Any problem in the relationship with a care giver should be promptly addressed. Unspoken concerns gradually erode the quality and trust in the relationship. A care giver's difficulty in constructively responding to appropriate concerns may indicate time for a change.

Adjusting to illness

1 Get a second or even third opinions for any serious condition. This is inconvenient but often avoids unnecessary intervention. A care giver who is affronted by the desire for a second opinion should be avoided.

2. Understand the limitations and changes required by your chronic illness and do the best you can to make the needed adjustments.

3. Decide on what is needed to meet the needs of your illness and what is possible that you can manage on your own and what help you will need from others.

4. Recognize that blame and judgment in coping with your illness makes it harder for those who want to help you. This takes energy better spent on things that can help you feel better.

5. The best approach to managing illness is to make the most out of what is possible rather than complaining about the limitations of your illness.

Individual Responsibility

Good medical care is a joint responsibility of you and your care giver. Assume responsibility for as much as you are able to do and to rely on the care giver when you have exhausted what you can do for yourself. Don't leave it all to the care giver. You should be helped to understand your options in dealing with a medical problem, It is up to you to decide which one to choose. You are the one who has to live with the consequences of a decision. Accepting advice from others without evaluation makes it too easy to hold others responsible for the outcome which is not good for anyone.

1. Have regular medical checkup as directed by your physician or other care giver.

2. Follow recommendations of nutrition, exercise, sleep, and other suggestions for optimal health.

3. When hospitalized learn to identify your medication and check to ensure the proper medication is being administered if you is able to do so. Otherwise, a family member's help may be enlisted.

4. Do not submit to procedures or medications without knowing their intended impact and side effects.

5. Get second opinions for any invasive procedures.

6. Get medical consultation for any unusual body symptoms that last for more than a couple of weeks.

7. Get medical insurance and look into getting long term care insurance after age 40.

8. Live a balanced life style between work, family, and individual interests. To accomplish this will require setting time limits on each of these activities.

Impact of Illness on Relationships

Illness does not happen in a vacuum. The chronically ill person's life may be changed forever. This may require a significant adjustment by the people close to you who will also be affected. The degree of changes required will be a challenge to both the chronically ill person and those close to you to manage the illness without unduly affecting the quality of relationships.

1. Negotiate with those people affected by your illness how you will work out

paying attention to your needs and those of others affected by it.

2. Notice how your attitudes and personality are affected by your being ill. Don't hesitate to ask for help when you find you are having a hard time developing a positive attitude in adjusting to your illness. This is in the best interest of all concerned. Doing this will make managing it easier.

3. Be aware you may seem surly and unappreciative in asking for or in receiving help. You need to let people know when it is their behavior or your feelings in coping with your illness that is causing a problem.

4. Don't take receiving help for granted. Care givers will be more disposed to be helpful when their efforts are periodically acknowledged. This includes not only regarding the help they give you, but also how doing this interferes with their normal activities.

References:

500 Tips for Coping With Chronic Illness, Pamela D. Jacobs, Reed Publishers, 1997, 238 pages, Paperback

Coping With Illness, Helen Garvy, Shire Press, 1995, 235 pages. Paperback

Living with Life-Threatening Illness: A Guide for Patients, Their Families, and Caregivers, Kenneth J. Doka, Jossey-Bass, 1998, 352 pages. Paperback

Coping With Chronic Illness: Overcoming Powerlessness, Judith Fitzgerald, F. A. Davis Company, 1999, 450 pages. Paperback

Helping Someone with Mental Illness: A Compassionate Guide for Family, Friends, and Caregivers, Rosalynn Carter & Susan Ma Golant, Three Rivers Press, 1999, 368 pages. Paperback

Coping with Long-Term Illness, (Overcoming Common Problems), Barbara Baker, Sheldon Press, 2001, 118 pages. Paperback

Anatomy of an Illness as Perceived by the Patient, Norman Cousins, W. W. Norton & Company, 2005, 192 pages. Paperback

PSYCHOTHERAPY:

What it is and How it Works

Paul was busy working on his career as a musician. It was an ongoing struggle for him. He had the talent but lacked self confidence. His short temper often created

problems in relationships, especially with his girlfriend. They shared strong feelings for each other. He was overly sensitive and jealous which led to many cycles of arguments and making up. This was similar to the struggles with his family who were unhappy about his choice of occupation and life style.

His mother vacillated between criticism and being loving. When she wasn't angry with him she was sensitive to his problems. She urged him to see someone to help with his struggle. Paul felt that psychotherapy was for people who were crazy and that wasn't him. His mother told him psychotherapy was useful for people who were struggling with problems and frustrations that don't seem to go away and that it had been useful to her when she was about his age. At first he rejected her suggestion. He thought about it over time. Eventually his continued frustrations led him to give it a try.

Psychotherapy is concerned with helping you when you have problems that elude your ability manage them in your personal life, in your family, at work or in pursuing your life goals. This is accomplished through help in understanding the source of what is in your way and learning how to overcome what is troubling you.

When to Go for Psychotherapy

There are times when managing your life feels overwhelming. The situation gets worse when you feel you should be able to manage your own feelings in any situation. This is unfair because everybody has a limit to what they are able to handle. We seem to live with a double standard. When your automobile isn't working properly, you have no hesitation about promptly going to a mechanic for help. No one expects to be able to fix their own car. You are likely to find it costly if you wait too long. Everybody sees this as the smart thing to do.

The same idea works for getting medical help. You don't expect to cure yourself when you are feeling sick. You do what you can to feel better: take aspirins, eat chicken soup, get rest or other things. When this doesn't take care of the problem you go to the doctor.

The same idea should apply when you are feeling bad about yourself and you don't seem able to overcome problems that won't go away. You may find it hard to control your emotions and wind up saying things that you don't mean. Things that you used to be able to easily manage seem to be so much harder to accomplish. There are days it is hard to get out of bed. You feel depressed and unloved most of the time. Nothing seems to be working out right. When you have done everything you can to feel better and you don't get better, see a psychotherapist after you have checked out you don't have a physical problem.

There are people who see going for psychotherapy as being weak. They grew up with the idea you should be able to solve your own problems. Yet, emotional problems can be far more complicated than dealing with most other problems. Seeking help should be viewed as a strength not a weakness in the same way that you view getting medical care.

1. Try to pinpoint what is causing your upset.

2. Do whatever you think will help solve your problem.

3. Don't put yourself down if you can't overcome your problem. It is natural to feel bad when this happens. Talking with family and friends may help.

4. Be careful in how you accept advice from other people. They will tell you what they think you should do. This might work for them but it doesn't mean it will work for you. You should accept advice only when it fits for you. Otherwise you will blame someone else for giving bad advice.

5. If your problems haven't been solved by these efforts, it time to seek help from a mental health professional: psychologist, psychiatrist, clinical social worker, or other qualified mental health professional.

Working with a psychotherapist

1. There are several ways to find a psychotherapist: Get recommendations from family or friends who have had a good experience, from your doctor, or from professional organizations as American Psychiatric Assn, American Psychological Assn, National Association of Social workers or from other professional organizations. You will find these organizations in the phone book or on the web. Go into Google and look for a therapist. One example is www,psychologytoday.org.

2. Do not just take the first name you get. Interview at least two and preferably three therapists. This is worth doing even if cost is involved. The selection of the therapist should be based on three things: comfort with credentials- education and experience, the type of therapy, and a feeling of trust and comfort with the therapist. This is needed to be able to share intimate thoughts and feelings. A therapist can only be of help when you are able to tell him/her all the things about which you are concerned. Talking about embarrassing things or difficult subjects may be hard to do but are necessary to overcome what is troubling you.

3. Most often psychotherapy starts with hourly meetings once a week or more if needed. Therapy sessions are usually fifty minutes to an hour per week. Some therapists will have longer sessions of two or three hour sessions depending on your need and desire. The therapy may be brief, lasting just a few sessions, or it may extend over months. The length of time depends on the nature of your problem and your willingness to work at it. The first few appointments are usually about the reason for wanting therapy and getting

background history. Weekly sessions may eventually give way to bi-weekly or monthly sessions as you get better and need more time to practice in between sessions.

4. There are times when being seen alone is indicated. There are other situations when you meet with one or more family members. This would be the case in marriage counseling or with a parent and child who are having difficulty in their relationship. Seeing people together recognizes that relationship problems are the responsibility of both people. It takes cooperation of both people to make it work or to have it be a problem. Best results are obtained when people are seen in whatever combination is needed to improve relationships.

5. The therapist will want to understand your problems and why they happened. The way feelings get expressed and managed will be considered. He/she will make suggestions on what to do next. You will be helped to learn different ways of dealing with things that bother you. Therapists are committed to confidentiality and respect for your privacy. They are not permitted to tell anyone anything you tell them without your permission.

6. The therapist will probably give homework to practice what is learned in the session. The therapy hour is similar to a classroom where you learn concepts. The real learning comes only when you practice outside the session. The success of therapy is largely dependent on how much effort you are willing to put in work on your new learning. Reluctance to do this is one of the major reasons that therapy doesn't work. Therapy involves learning better ways to cope with conflicted relationships and self confidence issues. There is no substitute for practice. You may desperately want to be a good baseball player or musician, but there is no way it will happen unless you do the practice to takes to get rid of old ways of behaving and replacing them with new effective ones. The same is true in therapy.

7. Therapy can be hard work. Old ways if behaving don't give way easily, Frustration at the process can sometimes be taken out on the therapist as the source of the problem. The therapist should not be judged until you have done your part in the therapy. Discuss any feelings that bother you about the therapist. This will help both of you and make good practice in how to help you improve your relationships.

8. Your success will depend on your being forthright both in talking about thoughts and feelings. This includes letting the therapist know about anything that bothers you about anything he says. Keeping things to yourself that bother you will only hold you back.

9. You have no responsibility for worrying about any feelings the therapist may have regarding what you say to him/her. Expect that the therapist can take care of his own feelings. This is part of what you can expect in seeing a professional mental health person. A good therapist will welcome knowing what you feel, especially if it is critical. This will help him to be better able to help you . If this is not the case, get a new therapist

10. In the past, successful therapy would end when the reason for coming is accomplished. Some therapists deal with this differently. They do the same thing as your medical doctor who doesn't stop seeing his patients. He works with them until they have recovered from their illness and then may not see him again until another problem happens . The same thing is useful in psychotherapy. The psychotherapist like the physician may suggest checkups to make sure you continue to be doing well.

References:

Mindfulness and Psychotherapy, Christopher K. Germer, Guilford Press, 2005, 333 pages.

A Consumer's Guide to Psychotherapy, Larry E. Beutler, Bruce Bongar, and Joel N. Shurkin, Oxford University, 2001, 224 pages, Paperback

The Psychotherapy Maze: A Consumer's Guide to Getting in and Out of Therapy, Otto Ehrenberg, Jason Aronson, 1994, 240 pages. Paperback

A Guide for Effective Psychotherapy, John, R. Morella, Helm Publishing, 2006, 184 pages. Paperback

Psychotherapy Today: A Consumer's Guide to Choosing the Right Therapist, Ronald W. Pies, Skidmore-Roth Pub, 1991, 232 pages. Paperback

Therapy Demystified: An Insider's Guide to Getting the Right Help, Without Going Broke, Kate Scharff, Marlowe & Company, 2004, 256 pages. Paperback

SURGERY

Francine was not looking forward to her annual physical. She always approached it with anxiety fearing what problems might be found. On one occasion her fears were realized. She was told that the chronic pain in her hip would require surgery and probably a hip replacement. The news frightened her even though she had been anticipating that it was going to be necessary at some point.

She did what she usually does when faced with a problem. She got all the pos-

sible information about her condition. This always helped her manage her anxiety. Francine quizzed her doctor about the surgical procedure, and what could be expected after the surgery and in recuperation. The internet also provided her with additional information which helped her approach the surgery with a positive attitude and also helped in her adjustment after the surgery.

Surgery of any kind is a shock to your system. This arouses anxiety about the uncertainty of any invasive procedure. There is always some risk, however small, in doing even the simplest procedure. It is a challenge to not let your fears get the best of you. This means learning all you can about what will be done. It is helpful to know what to expect before, during and after the surgery as Francine learned. Also important is knowing what to expect during the convalescence and how long it will likely take to get back to normal behavior. Learning what you need to do to get ready for surgery will make it easier for you.

Preparing for surgery

1. Get at least a second opinion when you are told you will need surgery.

2. Pick a surgeon who has a lot of experience in doing the surgery you need. Also helpful is a surgeon who will take the time to answer questions and who gives a balanced view of what may happen in surgery. This is done to make sure you understand the risk involved.

3. Prepare for surgery both physically and emotionally. Be in as good condition as possible, physically and emotionally. This involves good nutrition and being rested. Anxiety can be minimized by knowing what to expect both before and after the surgery. Don't hesitate to have all of your questions answered.

4. Make arrangements for coverage for what you will not be able to do because of having surgery. This might include making sure that concerns at work are covered, coverage is arranged for running your household and care of children, and any other responsibilities that would normally need your attention.

4. Work out a support system to make the experience as comfortable as possible. This may include: being able to discuss feelings before the surgery, someone to go with you to the hospital, and who you like for visitors after the surgery.

5. Have or update your health care proxy. You may not like to think about such things but it is a good idea in case decisions have to be made when you are unable to do so. Make sure this person understands your wishes. Go over your health proxy once a year to be sure it says what you want.

6. Following directions for behavior after surgery will give the best chance for avoiding complications after surgery. Trying to rush the process will likely complicate recovery.

Surgery: A Patient's Guide from Diagnosis to Recovery, Melinda Brubaker, Claire Mailhot & Garratt Slezak, University of California San Diego, 1999, 254 pages. Paperback

The Perioperative Experience of the Ambulatory Surgery Patient, Diane L. Layman, Storming Media, 2000.

Informed Consent to Surgery: Everything You Wanted to Know About Your Operation but Were Afraid to Ask, Simon Marinker, Trafford Publishing , 2001, 114 pages. Paperback

MARRIAGE

GUIDELINES FOR CHOOSING A MATE

At age 25, Bob enjoyed the dating scene but decided it was time to get serious about finding a wife. He had to shift from the attraction of the moment to qualities he wanted in a wife. This changed his attitude about the way he viewed women. He wasn't quite sure where to start. He thought it would be useful to talk to couples who seemed to have a good marriage and see the qualities they felt was important in a long term relationship. He found these discussions and his readings helpful. These efforts helped guide him to developing specific ideas of what to look for in women. It took him a couple of years and many dates until he met his soul mate, Karen.

There is no easy formula in choosing a marriage partner. Finding some one compatible is much easier for the moment than trying to guess whether the relationship will stand the test of time. Will the qualities: handsome or beautiful, smart, funny, considerate, and caring, and others, important in the beginning be the same over time. How to decide is one of the most important decisions of your life. Choices have to be made about which qualities are important with what priority both in the present and likely to be so over time. Keep in mind that relationships are 'package deals'. You have to be able to live with the qualities in your partner you don't like to gain the benefit of those that are important to you.

Choosing a mate

1. You are ready to begin choosing a spouse when you have a good sense of who you are and the values and behavior important to you.

2. Knowing how you are going to make a living and the life style that might be possible can help you concentrate on finding a mate.

3. Consider the qualities you want a spouse to have. A good starting point is a person who is self confident, has compatible values, likes the same things you do, and has an idea of what he/she wants to do with his/her life.

4. Keep in mind that the most important single quality for a successful relationship is the ability of two people who are able to settle their differences in a way that is acceptable to both people. This ability gives confidence that you will be able to solve any problem that might come up.

5. Date people of similar cultural background and values to yours. Mixing

cultural and value backgrounds are possible but bring added challenges in being able to develop a relationship that fits for both of you.

6. A good place to meet compatible people is around shared interests: church, business or professional meetings, sports interests, educational classes, cultural events, and more.

7. Getting along with someone under comfortable conditions does not give a good enough idea of how you will get along in difficult times. Get to know a potential spouse under as broad a range of conditions as possible: happy times, when ill, frustrated, and when angry. Add to this, how they deal with success, manage anger and respect different ways of thinking or doing things. Is prevailing in a disagreement more important than finding what fits for both of you? Knowing how a person deals with difficult times is a good way to see what is beneath the surface persona people project.

8. It is hard to get to know a person when you see them for short periods and when you are having a good time. Spending time with a person's family is one of the best ways to learn a lot about a person in a short time. One very informative way is around the family dinner table. This will give more information about a person than any other single experience. It will show you what values with which he/she grew up, what and how they speak, show respect for one another, whether people expect to be waited on or whether they all pitch in, how they express and manage feelings and much more.

9. The pressure of romance should not be permitted to shorten the period of exploring compatibility. The length of time this takes will depend on how much time is spent together under a broad range of circumstances. This generally takes several months at minimum assuming there is a lot of time together.

10. A relationship becomes committed when both parties feel satisfied they know each other well enough along the lines described above. This ultimately leads to the next step of engagement, which gives both people time to test out how they get along under more intimate conditions.

References:

Finding Your Mate Online: No Fear, No Embarrassment, Just Love!, Karin Sterling Anderson & Beth Roberts, BookSurge Publishing, 2006, 236 pages. Paperback

Date…or Soul Mate? How To Know If Someone Is Worth Pursuing In Two Dates Or Less, Neil Clark Warren, Thomas Nelson, 2002, 224 pages. Paperback

Falling in Love for All the Right Reasons : How to Find Your Soul Mate, Ken Abraham and Neil Clark Warren, Amazon Remainders Account, 2005, 256 pages.

10 Commandments Of Dating, Ben Young & Samuel Adams, Thomas Nelson, 1999, 192 pages. Paperback

Boundaries in Dating, Dr. Henry Cloud, Dr. John Townsend, Zondervanm, 2000, 288 pages. Paperback

The Harmonious Way: A Success Guide to Selecting A Compatible Mate, Aaron Turpeau, Pantheo, Inc., 2002, 154 pages. Paperback

DIVORCE

The first few years of Rebecca and Larry's marriage went well for the most part. They had their share of difficult times but were able to handle them. Their relationship began to deteriorate after their first child, Jonathan, was born. Larry felt their relationship became secondary to Rebecca's involvement with mothering. This became even more so with the birth of their second child, Zoe. Rebecca dismissed Larry's concern as nonsense and berated him for being jealous of the attention she gave to their children.

Larry's felt neglect eventually led him to having affairs. Initially, Rebecca welcomed his distancing since it reduced pressure on her. She presumed he finally recognized the children's needs should come first. She did not recognize how his felt neglect affected him and how it got expressed in increasing arguments. The distance between them grew as the frequency and severity of their arguments increased. Rebecca felt very unappreciated and abandoned. Larry felt taken for granted.

Rebecca accidently discovered that Larry was having affairs. She was furious and asked him to leave. Larry was angry at her insensitivity for any appreciation of his feelings. He got fed up and filed for divorce since he saw no prospect of things getting any better.

They went through two abortive attempts for reconciliation. Divorce seemed the only option which was accomplished only after a bitter struggle that left scars on all of them - parents and children.

Divorce is usually very trying. It is not easy to face that your marriage has ended. The degree of difficulty will depend on how much prevailing is put ahead of working out a settlement acceptable to both of you. There is the choice of using lawyers or mediation. Involving competitive lawyers, has a much greater chance of the divorce getting unpleasant. Mediation is less complicated because a mediator's job is to help the couple find common ground. He has no vested interest in either spouse.

Divorce isn't what you expected when you got married. It was supposed to be 'til death do you part' The decision to divorce can be almost as difficult as going through the divorce itself. Both of you face the painful and complicated job of untangling your emotional, material and financial connections. This gets considerably more difficult when children are involved. An added complication occurs when there has been a long marriage with many happy times. Another kind of difficulty occurs when two people share a strong emotional bond but find it too hard to live together. Divorce also will be especially difficult for a spouse whose life has centered around the career of other partner. In the past it was usually the wife who the one affected. In the present climate it could be either husband or wife whose interests become secondary.

Divorces that become a war take their toll on everybody, especially young children. Battles over custody, money, and property often mask efforts to attack and undermine credibility of one another. In the process the children suffer the most. Trips to court become a revolving door dance when the couple are able to solve little on their own.

There also are divorces that work out smoothly with minimal struggle. This happens when a couple recognize their incompatibility without blame and want to accomplish the divorce with as little struggle as possible. It happens when they put t a high priority on consensus that is in the best interest of their children. The divorce process gets more complicated when legal gladiators do their ritual dance in service of their clients. Sometimes it becomes hard to decide who is more argumentative – the opposing lawyers or divorcing couple. This happens when the couple's feel helpless, weary from the battle and delegate responsibility to their lawyers for making the divorce happen. This can become a problem when what makes sense to your lawyer may not be in your best interest. A client should not let his/her lawyer tell you what to do. It is his job to tell you what your choices are and to help you understand what goes with each one because you are one who has to live it. This makes you responsible for your choice and not to be able to blame someone else if you don't like the way it works out.

Enduring the divorce process

1. Do not make the decision to divorce in the heat of emotion. Decide to divorce when the marriage is not working out and you don't see any possibility that it can change enough to make staying in it workable. This conclusion should be reached only after repeated efforts to improve it have failed. Hanging on to a dead marriage is bad for all concerned.

2 Getting divorced will be much easier if you both want it. It will be far more difficult if one of you doesn't want it or if your marriage has been an ongoing battleground.

3. Ideally, it is helpful when the couple are able to mourn the loss of their marriage together. This is possible when the divorce is a joint decision. The mourning is not about blame but the recognition that it was not possible to save the marriage in spite of your best joint efforts. It is helpful to appreciate what was good about it and to learn from what made it too difficult to continue without getting into blame.

4. This joint assessment will probably not be possible in a marriage filled with anger, pain and blame. These feelings will have to be harnessed to avoid making the process far more difficult than it need be. Each partner should do his/her own review of how you got to this point. Consulting a therapist can help when managing the feelings becomes too difficult.

5. One of the first decisions to make is whether to use lawyers or go for mediation. It is the difference between working together or getting into a boxing match. There are two possible problems in working with lawyers.

   A lawyer thinks it is his duty to get the most favorable outcome for his/her client. This sometimes invites a gladiator contest that can end in a long drawn out expensive struggle. The attorney's measure of success is how well he does for his client. His success is not necessarily in your best interest. Problems may result the couple will have to face in the future, especially when children are involved. An angry divorce will be the outcome when the settlement is too one sided which happens when the lawyers are not equally matched.

6. Great care should be exercised when selecting an attorney. There is no simple way to do this. Often the choice is made by word of mouth from family or friends. It is a good idea to interview two or three attorneys before choosing one. The choice should take into account his/her level of experience in divorce, how he/she handles divorces, and whether associates will do the work. Also important is whether there is a commitment to respond to phone calls, fees, and whether you feel comfortable working with the attorney. You should meet and find acceptable anyone else working with your lawyer on your behalf. The same qualifications should apply as those you used on the lawyer with whom you first spoke.

7 Always remember that the lawyer works for you. This means you do not let him talk down to you, hold him to his promises, and do not let him tell you he knows what is better for you than you do. Getting as big a settlement as possible will not be good for you if it creates acrimony with your soon to be ex-spouse. An example would be to tell him to show consideration for fairness rather than getting all that is possible. When possible, you should be treated as a partner in making decisions and not delegate them to your lawyer.

8. Mediation has a very different approach. The couple meet with a mediator who treats you both the same. He has no vested financial interest in the outcome. His job is to help both of you work out a mutually acceptable agreement on terms of the divorce. Attention is on working out finances, division of property, and custody issues. Mediators are not equipped to deal with the emotional issues. Consulting a mental health professional will help if this becomes a problem.

9. An attorney may be needed after mediation to handle the paper work. He would not get involved an having anything do with the settlement you reached with the mediator.

10. Divorce is very upsetting for children under the best of circumstances. Often they are victims when parents are involved in an angry divorce. The situation becomes even more difficult when they are used as pawns in the parents struggle. They need to be protected from this abuse.

11. It is better for both parents to jointly tell children that there will be a divorce. They need to be able to do this without getting into an argument. The parents should share in giving an explanation. If this is not possible they should do it separately and agree to do it without blame.

12. Make very clear to your children they are not responsible for the divorce.

13. Children need to understand that though their parents are divorcing, they are not divorcing from being parents. They are both committed to seeing that they will get the needed love and care.

14. It is essential for the children's welfare that they not be used as messengers between parents. Agree not to say nasty things about each other to the children.

15. Scrupulously honor alimony and visitation agreements. Children will be the ones to suffer if parents use alimony or visitation in their arguments.

16. The custodial parent sometimes is faced with a child who balks at visitation with the other parent. This presents the dilemma between paying attention to the child's desire and obligation to the other parent. The custodial parent should opt out from making that choice because it creates a problem with either choice. A better approach is to leave it to the other parent to work it out directly with the child. This is the same thing that would apply in an intact family. The custodial parent should not be put in the position of pressuring the child to conform, nor should he/she interfere with visitations.

17. Consult a mental health professional when there are problems in making the adjustment to divorce. Children may have trouble talking to either parent about some of their concerns. The therapist can give them a safe place to talk about their fears, concerns, and any problems with a parent and how to manage them.

References:

Your Divorce Advisor: A Lawyer and a Psychologist GuideYou Through the Legal and Emotional Landscape of Divorce, Diana Mercer & Marsha Kline Pruett, Fireside, 2001, 361 pages. Paperback

Getting Divorced Without Ruining Your Life: A Reasoned, Practical Guide to the Legal, Emotional and Financial Ins and Outs of Negotiating a Divorce Settlement, Sam Margulies, Fireside, 2001, 368 pages. Paperback

Too Good to Leave, Too Bad to Stay: A Step-by-Step Guide to Help You Decide Whether to Stay In or Get Out of Your Relationship, Mira Kirshenbaum, Plume, 1997, 304 pages. Paperback

Can Your Relationship Be Saved? How to Know Whether to Stay or Go, Michael S. Broder, Impact Publishers, 2002, 160 pages. Paperback

Should You Leave?: A Psychiatrist Explores Intimacy and Autonomy--and the Nature of Advice, Peter D. Kramer, Penguin, 1999, 320 pages. Paperback

Making Divorce Easier on Your Child: 50 Effective Ways to Help Children Adjust, Nicholas Long & Rex L. Forehand, McGraw-Hill, 2002, 256 pages. Paperback

The Truth About Children and Divorce: Dealing with the Emotions So You and Your Children Can Thrive, Robert Emery, Plume, 2006, 336 pages. Paperback

Dividing the Child: Social and Legal Dilemmas of Custody, Eleanor E. Maccoby & Robert H. Mnookin, Harvard University Press, 1998, 416 pages. Paperback

INFERTILITY

Meg and Sam enjoyed fantasizing on their honeymoon about the children they were going to have. They returned to the pursuit of their respective careers. Two years later they started to look at purchasing a house. As they looked at prospective homes, Meg envisioned the room suitable for a nursery and would fantasize how she would decorate it.

Getting their own home was preparation for starting a family. They anticipated that pregnancy would happen on demand. Optimism gave way to concern when a year of trying did not yield any results. They each began to vacillate between fearing he/she was the problem and being angry at the other one for being the problem. Eventually they sought medical help. After seemingly endless tests they found that having their own child was not to be. This was devastating news and resulted in a test of their commitment to one another that took them to the brink of divorce. Eventually they decided their commitment to one another would prevail and turned to consider adoption.

Devastating is a couple's experience when they realize they are infertile. Eventually the question is, Whose fault is it? This realization is an attack on any good feeling you have about being a man or woman. You search for medical help to find out what is wrong. This takes time which only adds to your anxiety. You get a little encouraged by the possibility fertility treatments might help. Frustration again sets in

possibility is a donor. There is worry that the money might run out before you will be able to find out what is possible. The upside of getting a donor is that you will have a biological child of at least one parent.

Finding out why pregnancy isn't happening has its own problem. The spouse who has the problem might have a struggle with guilt because of not being able to make pregnancy possible. It feels like you are letting your partner down even though you couldn't do anything about it. Some couples are able to get over this while others are not. Sometimes couples divorce when it gets too hard to cope with the problem. Couples that eventually accept that they won't have a child of their own turn to adoption.

Coping by the infertile spouse

1. Allow time for both of you to get used to realizing you will not be able to get pregnant and to express the feelings of frustration and anger. Realizing that the problem is out of either of your control only makes it worse. Make sure your feelings of anger and disappointment get put on the problem and not on each other.

2. Jointly decide on how you will tell family and friends. They will want to help but won't know how. Let them know what will help whether it is sympathy, listening to your feelings, saying nothing, or anything else that might be useful. Also let them know what will not be helpful.

3. Whichever one of you that has the fertility problem will need time to deal with his/her disappointment to what is out of his/her control. The other spouse will also need time to make the adjustment

4. You will need time to consider how infertility will affect the marriage and how you will manage it if will be a problem.

5. It takes two to make a marriage work. If this fertility problem is too much for the marriage to survive, take some comfort that you did all you could to make it work. The thought of not being able to have your own child may be too much to overcome.

Coping for the other spouse

1. You may have a lot of feelings about not being to have your own child. Some of them will be at the problem and some maybe at your spouse. Have time to allow yourself to vent whatever feelings you may have without judging whether you are entitled to have them. It is difficult to give free expression to what you feel and pay attention to how it affects anyone who hears you. This is why you probably need to do this safely by yourself. You may find

you are having a lot of different feelings anger, resentment, guilt, sympathy, empathy, frustration and more. You also may feel cheated or betrayed for something out of your control. Keep in mind that you cannot control what you feel but you do have responsibility for how you express them.

2. Once you both have had time to express your feelings privately, talk about them together. It will be hard but necessary to listen to one another with sympathy and acceptance. You will need to manage not to get angry at hearing things you don't like. Once you have been able to understand each other's feelings without judgment you will be in a better place to decide how to move ahead.

3. Focus on how to make the most of available possibilities, whatever they may be.

4. Addressing your disappointment together can make the relationship stronger. This will be necessary before you consider the possibility of adoption.

References:

Infertility Sucks! (Keeping it all together when sperm and egg stubbornly remain apart), Beverly Barna, Xlibris Corporation, 2002, 140 pages. Paperback

Infertility Survival Handbook, Elizabeth Swire-Falker, Riverhead Trade, 2004, 320 pages. Paperback

What to Do When You Can't Get Pregnant: The Complete Guide to All the Technologies for Couples Facing Fertility Problems, Daniel A. Potter & Jennifer S. Hanin, Marlowe & Company, 2005, 288 pages. Paperback

Conquering Infertility: Dr. Alice Domar's Mind/Body Guide to Enhancing Fertility and Coping with Infertility, Alice D. Domar & Alice Lesch Kelly, Penguin, 2004, 320 pages. Paperback

Riding the Infertility Roller Coaster: A Guide to Educate And Inspire, Iris Waichler, Wyatt-MacKenzie Publishing, 2006, 268 pages. Paperback

INFIDELITY

Max and Joyce had been married for eight years when he began to feel their relationship was getting stale. Joyce was very absorbed in her job and looking after the children. Sex became routine with decreasing frequency. He felt neglected and taken for granted. His attempts to talk to Joyce about his feelings always seemed to get interrupted, besides which he didn't sense it was a concern of hers.

with women colleagues who found him attractive. He got into a discussion with a
female colleague on a project they were sharing that carried over into lunch. This led
to further lunches as the discussion gradually shifted from business to personal as
Max became aware of a budding physical attraction. She sensed the same. This led to
more frequent business lunches and less to business interest and increasingly more to
personal topics which became better suited to a hotel room. Max found this and other
affairs that followed filled the void he felt in his marriage.

Everyone involved gets hurt when you or your marriage partner has an affair which violates marital trust. The spouse affected by the infidelity feels betrayed. The marital relationship faces a crisis that raises questions: Is this the first time? What does it mean? Will it happen again? What commitment is their to the marriage? How to respond to it? It is tempting to focus on being furious and to want to cast out the violator of the marriage. It is one thing to feel something . It is quite another thing to act on it. It is not useful to react on what you are feeling until you have cooled down. Otherwise you are likely to make decisions you may regret. You need to know what and why something has happened in order to make a decision with which you can live.

Coping by the injured spouse

1. Allow time for venting your feelings without making any quick decisions.

2. Let your spouse know how you feel. Once the shock of the affair has died down, let your spouse know what the affair meant to you. Tell how you feel in "I" statements rather than "you are" statements. For example, "I feel betrayed". instead of "You have violated our marriage." This will have a better chance of getting through than if you attack the person's character.

3. Give your spouse a chance to tell you how the affair happened. Don't let it be made your problem. Any problems with your behavior should be talked about at another time. Keep on the subject. Affairs need to be understood not justified.

4. Determine if the affair is an indirect way of expressing unhappiness or an indirect way of wanting out of the marriage.

5. Any expressed desire by the offending spouse to stay in the marriage should be accompanied by accepting responsibility for the affair and demonstration in behavior that there is a commitment to it. Any attempt to put the responsibility elsewhere should question whether accepting responsibility is really sincere.

6. Consider whether professional help would be useful to assess the viability of the marriage or whether to focus should be on how to divorce in a constructive way.

Marvin Snider, Ph.D.

Application for the spouse who had the affair

1. Accept responsibility for the affair. Don't make excuses for why you did it.

2. Allow your spouse to vent feelings at learning of the affair without getting reactive. Saying hurtful things is a way of letting the pain out. The message to get when someone is angry at you is that they are really hurting. That's why you should pay attention to the feeling message and not to the nasty things that are said. The more a person is hurt the nastier will be what they say.

3. Do not make your having an affair the responsibility of your spouse. An affair is not the way to deal with complaints about the marriage.

4. Be forthright in telling your spouse how you feel about the marriage. Don't play games to get by the moment. It will only make things worse.

5. Tell your spouse what you are willing to do if you want to stay in the marriage and be prepared to act on it if this is accepted. Otherwise, negotiate how best to end the marriage.

6. If staying in the marriage is not what you want, say so without blaming. Take responsibility for using your affair to give this message. Jointly consider how to end the marriage with the least amount of conflict.

References:

NOT "Just Friends": Rebuilding Trust and Recovering Your Sanity After Infidelity, Shirley Glass & Jean Coppock Staeheli, Free Press, 2004, 448 pages. Paperback

Emotional Infidelity: How to Affair-Proof Your Marriage and 10 Other Secrets to a Great Relationship, M. Gary Neuman, Three Rivers Press, 2002, 320 pages. Paperback

After the Affair: Healing the Pain and Rebuilding Trust When a Partner Has Been Unfaithful, Janis A. Spring, Harper Paperbacks, 1997, 304 pages. Paperback

Infidelity: A Survival Guide, Don-David Lusterman, New Harbinger Publications, 1998, 207 pages. Paperback

My Husband's Affair Became the Best Thing That Ever Happened to Me, Anne Bercht, Trafford Publishing , 2005, 334 pages. Paperback

First Aid for the Betrayed, Richard Alan, Trafford Publishing, 2006, 168 pages. Paperback

Natasha and Horst had been married for forty-five years when she died of cancer. They had a very happy marriage in which they shared many interests in music, theater, politics, the outdoors, and others. The one shared disappointment was their inability to have children which brought them closer. They compensated by being able to do extensive traveling and other activities that they might not have been able to do with a family. They adored each other and became very dependent on one another, often being able to anticipate what the other one needed without having to speak.

The tragedy of her death was made more difficult because she developed a particularly virulent form of cancer which took her from him in just a few months. Horst was devastated beyond words. The suddenness hadn't given him enough opportunity to adjust to what was happening. He felt as though he too had died but for some reason seemed to still be living. He was depressed, forlorn and walked around in a stupor. His sister forced him to come live with her family. He was uncomfortable with the idea but didn't have the energy to resist. He and his sister had been on good terms over the years though not very close.

Facing the loss of your spouse is also losing a part of yourself. All too sudden there is a gaping hole in your life. The person with whom you spent so much of your life is no longer there. While the physical being is gone you have your spouse's spirit and a life time of memories to keep him/her alive in your mind and heart.

You now have to decide how to move on with your life. What to change? What to keep the same? How to fill the empty void that was left by your spouse? It will take time for your emotions to fully accept that you no longer have a spouse. The suddenness of Natasha's death made this adjustment all the more difficult.

How to cope with loss of spouse

1. Don't rush your grieving. It will take time. Don't go with ought to's. Each person has his own way of dealing with grief. Don't judge the way you express your grief. There is no right or wrong way. Your grieving will gradually begin to lighten. It will kick up whenever anything happens that reminds you of your loss. This will soften with time but always be there in the background. Your success in coping will depend on how well you are able to go on in developing a new life style on your own.

2. The sudden and unexpected death of your spouse will be an even greater challenge to your grieving. You are likely to feel thunderstruck with a sense of unreality. One moment your spouse is there and the next moment he/she is gone. It may take some time for the numbing to wear off before you can begin to grieve.

3. You will likely experience many different feelings in your grieving: anger,

guilt, blaming, bargaining with God or no one in particular. Don't judge these feeling, just respect them and allow them to be expressed.

4. Mourning will begin when you know that your loved one is going to die. This may be weeks or months before it actually happens and sometimes it may even be years. It starts with the time you begin to think of that person not being in your life and is likely to begin to affect your relationship with that person.

5. Sometimes you may feel you have done something that played a part in your loved one's death. Don't go that way! It won't bring the person back and will only make your grieving all the harder on you and those around you.

6. Every religion has its own way of dealing with observing a mourning period. It may place restrictions on what you should and should not do during this time. Do what is comfortable for you and respect what other people need to do for themselves.

7. Many people have different ways of observing the anniversary of a death. Some light candles, go to a religious service, or other important rituals. This may stir up your grieving. Do what feels right for you, but don't impose it on others. Respect what other people need to do to grieve in their own way or seemingly nothing at all. In this case you should not assume the loss means any less to them. They just prefer to manage their anniversary privately.

8. Sometimes anniversaries sneak up on you. You may find yourself feeling down for no particular reason only to realize that it is the anniversary of a loved one's death.

9. Many people find it comforting and meaningful to set up a memorial in memory of the death of a loved on. This takes many forms depending on what is available to you. It could be naming a program, building, scholarship, a foundation and many other possibilities in that person's name.

10. There comes a point when you should begin to recognize that you need to start to pay more attention to how you will go on with your life. This is not a disrespect to your lost loved one. It recognizes that you are living and you need to make a new life for yourself. You know this is what your spouse would have wanted.

11. Your mourning will be made easier when you start to get back to doing the things that have been meaningful in your life: work, hobbies, socializing, and whatever else has meaning for you.

12. At some point you may get remarried. This doesn't mean disrespect to your first spouse. Nor does it mean you have to pretend he/she never existed. You

may still observe anniversaries of his/her death but do it in a way that is respectful of your new spouse. This will require your working out how to pay attention to what you need to do that also fits for your new spouse. He/she will be able to support your doing what you need to do as long as he/she feels you are committed to building a new life the rest of the time.

13. Some people find it useful to be in a group of other people who have lost loved one. People help one another in their adjustment. It can be comforting to share experiences and learn from one another.

References:

Finding Your Way After Your Spouse Dies, Marta Felber, Ave Maria Press, 2000, 160 pages. Paperback

When Your Spouse Dies: A Concise and Practical Source of Help and Advice, Cathleen L. Curry, Ave Maria Press, 1990, 128 pages. Paperback

Lost My Partner-What'll I Do? A Practical Guide for Coping and Finding Strength When Your Spouse Dies, Laurie J Spector, McCormick Press,1999, 152 pages. Paperback

Living with Grief: A Guide for Your First Year of Grieving, Brook Noel & Pamela D Blair, Champion Press, 2004, 62 pages. Paperback

When Your Spouse Dies, Mildred Tengbom, Augsburg Fortress Publishers, 2002, 48 pages. Paperback

MARRIAGE

Janice and Jim's plans for their wedding also included thoughts about how their relationship might work after they were married. Janice had already established she wanted to continue in her career. They agreed it was important for her to be able to self-supporting if something happened to Jim. They also considered how this would impact their relationship. They began to consider a preliminary division of labor for what it would take to run a home, where they wanted to live, how they would furnish their home, and most of all being clear on what they expected of each other.

They recognized that getting married involved making a transition from being accountable only to one's self to having to take into account how one's behavior affects the other person. They understood that this involved joining the lifestyles that each one brings to the marriage to form a new one that fits for both of them.

They approached these considerations with the presumption that it would be easy since they cared so much for one another. Once they got beneath agreement on the values that would guide their marriage, they found that translating them into specifics was

more difficult. They found they had strong differences of opinion about how to manage money, where they would live, how they would deal with their families and others. It didn't take them too long to recognize that winning a point at the expense of the other eventually meant both would be unhappy. They agreed that they could resolve their differences by being committed to making decisions acceptable to both of them.

It didn't take Jim and Janice long to recognize that marriage is a partnership that involves merging two life styles that form a new one out of a combination of individual and joint needs and interests. This included values, attitudes, customs, beliefs, and rules of conduct that guided their lives to date.

Any partnership can be successful when both people agree on what they expect from one another and behave accordingly. Marriage is a special kind of partnership that has legal, physical, and emotional parts. The first two are familiar. A marriage ceremony is the legal part and sexual relationship is the second part. Unlike the first two parts, you can't point to a particular behavior and say that's what makes it an emotional marriage. Yet, the success of a marriage depends on a couple's ability to develop an emotional connection and keep it going in spite of all the problems they will face over time. You know you have an emotional connection when you are as concerned about your spouse's welfare as you are of your own.

A partnership also requires an ongoing division of labor to manage the day-to-day needs of tending to the emotional and physical needs of your marriage and home. This division should be a flexible one that works for both partners and changes over time as needs and circumstances change.

The success of the marital partnership will depend in large part on the couple's ability work out their differences in a way that fits for both people. This is more likely to happen when both partners see compromises as an investment in a relationship rather than focus on what they have to give up.

Marriage also depends on the trust that they will honor whatever they promise to one another. This builds emotional security that strengthens a relationship. The marriage suffers when there is breech in this trust. An affair is a very serious example of how this breaks down.

Period of engagement

1. Start the discussion of the life style you both want your marriage to have during your engagement. This is not a one time decision but an ongoing process as needs and interests change. This process provides an opportunity to explore your compatibility and ability to work together. Include in this discussion the individual goals important to you separately and jointly and how this will impact your marriage.

2. This also will be the beginning of an ongoing discussion about what will be involved in setting up housekeeping: how your jobs might affect the marriage, how you will manage money, where you will live, interests you want

to follow, if and when you want to have children, and more. This will work out well as long as you have the commitment to put agreement above individual preferences.

3. You will also have the opportunity to begin to work out your relationships with your respective families. This will involve benefitting from their experiences and defining how you would like the relationship to be after you are married. Your families may want to be more involved in your lives that you would like. You will do well to begin negotiating what is acceptable for all concerned.

Working out a division of labor

1. Develop a division of labor about who will do what and when. This often works well when each of you have chores that are a combination of likes and dislikes. Some couples find it useful to periodically rotate responsibilities. Other couples find it easier to stick to familiar responsibilities.

2. The quality of marital life will be happier when both you and your spouse are committed to follow through on your agreement. This will avoid many arguments that are so common in marriages.

3. Have weekly or regular meetings to deal with day-to-day problems and go over schedules for the following week. This will help to avoid problems, misunderstandings, and negotiate needed changes.

Managing Family Finances

1. Go over your finances together every month so that you both know where your money is going. Both spouses should have full knowledge of the families finances and how to manage them in case something were to happen to one of you. Working together will help keep the relationship in a good place.

2. Long term finances should be looked at on a regular basis. How often you do this will depend on changing conditions and your need to check on the status of your assets. You will also need to plan for long term expenses in planning for college tuition, retirement, and any other things you will eventually need over time.

Resolving Disagreements

Disagreements are part of every relationship. They can be an asset when resolving them leads to improvement and confidence in your relationship or a liability when you are not able to do so. A useful approach to resolving conflicts can be achieved in the following way.

1. Be sure you have adequate information before you try to resolve your differences. Insufficient information makes it harder if not impossible to work out disagreements.

2. Assume each disagreement has a solution that can fit for both of you. The chance of a meaningful resolution is diminished if one has an attitude that an agreement is not possible. This leads to a self-fulfilling prophecy of having a problem. Your chances of good resolution are much better when you each of you show as much interest in getting your own needs met as you do your spouse's needs being satisfied.

3. Sometimes arguments are not about differences of opinion but who is going to win or be in control. A couple may be arguing about what a child's bed time should be. That may be less important than who has the last word. Arguments are easier to resolve when they don't involve struggles about conflicts in personality. Working out a disagreement gets difficult when the problem is more about wanting to win than it is about whether you actually disagree about the subject of your argument.

4. Be aware when you are arguing about the difference between who will pay the bills and not liking the disrespectful way your spouse is speaking to you. Keeping the two issues separate will make it easier to work out your differences

5. You also should decide whether the disagreement is on a general principle or about a specific behavior Two parents may be disagree on how to handle disciplining a child for something he did. Whereas, the greater concern is on the question of whether your child is doing something wrong. A couple may disagree on whether to buy a particular house when the underlying issue whether to live in the city or the suburbs

6. Timing of negotiation: Disagreements have a better chance of being resolved when enough time is available. Rushed agreements have a greater chance of not working out. Try to settle disagreements as close as possible to when they first became a concern that provides enough time for adequate consideration.

7. An agreement doesn't become meaningful until it can be put in practice. Don't assume that agreement means things will automatically happen. Doing something new needs conscious effort to make it happen. Agreeing to do something is easier than acting on it. Set up an agreed upon time table for commitments to be carried out. Hold one another accountable for following through as promised. Review the status of commitments at regular family meetings. Issues of losing trust can be avoided if each of you agrees to let the other one know when you aren't going to be able to fulfill your commitment by the promised time. A new time for completion needs to be negotiated and tracked.

1. Don't assume you are able to read each others mind. Checking out assumptions can avoid misunderstandings and arguments.

2. Take time on a weekly basis to review your joint comfort level in the marriage separate from any particular issue. This also gives you a chance to take care of any problem that came up that you didn't have time work out.

3. Make time on a weekly basis to focus on doing something enjoyable together that leaves out any kind of family business: money, children, chores, and others. Having regular fun times makes it easier to deal with difficult times.

4. Don't try to work out problems when you are emotionally upset. Keep in mind that when a person is upset, he will have difficulty paying attention to logic or reason. Waiting until you are in a more comfortable emotional place will give you a better chance of finding a solution acceptable to both of you.

5. Things said in anger to you should be understood as your spouse letting you know he/she is hurting about something. It may be hard to think of it this way when somebody is bellowing at you with venom, but this is often the case. Usually the more nasty the comments the greater is likely to be the amount of hurt that is felt. Don't assume that things said in anger are really meant. When people are angry they tend to get back by saying things they expect will hurt the person at whom they are angry. Take seriously what someone says to you when they are calm.

References:

The Seven Principles for Making Marriage Work, John M. Gottman, Orion mass market paperback, 2004, 288 pages. Paperback

Why Marriages Succeed or Fail: And How You Can Make Yours Last, John Gottman, Simon & Schuster, 1995, 240 pages. Paperback

Getting the Love You Want: A Guide for Couples, Harville Hendrix, Owl Books, 2001, 303 pages. Paperback

How to Improve Your Marriage Without Talking About It: Finding Love Beyond Words, Patricia Love & Steven Stosny, Broadway, 2007, 240 pages.

The New Rules of Marriage: What You Need to Know to Make Love Work; Terrence Real, Ballantine Books, 2007, 320 pages.

The Intimacy Factor: The Ground Rules for Overcoming the Obstacles to Truth, Respect, and Lasting Love, Pia Mellody & Lawrence S. Freundlich, Harper,San Francisco, 2004, 240 pages. Paperback

7 Stages of Marriage: Laughter, Intimacy and Passion Today, Tomorrow, Forever, Rita M. DeMaria (Author), Sari Harrar, Readers Digest, 2006, 352 pages.

Boundaries in Marriage, Dr. Henry Cloud & Dr. John Townsend, Zondervan, 2002, 256 pages. Paperback

MIXED MARRIAGES

Alice and Edgar were a mixed racial couple. He was black and she was white and Jewish. She was a teacher and he a computer analyst. They had too children, Alex and Martha. They met in college, fell in love, and married to the displeasure of both their families. His family became grudgingly accepting after the children were born. Her family disowned her with the traditional Jewish ritual of sitting Shiva conducted after the death of a family member. She knew her parents would be unhappy but didn't think they would go to that extreme. Alice has feelings of remorse for having hurt them. She was hurt and angry and at being abandoned even though it was her own doing. Hope led her to feeling they would put seeing her happy and move past their prejudice.

Alice and Edgar had to face their illusion of idealism as they encountered society's prejudice once they left the liberal confines of college life. Helping their children cope with prejudice from their families and both the black and white communities was very trying for them as a family. They persevered and gradually evolved a workable life style for all of them.

Marriages have problems even when the partners have the same background. Couples who have quite different backgrounds face added risks in working out a good marriage. This is especially true in mixed religions and mixed races when orthodoxy is involved. In these cases, couple run the risk of being cutoff from being accepted in their religion. In orthodox Judaism, violators are considered dead. Mixed marriages have the added issue of how to raise your children when your religions or different cultures are involved.

Marriages between races has the added handicap that just seeing the difference between white, black, Latino or Asian backgrounds doesn't even give you a chance before prejudices kick in. This is especially difficult for young children who may not understand the treatment they receive is not about them personally. All mixed marriages face two kinds of adjustment problems. The first is the added pressure that comes from different racial or religious backgrounds. This places added stress over what any couple faces as they try to breathe life into their fledgling marriage. The second problem is with families having a hard time deciding how to deal with the marriage they didn't want to happen. Each partner has to manage being caught between allegiances to their new spouse and their families

Adjusting to a mixed religious or cultural marriage

1. Consider the attitudes and acceptance of both families and your ability to deal with them if you are thinking of getting into a mixed marriage.

2. Get some idea of how big a problem family resistance to a marriage will be. See if you can find out to what length your families would go to express their unhappiness with a prospective marriage.

3. Each of you consider whether you will be able to deal with your family's resistance to the idea of your marriage. Then you have the added question of whether you can deal with the objection of your spouse-to-be's family.

4. Your engagement should be long enough to test out your respective family's ability to eventually accept your marriage. This will also give both of you time to see whether you can overcome these problems and achieve a workable marriage.

5   Talk to couples who are in a mixed marriage about the problems they found and how they managed them. Include relatively new couples and those who have been married for many years. This will give some sense of the long and short term problems you might have to face and how to deal with them.

6. Work out how you will raise your children with respect to problems of a mixed marriage. Consider how your children will be raised with respect to religion and what efforts are you going to make for your children to know both of your religions and/or cultures.

Adjusting to a mixed racial marriage

1. Dating experiences will give some idea of how other people will react and your comfort level in managing any problems you may encounter. This will be more difficult if the respective families are not aware of the dating.

2. Consider making your families aware of the dating no later than the point when the relationship shifts from casual to potentially more serious.

3. Be prepared to expect and plan how to manage resistance from both sides.

4. Test reactions in environments that may be more hostile to a mixed racial relationship compared to a relatively forgiving one. This will give some idea of the range of reactions you might come across and your comfort in coping with them.

5. Anticipate how you would feel helping your children cope with the same issues with which you have had to cope. Talk to parents who have been through this to see if this is something you would be able to handle.

References:

Do Opposites Attract Divorce? Dimensions Of Mixed Marriage, Jacques Janssen, Purdue University Press, 2003, 210 pages.

Mixed Blessings: Marriage Between Jews and Christians, Paul Cowan, Doubleday, 1987, 275 pages.

Mixed Matches, Joel Crohn, Ballantine Books, 1995, 352 pages. Paperback

Intercultural Marriage, Dugan Romano, Nicholas Brealey Publishing, 2001, 250 pages. Paperback

How to Survive in International Marriage, Oksana Leslie, AuthorHouse, 2004, 216 pages. Paperback

Guess Who's Coming to Dinner: Celebrating Interethnic, Interfaith, and Interracial Relationships, Brenda Lane Richardson,Wildcat Canyon Press, 2000, 216 pages. Paperback

Multiracial Couples: Black & White Voices, Paul C. Rosenblatt, Terri Karis, & Richard R. Powell, Sage Publications, 1995, 320 pages.

Mixed Blood: Intermarriage and Ethnic Idenity in Twentieth-Century America, Paul R. Spickard , University of Wisconsin Press, 991, 544 pages. Paperback

PRESENT FUTURE BALANCE

Ken recently came home from a fishing trip all charged up to get a small boat of his own. He mentioned this to his wife, Ida, when they had their monthly meeting to review family expenses. She was sympathetic but reminded him of their agreement to save money for their children's education and retirement. He resented her putting a damper on his excitement. It also got him to recognize that they were always thinking about saving for the future for one thing or another. That was all fine and good but what about the present? Were they supposed to keep depriving themselves living in the present for a future they may or may not ever reach? He concluded that they needed to strike a better balance between living in the present and planning for the future.

How to divide your attention between planning for the future and living in the present? This is a much harder question for a married person than for the single one. Both married and single have to provide for old age, medical care, and how they would like to spend their retirement. Both have to worry about how they will support whatever life style they want to have and what it will take to get it. Addressing these questions will force attention to how to balance current life style needs with anticipated future needs. This has to be repeated periodically to consider changing needs and interests.

A married person has more uncertain questions to consider that take into account the needs of all family members. Having children presses you to think a lot more about providing for the future for a home, taking care of the every day needs of his family, the education you want to provide your children, retirement, any other needs of your children, and the importance of building an estate. Answering these questions will help you decide how to divide your attention between living in the present and the future.

Reluctance to ask this question invites unhappiness. This occurs when you get too busy living in the present and too much assumption the future will take care of itself. When life catches up and you have to face medical or financial problems you can't handle, you will be overwhelmed with difficulties out of your control.

To avoid getting in this kind of situation requires time and attention to working out some form of plan. Getting help from a financial planner can be useful in deciding how to strike a reasonable balance with regard to finances.

Balancing the present and the future

1. Work out answers to the questions raised above that take into account both individual and couple needs.

2. Couples should also consider present-future balance on individual interests. This includes work, leisure activities, community involvement and others. Pay attention on how to work out these interests so that plans in one area don't cause problems in another one.

3. These present-future balance views are not static and will need to be reviewed on an ongoing basis as needs and circumstances change.

4. Whenever possible, children should be consulted for their views. This will improve the probability of finding conclusions that create the least amount of friction. On the positive side, they will improve the quality of relationships and provide a model for your children to follow.

5. Keep in mind that conclusions may be less important than the way you approach them. Being consulted about things that affect you will get a lot better hearing when this is not the case. This happens even when the conclusions are not to your liking.

References:

The Present: The Secret to Enjoying Your Work And Life, Now!, Spencer Johnson, Doubleday, 2003, 112 pages.

Next Places: Seeing Yourself, Seeking Your Future, Harvey Sarles, Syren Book Company, 2006, 214 pages. Paperback

Creating Your Future, David B. Ellis, Houghton Mifflin, 1999, 240 pages. Paperback

Falling Awake: Creating the Life of Your Dreams, Dave Ellis, Breakthrough Enterprises, 2002, 304 pages. Paperback

Living in Balance: Reshaping the You Within, Jerry Jonnson Ph. D, Author House, 2006, 188 pages. Paperback

IS MARRIAGE FOR YOU?

Bob was happy! He was 33, a successful bank manager, had many friends, dated frequently, had no serious attachments and wasn't sure he wanted one. In his spare time he enjoyed sports and golf in particular, and traveled whenever he got the chance.

His complacency came to a halt as more and more of his friends succumbed to marriage. This got him thinking whether that was a route he wanted to follow. He enjoyed his freedom and not having to be accountable to anyone for what he did. A mixed message came from observing his married friends. There was the joy of long term companionship and the pleasure from their children and the satisfaction in raising them. On other hand, they had financial pressures that would only increase over time and family needs that often conflicted with those of work. This left very little time for themselves. These obligations also left little time for the couples to enjoy the relationship they had before having children.

Thinking about the future got him wondering about what it would be like to be a bachelor when he was older. He could see that he might not enjoy growing old without having a family. He became acutely aware of the many trade offs that needed consideration.

Bob felt flooded and decided to put the subject of marriage on hold and let his thoughts simmer in the background. He found these thoughts creeping into his mind increasingly over the next few months. The answer came to him in a way he hadn't expected. He met a woman to whom he felt an instant attraction in a way he had never felt before. This was the beginning of finding the answer to whether marriage was for him.

Getting married isn't like buying a new car when you have a pretty good idea of what you want and you don't worry about whether the car wants you. Marriage is something else. You aren't sure what is really involved or whether it is for you. Neither are you clear about what to look for in a mate. Dating has been easy because you don't have to make any long term commitment. Marriage is for the long haul and that seems a little scary especially when it involves having a family. Thoughts of matrimony become less uncomfortable as your friends begin to marry and see what is involved. The idea of having a family also begins to become more attractive.

Marriage gets attractive with the prospect of having a life long companion with whom to have a family. Getting married also has its challenges. For a man it means taking on the responsibilities of marriage that include: mortgages, responsibility for the lives of others, and foregoing the pleasures of being single. The thought of having children is both exciting and daunting with the responsibility that goes with it. This can be more than offset by the pleasures of a loving and supportive relationship, having children and the satisfaction of playing a part in shaping their lives.

The situation may be more complicated for women who want both a career and a family. Having children will mean having to interrupt your career. This is followed by having to constantly juggle career and family. This is made easier with a mate who is able to share the responsibilities of parenthood and respect what it takes for her to have her own career. The upside of this for the husband is that her income lessens the pressure on him.

The situation is easier for women whose primary goal is having a family. She fulfills the traditional role of maintaining a home and raising the children. With this role is financial dependence on her husband and having to trust he will do his part. This works well in a good marriage but can become a major problem in a divorce. For both men and women marriage involves the anxiety of going into a new situation with uncertainty of what it will be like and your ability to manage it. Marriage works when you think of it as an investment in a relationship and family not the sacrifices you have to make.

The way you go about dating changes as the idea of marriage becomes more serious. It shifts from seeking an attractive and enjoyable companion to include the choice of a life-long companion with whom to have a family. You become more sensitive to looking for someone to share the responsibilities of being a good parent and help in having a home. The idea of who would make a good pre-marriage date becomes different when you are looking for a marital partner. Whether or when marriage happens depends on having the time to explore relationships, find a suitable mate, and the have the means to support a marriage and family.

Exploring marriage as a possibility

1. Becoming an adult involves making decisions about how you are going to support yourself, whether you want to get married, have a family and what other interests you want to follows. Decide whether you want to live a single or married life.

2. Any thought of marriage will be affected by how it impacts your career or others things you want to do.

3. Give thought to how comfortable you will be being accountable to another person and not always be able to do the things you like to do. Think about the ups downs of having a life long companion compared to bouncing from one relationship to another.

4. Make a decision about whether the benefits you get will be worth what it takes to get them. This gets easier when you find the love of your life.

5. Consider whether you want to have a family and all that goes with it.

6. Can you think about marriage as an investment in a relationship rather than what you have to give up to get it.

7   Making a decision to marry is not something you do in a moment. It is best done by letting it simmer over time until it becomes clear which way you want to go. Then it depends on finding the right person.

References:

Should We Marry? Joseph M. Champlin, Ave Maria Press, 2001, 159 pages. Paperback

Here Lies My Heart: Essays on Why We Marry, Why We Don't, and What We Find There, Amy Bloom, Beacon Press , 1999, 209 pages. Paperback

Why Men Marry: Marriage/Re-Marriage, H. William Schmitt, Author House, 2006, 408 pages. Paperback

Why Women Marry: An Odyssey of Women That Have Walked the Aisle, H. William Schmitt, 1st Books Library, 2004, 252 pages. Paperback

Why You're Still Single, Evan Marc Katz & Linda Holmes, Plume, 2006, 208 pages. Paperback

WORK

CAREER FATIGUE

Erica grew up in a family where she was the youngest and only female of four children. Her father and all of her brothers were aggressive, high achievers, competitive in the family and in their careers. They competed with one another in accomplishments and in sports. Erica, her brothers, and father enjoyed family times playing touch football, golf and tennis. She always felt pressed to show that she was as good as her brothers. Her mother tried unsuccessfully to moderate her intense need to compete with them.

Erica got her MBA degree and worked in corporate America. She was bright, competent and advanced quickly up the corporate ladder. She readily accepted any challenge that came her way. She worked very long hours that left little time for any social life or to enjoy her love of skiing and tennis. By the time she hit forty she found her energy and enthusiasm waning. Work and things she enjoyed doing didn't interest her any more. Work began to feel tedious. This frightened her because this was unfamiliar. She started to wonder whether she was burned out and maybe needed to be doing something different.

Career in common usage refers to work in a profession or business that is usually achieved through formal education and extends beyond a particular job. In contrast, a job usually refers to work done to earn money without any particular commitment beyond required performance.

Your career can become your prison. Erica was doing well until her work has lost its attraction. You may feel trapped into staying with your job either because your fear of the unknown if you leave it or for financial need. You have two options in both cases. You can either find a way to re-energize your interest, focus on how to make the most of what is possible, or you can explore whether pursuing a new career is feasible and economically possible. This latter option is more challenging and should not be dismissed without determining whether it is a possible option.

Coping with lost attraction

1. List the specific ways you feel trapped

2. Look at the possibilities that might improve for each of these items . Include continuing education possibilities.

3. Attempt to put into practice each of the possibilities in item 2.

4. Evaluate the outcome. If this does produce renewed interest, consider exploration on your own or with a career counselor for new career opportunities on how to make the most out of what is possible.

Making the most out of what is possible

1. Recognize that complaining or blaming about being in a bad place doesn't solve the problem and adds to the already existing unhappiness. It also uses intellectual and emotion energy (psychic energy) that would be better spent in finding solutions.

2. Psychic energy should be invested in improving the situation not in blame. For example, if one of the problems is a difficult boss, focus on how to deal with him differently rather than on how to get him to change.

3. Have a clear understanding of the existing situation. This requires checking out assumptions. It is easier to assume that something is the case than to check presumptions out. This can help avoid problems that don't have to happen. Not getting an expected promotion may not be about you. There could be many other reasons why this might happen. Find out before you come to any conclusion.

4. Don't view efforts that don't work out as failures. Recognize that efforts that don't work out, while disappointing, do provide the opportunity to learn from your mistakes. Failure is not learning from experience.

Reviewing Financial Need

Making a career change will likely have financial implications, at least in the short run. Assess your financial situation to see what is possible.

1. List financial assets.

2. List possible financial resources that might be utilized on a short term basis.

3. List financial obligations. Divide the list into two categories: those that relate to basic essentials and those that are desirable but not essential.

4. Evaluate how you could manage to live on bare essentials for the limited time it might take to get established in a new occupation. Make this evaluation in consultation with affected family members.

5. Determine how workable making any of these changes might be and develop a plan for making them happen.

1. Review your interests, abilities, and experiences for application to a new career.

2. Review what experiences and interests you enjoy.

3. Consider in what occupations these might be useful.

4. Talk to people in these occupations to see what it would be like to be working in them.

5. Find out if there is any way to gain actual experience in pursuing possibilities that are of particular interest before having to make a commitment.

6. Determine what training would be needed to perform in these occupations and the feasibility of gaining it.

7. Evaluate whether pursuing one of the new career possibilities is workable financially and emotionally.

References:

Banishing Burnout: Six Strategies for Improving Your Relationship with Work, Michael P. Leiter & Christina Maslach, Jossey-Bass, 2005, 208 pages.

Overcoming Job Burnout: How to Renew Enthusiasm for Work, Beverly A. Potter, Ronin Publishing, 2005, 238 pages. Paperback

Reclaiming the Fire: How Successful People Overcome Burnout, Steven Berglas, Random Hou se, 2001, 256 pages. Paperback

Career Burnout: Causes and Cures, Ayala Pines & Elliot Aronson, 1989, 257 pages. Paperback

Toxic Work: How to Overcome Stress, Overload and Burnout and Revitalize Your Career, Barbara Bailey Reinhold, Plume, 1997, 256 pages. Paperback

ENTREPRENEUR OR EMPLOYEE

Brad was about to graduate from college with his Master's degree in Business Administration. He had a couple of interesting job offers but was undecided about what he wanted to do. He had always wanted to follow in his father's foot-steps and have his own business, since he was a kid working for him. His father hoped he would take over his business some day but this was not to be. His father had a heart attack and died when he was in high school. To his disappointment the business was sold.

Brad was trying to decide whether to get a job or start his own business after getting his business degree. His father had left him enough money to get started in a small business. He considered both possibilities. It came down to deciding whether he wanted to have a job with a steady income and time for a life outside of work or whether he want to do his own thing with a lot of financial insecurity and little time for himself until he got the business up and running.

He remembered what it was like watching his father start his business. He decided to take a job to see what it was like working for someone else before deciding whether he wanted to work for himself. After awhile he found the challenges of working for someone else too limiting and launched into following in his father's footsteps to start his own business.

Being an entrepreneur or an employee requires two different mind sets. Being and entrepreneur has many attractions: profits and how they are used, being one's own boss, make decisions, work with people by choice, no restriction on creativity, control over work environment among others.

Being an entrepreneur also has a downside, financial responsibility, long hours, having to manage all administrative details, hiring, firing, managing personnel issues, having to be responsible for other people's welfare, limited personal time and the possibility of losing your shirt.

An employee has a greater chance of doing work of choice without having financial responsibility or responsibility for other people's welfare. Income is more predictable with established fringe benefits but has lower income potential. There are usually opportunities for additional training at no expense and working in an established community.

The downside has its limitations: being managed by others, limited compensation, defined work hours, and benefits determined by others.

Being an entrepreneur

1. Define a vision on which you are willing to risk your occupational and financial future.

2. Evaluate the financial, physical, emotional, intellectual, and business acumen resources needed to achieve your vision.

3. Determine whether these resources can be accomplished.

4. Prepare a business plan that is reviewed with an accountant that will acceptable to a bank or financial backer.

5. Talk to at least two or three successful entrepreneurs, preferably in businesses that parallel the one that is being considered. The objective is to gain insight into the realities that go with starting a business. It will also be helpful to learn from entrepreneurs who did not succeed.

6. Experience suggests you be prepared to spend at least 18 months to two years to become profitable.

7. Determine if you have the needed traits for being an entrepreneur.

8. Evaluate your comfort level in living with high risk.

In the May and June 2007 Newsletter of AARP, Brent Bowers discusses the case of Barbara Thornton who had the where-with-all to start her own business at age 48. He also discusses the traits it takes to start your own business.

"All her life, Barbara Thornton put up with a nagging problem: her shoes. Why, she wondered, could she never find size 11½ shoes? She knew many women in the same predicament who either put up with tight fits or did their shopping in the men's department.

In 1995—at age 48, fresh out of Harvard Business School, after a long career in public policy, she saw a business opportunity in her fellow sufferers' frustrations. Two years later, she launched DesignerShoes.com, which sells more than 50 brands of footwear in hard-to-find sizes up to 15WW. "

Older entrepreneurs have a huge advantage over their younger competitors can only envy. They have wisdom forged by experience. Having skills is one thing; being able to use them successfully to launch a business is another.

Brent Bowers interviewed some 500 business owners over a period of 15 years. He found that highly effective entrepreneurs are shrewd judges of strengths and weaknesses, most especially their own, and they share an important set of traits.

1. *An Eye for Possibilities:* spotting opportunities others miss is a signal trait of entrepreneurs of any age.

2. *A Take-Charge Attitude:* The second most common trait among entrepreneurs is their compulsion to run their own show. They have the initiative and had it even as employees.

3. *Comfort With Chaos:* As much as they relish their independence, entrepreneurs anticipate and even enjoy the curve balls that life throws. They fully expect to scramble to survive. They thrive on chaos and see advantage in every messy situation.

4. *The Tenacity of a Pit Bull:* Without tenacity—a term used to encompass persistence and passion—most businesses would never come to be. There are just too many unpleasant jolts in starting a company to keep on going unless you are the human equivalent of a pit bull.

5. *Creative Instincts:* There's no evidence, yet, of an entrepreneurial gene, but most business owners interviewed showed entrepreneurial flair as children, and many had business in their bloodlines.

6. *Enormous Self-confidence.*

7. A case in point has been reported by William J. Dennis, a researcher at the National Federation of Independent Business in Washington, D.C.

    "Entrepreneurs are dreamers. But they can also be as logical as Mr. Spock. While real-estate agents talk "location, location, location," the start-up mantra is "research, research, research." Before Barbara Thornton launched DesignerShoes.com, she quit her job as a management consultant and sold shoes in a mall for six dollars an hour. The experts say entrepreneurs are a rational breed, better described as risk managers than risk takers. "They don't roll the dice," says" They don't pursue wild schemes. They take calculated risks.""

8. *Super Resiliency:* Learning from failure is a lesson every entrepreneur eventually learns.

Being an employee

1. Find a suitable job for your skills, long term career goals, and desired life style.

2. Determine suitability of work conditions and benefits.

3. Evaluate your work environment for how you can make it a meaningful experience for you.

4. Evaluate your job performance on a regular basis that includes both positive accomplishments and areas that need improvement.

5. Don't let bothersome situations pass without addressing them. Let whomever is involved know what is bothersome in a way that focused on a problem situation not a judgment about what another person's behavior. Letting frustrations fester only creates problems that grow the more there is a delay in addressing them.

6. Be diligent in meeting expectations that you accept. Let the person to whom you report know when it becomes clear the expected deadline will not be met and why this is so. Indicate expected completion time when that can be determined.

7. Have a plan for keeping up to date in your job skills.

    Brad solved his problem about whether to be an entrepreneur or an employee by trying out both possibilities. He found it was more satisfying to have his own business and was worth the risk that was involved.

- The Kauffman Foundation in Kansas City, Missouri, has a website with information and advice by and for entrepreneurs. The foundation's FastTrac business-development program is offered across the country for aspiring and established entrepreneurs.

- SCORE is a national network based in Washington, D.C., with more than 10,500 volunteer counselors who give free advice to entrepreneurs.

- The Small Business Administration, a federal agency, provides a wide variety of services and funding to entrepreneurs. It also operates Small Business Development Centers in every state.

- Angel-investor groups take stakes in start-ups that more traditional financiers might shun. For a list of groups see the Angel Capital Education Foundation's website.

- Colleges and universities offer courses in entrepreneurship. More than 2,000 schools have such programs, up from just a handful when boomers first entered the workforce.

- Websites and magazines such as www.vFinance.com, Inc., and Entrepreneur.

References:

How You Can Start and Manage Your Own Business: Complete Step-by-Step Guide, Dr. N. O. O. Ejiga, Trafford Publishing, 2006, 324 pages. Paperback

Are You Ready to Be Your Own Boss?, Carol Denbow, Plain and Simple Books, 2006, 144 pages. Paperback

Starting Your First Business: Gain Independence and Love Your Work, American Jim Sapp, Rylinn Publishing LLC, 2004, 280 pages. Paperback

Employee to Entrepreneur, Suzanne Mulvehill, Business Publications, Incorporated, 2003, 288 pages. Paperback

Entrepreneur Or Employee? Should You Get Out Or Stay In Your Current Job?, Ken Chane, Agathos Publications, 290 pages.

How to Succeed on Your Own: Overcoming the Emotional Roadblocks on the Way from Corporation to Cottage, from Employee to Entrepreneur, Karin Abarbanel, Henry Holt & Co., 1994.

FAMILY BUSINESSES

Marvin Snider, Ph.D.

Howard ran a successful business that manufactured various rubber products. His wife, Sally, managed the business office. They had two sons, Mark, 30, and Jerry, 27, who each entered the business when they were old enough. They both eventually worked up to middle management positions. Mark was responsible for production of one product and Jerry was responsible for marketing of Mark's product.

The brothers had a stormy time growing up. They were always competing with one another. Jerry always wanted to do what Mark did. This often created arguments. It got more difficult when Jerry was able to do better than his brother as often happened in sports and at times in their studies.

Family relationships spilled over into the business. When problems developed on the product in Mark and Jerry's department they would blame one another and then try to get their father to support their views. Howard tended to favor Jerry who seemed to have a better grasp of the business. Mark resented this which only added more ammunition in their battles. Mark would try to even things out by getting his mother involved. She would be sympathetic to Mark and try to intercede which annoyed both Howard and Jerry and led to some struggle between the parents. Howard had a hard time getting Sally to stop acting on her motherly instincts when they interfered in the business. They all had trouble keeping work relationships separate from family relationships.

This struggle created another problem for Howard. Employees, not part of the family, resented Mark and Jerry being given their responsibilities before they were ready because they were family. This created some concern among Howard's senior executives regarding their future when Mark and Jerry became more experienced. They wondered whether family ties would trump loyalty, experience and competence.

A family business is a mixed bag. On the one hand it provides an opportunity for a family to enjoy their relationship while generating their financial support. Family relationships suffer when the needs of business conflict with family needs. It is very difficult to keep clear the distinction between the structure of family relationships and those that are needed in business as Howard found out. It gets all too easy to confuse the two. A mother who is committed to emotionally nurturing her children in the family environment may have a hard time making decisions in work that are unpleasant for her children. It was very hard for Sally to keep family relationships between family and business separate. A father who will tolerate incompetence in work from a son that he would not tolerate from other employees, creates problems both for his business and in his family. Children can learn to take advantage of their parents in the work place in ways they learned growing up.

Family members are likely to have different views and priorities and often not have productive ways of resolving differences. They all have difficulty separating out their roles as family members from those as employees. Firing an employee is always unpleasant but near impossible when parents disagree about a child's behavior in the business. Favoritism often gets confused with competence. It takes maturity and clarity to keep separate what is appropriate in the home from that of the work environment.

Making a family business workable

1. Parents should not involve family members in their business unless they are prepared to implement clear boundaries between family and work relationships. This applies as much for themselves as for family members as was the case with Mark and Jerry.

2. Everyone should understand family relationships will not make up for incompetence. To ignore this is a problem for all concerned: the business, family relationships, other employees, and the self esteem of the individuals involved.

3. Do not involve family members in the business unless they are able separate accountability as family members from that as employees.

4. A business cannot serve two masters.

5. Have family members report to a non-family member. This will reduce the potential for emotional conflict in the work environment. This can only work if the designated employee has the same authority he would have with any other employee.

6. Parents should maintain ownership control to avoid legal and emotional problems. Parents and children need to learn that becoming a partner is earned not a birthright.

7. Define an explicit statement on advancement and reward possibilities for non-family members if you are to retain valued employees. Morale will be undermined if family connections supercede competence.

8. Do not hire any person who cannot be fired, family or otherwise.

References:

Generation to Generation: Life Cycles of the Family Business, Kelin E. Gersick John A. Davis, Marion McCollom Hampton, & Ivan Lansberg, Harvard Business School Press, 1997, 302 pages.

The Survival Guide for Business Families, Gerald Le Van, Routledge, 1998, 256 pages.

Keeping The Family Business Healthy: How to Plan for Continuing Growth, Profitability and Family Leadership, John L. Ward, Business Owner Resources, 1997, 266 pages.

Perpetuating The Family Business : 50 Lessons Learned from Long Lasting, Successful Families in Business, John L. Ward, Palgrave MacMillan, 2004, 178 pages.

Making Sibling Teams Work: The Next Generation, Craig E. Aronoff, John L. Ward, Business Owner Resources, 1997, 72 pages. Paperback

Family Meetings: How to Build a Stronger Family and a Stronger Business Second Edition, Craig E. Aronoff, John L. Ward, Business Owner Resources, 2002, 61 pages. Paperback

TEAMWORK

Harry was the owner of an advertising agency. His employees worked on accounts in teams. He was faced with improving the poor performance of one team. The five members of the team seemed to spend more time arguing with one another than getting their work done. Evaluation of the group's performance revealed that Barry, the team leader, did not have the group's respect. There also were problems in the lack of a coordinated focus. Their effectiveness also suffered from Barry's leadership in guiding them to work together in a respectful and supportive manner. The result was competition for dominance in the vacuum resulting from his limitations. Jockeying for power significantly reduced their productivity.

Harry replaced Barry with Jack, a new hire, whose personality and experience suited him for the leadership role. Jack started by interviewing each member of the group to get a reading on their personality, skills, and personal goals. His other purpose was to let them know his leadership would be different than Barry's had been. He met with the whole group to get their collective view of how they understood the problem they had working with Barry. Jack also guided them in revising their account strategies and how this fit their individual agendas. He made sure he acknowledged their contributions and welcomed their ideas. The team's productivity showed marked improvement within a short period.

Teamwork is about the collected efforts of a group to achieve a common goal. As a member, you will be productive and satisfied when you are able to achieve your own goals as you participate in reaching the group goal. You recognize a way to move up the corporate ladder is enhanced by being a cooperative and productive member of team. This effort gets undermined when personal agendas of the group interferes with the group's other responsibilities.

Team efforts are successful when the leader has a clear vision of the goal to be achieved and has personality and charisma that motivates team members to follow his direction. This will happen when the leader is able to have team members feel respected and welcomed for their contributions. Another essential quality is the leader's ability to provide an atmosphere where people are able to respectfully explore their different perspectives and have the common goal of finding a resolution that best meets the objectives of the group. This requires team members to put finding resolution of differences over needing their own views to prevail. This permits the team members to share satisfaction in their individual accomplishments secondary to their joint accomplishments.

Effecting a productive team effort

1. Put a team leader in place who has the required skills to lead the group.

    I. Good relationship skills

    II. Able to motivate group members to follow his lead

    III. Respects and invites contribution of others.

    IV. Has needed technical knowledge and experience for the groups mission.

    V. Has self confidence

    VI. Skilled in conflict resolution

    VII. Pays as much attention to affirmations as criticism

2. CEO demonstrates support for team leaders

3. CEO provides necessary administrative support for the group to accomplish its mission.

4. Keeps the group informed of matters that affect them such as status of the company, changes in personnel polices, and monitoring of their efforts - acknowledgment of their achievements and accountability for unacceptable performance.

5. Team members are acknowledged as individuals and not just as a member of a group.

References:

Making Teams Work : 24 Lessons for Working Together Successfully (The McGraw-Hill, Michael Maginn, McGraw-Hill, 2003, 64 pages. Paperback

Overcoming the Five Dysfunctions of a Team: A Field Guide for Leaders, Managers, and Facilitators, Patrick M. Lencioni, Jossey-Bass, 2005, 180 pages. Paperback

When Teams Work Best: 6,000 Team Members and Leaders Tell What It Takes to Succeed, FrankM. J. LaFasto & Carl Larson, Sage Publications, Inc, 2001, 221 pages.

The Wisdom of Teams: Creating the High-Performance Organization (Collins Business Essentials, Jon R. Katzenbach & Douglas K. Smith, Collins, 2003, 352 pages. Paperback

Marvin Snider, Ph.D.

Team Players and Teamwork, Glenn M. Parker, Jossey-Bass, 1996 ,208 pages. Paperback

Group Dynamics for Teams, Daniel Levi, Sage Publications, Inc, 2007, 384 pages. Paperback

UNEMPLOYMENT

Eric was happy in his job of ten years as a manager in a computer firm when a downturn in the economy resulted in being laid off. He experienced a range of emotions: surprised, upset, angry and betrayed. He was surprised because he had good reviews, he was well liked and his department was doing well. Logically, he could understand his being laid off because his department was merged with another one and they needed only one manager, they chose the one more experienced.

Emotional acceptance was much more challenging. He couldn't help feel that the dismissal reflected something lacking in him. Once he got over the shock , he was able step back and view what happened in a broader perspective. After reviewing his job history and the existing state of the computer industry, he was able to see that what happened was not about him. He was reminded of the regret and positive recommendation his boss gave him as he was being laid off. His wife, Linda, was angry and upset. She thought he got a raw deal. He knew she meant to be helpful but it had the opposite effect. One more concern to be managed.

He was optimistic he would find a new job. In the meantime, he had to reorganize his life and get prepared for the drudgery of looking for a new job: networking, rewriting resumes, interviews and more. They would also have to rethink their finances on the possibility it might take awhile before he found a new one. The upside of this happening is that he was able to spend more time with Linda and their son, Jason.

Getting laid off is likely to be very upsetting under the best of conditions. It upsets your established life style, adds anxieties about finding a new job, shakes up your self confidence, and raises uncertainty about how it will affect your finances. It gets even worse if you were fired. Also needing attention is the effect being unemployed will have on your family.

It may be tempting to 'keep a stiff upper lip' in minimizing your loss. This does not serve either for you or your family. Being upbeat and realistic about what has happened and sensitive to how it affects them will help them adapt. It will model a constructive way to deal with problems. It will also avoid arousing anxiety that comes with the double message everything is OK when your behavior says otherwise. Your children will benefit from feeling that they can be helpful in coping with a period of unemployment.

Rejection of any kind, and being laid off or fired, in particular, will challenge self confidence. You can minimize this happening, as Eric did, by taking inventory on your strengths, areas that need improvement, your work experience, interests, and the type of work you might enjoy. This assessment will buoy up your self confidence in developing a strategy for finding a new job.

Be prepared to modify your life style if being unemployed looks like it goes on for an extended period. Being conservative in managing your finances may be uncomfortable but it beats the alternative of getting over-extended on the expectation of quickly finding a new job.

A long period of unemployment can give rise to increasing tension and anxiety for you and your family. The tension increases after you have done all the prescribed things for an unemployed person. It is very desirable not to let disappointment leak out increasing tension between family members. This can be accomplished by family meeting where everyone's concerns can be discussed, respected, and solutions found that work for everybody. Feeling one another's support can be very helpful in keeping the focus on coping with ongoing problems rather taking frustrations out on one another. It is also helpful to engage in doing pleasant activities together that don't involve spending money: playing games, outdoor activities, visits to libraries, and more. The upside is that it gives families time to spend together they might not otherwise have.

Don't allow resumes that go unanswered, interviews that are not productive, or phone call not returned undermine your self confidence. These events should not be viewed as a measure of your competence, but of the need to find the right match between what a prospective employer needs and your skills and experience.

Adjusting to unemployment

1. Allow yourself time to vent your feelings at becoming unemployed. It doesn't have to have anything to do with logic, only an opportunity to release the pent up feelings which are likely to reflect the degree to which you feel it was unjustified.

2. Do the same in giving your family an opportunity to understand what happened and how it may affect them. Hearing first hand your view and an opportunity to be heard will minimize any difficulty they may have. Otherwise, if the event is unspoken, they are left to draw their own conclusions from the presenting ambiguity.

3. Taking time off before launching into a job search is likely to be helpful in gaining a more balanced perspective on what has happened. This will help you to present yourself to prospective employers in a more positive manner.

4. Update you resume. Decide on how you will respond to inquiries about why you left your last job. Develop a list of people to use as references. The ones you use may depend on the job you are considering. Tailor your resume to fit the job you are considering.

5. Develop a plan for how you will look for a new job.

6. Treat looking for new job as though it was a job in itself. This involves scheduling defined work periods, perhaps on a daily basis. This will enable you to take time off without feeling you are being negligent.

7. Prepare for job interviews with mental rehearsal. Learn what you can about your prospective employer. Anticipate the questions you might be asked. Prepare answers to these questions. Rehearse them often enough so that the answers come easily to you. This minimizes awkward silences of having to come up with answers to difficult questions in the moment.

8. Keep your family abreast of your progress. These discussions help them be aware of what is happening and be less subject to making erroneous assumptions that invite needless anxiety. This is also helpful in showing respect for what they think or feel. This is helpful in their being able to be supportive to whatever you need from them.

References:

Landing on the Right Side of Your Ass: A Survival Guide for the Recently Unemployed, Michael Laskoff, Three Rivers Press, 2004, 256 pages. Paperback

Career Comeback: Eight steps to getting back on your feet when you're fired, laid off, or your business ventures has failed--and finding more job satisfaction than ever before, Bradley Richardson, Broadway, 2004, 336 pages. Paperback

The Job Loss Recovery Guide: A Proven Program for Getting Back to Work -- Fast!, Lynn Joseph, New Harbinger Publications, 2003, 154 pages. Paperback

Unemployment Survival Guide, The-OSI, Jim Stringham & David R Workman, Gibbs Smith, Publisher, 2004, 96 pages.

We Got Fired!:...And It's the Best Thing That Ever Happened to Us, Harvey MacKay, Ballantine Books, 2004, 368 pages.

Surviving a Layoff: Managing Stress, Family, and Finances--Discovering New Opportunities and New Potential--How to Package, Market, and Sell Yourself--Tips for Starting, Harry Dahlstrom, Dahlstrom & Co, 1998, 48 pages.

Section II

TOOLS FOR ANY SUBJECT

COMMUNICATION

ACTIVE LISTENING

George was a graphic designer in an advertising company. The company held weekly staff meetings to review ongoing projects. His boss, Tom, ran the meetings. George was called into Tom's office after one meeting. He got apprehensive as he noticed that George looked angry. He wondered what he had done wrong but couldn't think what it might be. Once he sat down, Tom blasted him for his attitude at staff meetings. George didn't know what he was talking about. He hardly said anything at meetings. That was the point! Tom was angry at George's lack of contribution in these meetings. He seemed bored, doodled, looked out the window and didn't seem very involved. His behavior seemed to say he wasn't interested in what was going on. These observations surprised Tom. He felt interested and involved and followed what was going on. He apologized to Tom for how he come across and assured him he was more interested and involved than he appeared. He asked Tom to tell him what observations gave him that impression. Tom described the nonverbal behavior that led him to his conclusion.

Active listening may sound like a contradiction, but it isn't. In passive listening, the speaker has no idea whether what he says is heard or understood. In active listening, the listener gives cues that tells the speaker that he has the listener's attention. This attention is communicated in the following ways.

- *Regular Eye Contact:* The way a person looks can communicate warmth, interest, or boredom. A glazed look, for example, signals boredom and, "I'm somewhere else." In addition, attention focused on other objects than the speaker is distracting and is likely to suggest disinterest.

- *Sympathetic Facial Expression:* A pleasant facial expression accompanied by a smile, as appropriate, communicates interest. This interest must be genuinely felt, however; a smile can be offensive when the speaker hasn't said anything to warrant a smile. A fixed frozen smile also conveys a negative message. The attentive listener will know that he is doing something wrong when the speaker gives cues of discontent: irritation in his voice or facial expression.

- *Body language:* Periodically nodding the head in affirmation, sitting in an upright alert position, or slight leaning in the direction of the speaker are also positive signs to the speaker. Avoid distracting audience behaviors such as doodling, foot rocking, finger tapping, picking at finger nails, and toying with objects.

- *Periodic vocal affirmation:* Periodic statements such as uhuh, yes, good point, are welcoming, but they should not be made so often that they become distracting.

- *Request for Information or Clarification:* Such requests carry a message of interest, though they can become distracting to the speaker if too numerous. However, if the listener anticipates that frequent interruptions may be necessary, he should negotiate with the speaker the best way to relate to this concern. This is respectful to the speaker and helps to preserve a mutually positive relationship.

- Asking thoughtful questions: These questions tell the speaker that he has been heard and to what degree he has been understood. This also gives the speaker information that helps know how well he is coming across and how he might need to modify his comments. Usually a speaker will indicate when he is open to questions. A respectful listener guides his questions by this request.

Once Tom told George about his observations, George understood the basis for Tom's anger. He made a mental note to do something about each of the bothersome behaviors that Tom mentioned.

How to be an active listener

1. Be mindful of your nonverbal cues that you give in conversation, listening to a lecture or presentation. Intentional use of these cues will help improve the quality of your relationships.

2. Requests for information and thoughtful questions are useful to the person speaking and are ways for the listener to gain the most from the experience. Doing this tailors the experience to your needs.

References:

The Gift to Listen, the Courage to Hear, Cari Jackson, Augsburg Fortress Publishers, 2003, 109 pages. Paperback

How to Speak and Listen Effectively, Harvey A. Robbins, American Management Association, 2003, 77 pages . Paperback

A Little Book of Listening Skills: 52 Essential Practices for Profoundly Loving Yourself and Other People, Mark Brady & Jennifer Austin Leigh, Paideia Press, 2005, 103 pages. Paperback

Wisdom of Listening, Mark Brady, Wisdom Publications, 2003, 350 pages. Paperback

Listening: The Forgotten Skill: A Self-Teaching Guide, Madelyn Burley-Allen, Wiley, 1995, 208 pages. Paperback

ACTIVE SPEAKING

Sally was president of the Parent Teachers' Association of her children's elementary school. She worked very diligently in preparing next year's program. She wanted to be sure she got a good reception for her plans. She rehearsed her talk several times and once in front of a mirror.

She felt she the presentation went well, but was disappointed at it's cool reception. She asked one of her good friends, Gail, who also had children in the school how her proposal came across. Gail seemed uncomfortable as she gave some general platitudes. Sally picked this up and told her not to worry about giving her an honest assessment because she knew she was missing something. With that encouragement, Sally told her that she had a lot of good things to say but there was a problem in the way they were said. She tended to talk in a monotone and didn't make sufficient eye contact with the audience. When she did look up, she tended to talk to the ceiling. This distracted the audience from paying more attention to the merit of what was being said.

Active speaking isn't as redundant as it would seem. An active speaker continually monitors his impact whether with one person, a group or an auditorium full of people. The object of speaking is to be heard in a desired fashion. A speaker can do several things to encourage a positive response from his audience as Sally learned from her friend Gail.

- *Eye Contact:* Eye contact is just as important for the speaker as it is for the listener. A person who speaks while glancing around the room or who talks to the walls or ceiling is likely to gain the irritation of his audience. This will be especially problematic when discussing critical issues or when there is conflict.

- *Manner of Speaking:* Speaking at a pace that is comfortable to follow with appropriate expression of feeling and emphasis encourages the listener's attention. Periodic pauses should be included to give the listener time to absorb the significance of what is said. Also helpful is repetition for emphasis. Speaking too fast, too slow, or in a monotone will lose the audience's interest.

- *Periodic Feedback:* A speaker should periodically ask for feedback unless the listener volunteers comments along the way. The feedback gives the speaker some indication about how his comments are being received. This is especially important in one-on-one conversations. When one person dominates the communication, it becomes a lecture.

- *Balancing the Conversation:* Communication is mutually beneficial when views are exchanged. The speaker should present his views in a manner that will acknowledge the listener's interests, knowledge and perspective.

- *Validation of Listener*: Validation of the listener's comments will communicate the speaker's interest in what his listener thinks. This is likely to invite continued attention to the speaker. When the listener's comments approach being disruptive, the speaker should request that comments be postponed until he has completed his thought. Then, the listener should be given time to be heard.

- *Use of Stories:* Stories engage the attention of any person. The presentation of even the most boring material can be made interesting when laced with anecdotes or a story. This taps into people's natural love of stories, which is fostered by what they read, and why they go to the theater and movies. This provides a familiar context for new material that enhances understanding.

Being a Good Speaker

When talking to a group

1. Shift gaze from one side of the group to the other as you speak. Make momentary eye contact with individuals while scanning the group. Walking from one side of the stage helps with eye contact. Be careful to limit the amount of moving back and forth so that it doesn't become distracting.

2. Presentation language should be familiar to audience. Use of jargon will result in rapid loss of audience.

3. Use of stories and anecdotes can keep an audience engaged even with the dullest topic.

4. Don't speak in a monotone. Varying the speed and volume of speaking will help keep the audiences attention. Periodic brief pauses when making a difficult point will give the audience time to digest the point.

5. Being receptive to questions or comments can help keep an audience engaged. Manage these comments so that they don't become too disruptive or distract from your reason for speaking. Interrupt comments that go too long by suggesting private discussion after you have finished speaking.

6. Asking an audience to hold questions till the end of the presentation can invite audience to drift. An alternative is to take questions on an ongoing basis is to pause at a few times for questions or comments, instead of having to wait till the end of your presentation.

7. Repeating a point twice or more gives added emphasis and time to consider what is being said. It also helps to vary the pattern of presentation in how you use speed, volume of speaking, pauses and repetition.

8. Humor is a powerful in making presentations. It can help to get a point across as well as keep an audience alert.

9. Give affirmation to meaningful comments from the audience.

10. Appropriate use of hand gestures can be very effective in making a point. Use of hands can also be useful in giving visual image to a point. Examples include using fingers to tick off a number of points, show closeness or distance by moving hands together or far apart.

11. Props may also be useful in adding clarification to what is being said.

When in conversation with another person.

1. Maintain eye contact as much as possible

2. Avoid glancing around the room giving the impressions of surveying the crowd for better prospects.

3. Avoid getting into a monologue. Interrupt another person's monologue with questions.

4. Strike a balance between sharing one's thoughts with interest in the other person's thoughts.

5. Respect difference by avoiding judgments as "You are wrong." This kind of statement presumes superiority over the other person. When discussion does not resolve differences, the topic may end with an agreement to disagree.

References:

The Elements of Great Public Speaking: How to Be Calm, Confident, And Compelling, J. Lyman Macinnis, Ten Speed Press, 2006 ,148 pages. Paperback

The Quick and Easy Way to Effective Speaking, Dale Carnegie, Pocket, 1990, 224 pages. Paperback

10 Days to More Confident Public Speaking, The Princeton Language Institute &Lenny Laskowski, Grand Central Publishing, 2001, 224 pages. Paperback

Speaking Without Fear or Nervousness, Secrets of Successful Speakers, Helen Sutton Audio Cassette

How You Can Motivate, Captivate, and Persuade, Lilly Walters, McGraw-Hill, 2003, 368 pages. Paperback

Unlocking Speaking and Listening, Pam Hodson & Deborah Jones, 2006, 164 pages.

ASSUMPTIONS

Marvin Snider, Ph.D.

Edward and Linda consulted a couple therapist because they felt their marriage was in trouble. Their arguments were getting more frequent and more intense. They didn't understand what was happening because they often got along well. A typical example was given to their therapist. It happened when Edward expressed concern about how high their expenses were as he was going over the monthly bills. Linda got angry at Ed for blaming her for spending too much money. She fired back that he ought to look at the money he was spending. This led to an increasingly heated argument that went nowhere and left two frustrated and angry people. They learned in therapy that the source of their problem came from each of them making assumptions about the other and treating them as what actually happened. The stress in their relationship was greatly reduced once they learned to check out their assumptions before reacting.

The same problem occurs in other relationships. Jacob was a supervisor in a plumbing company for the past eight years. He got angry when he didn't get the raise he expected. He assumed this happened because his boss was angry at him for the problem he caused in not getting an important job done on time. He talked to his boss to protest the unfair treatment because it wasn't his fault the job didn't get done as expected. He was embarrassed at the way he expressed his anger when he learned the delay in his raise had nothing to do with the job being late. This embarrassment wouldn't have happened had Jacob checked out his assumption before acting on it.

Making assumptions in relationships occurs when one person treats his understanding as an accurate reflection of what another person meant by his word or behavior.

This can happen for different reasons:

- You are not aware you are making an assumption and are responsive to correcting your misperception once you are aware of your error.

- You are not sure your perceptions are correct because it is not possible to check them out. This happens when you have to make a decision and you don't have the necessary information to make it.

- You are not sure your perception is correct and it might be unpleasant to find this out. This could happen when you are expected to know the answer and don't have it and you are embarrassed to admit it. It could also be the case that if you check out your perception you will have to behave in a way you won't like.

- You are not interested in being correct because you just want to let someone know how you feel. This could happen when someone made you angry and you want to let them know that even if you are wrong.

- You don't need to check your assumption out because there is no consequence in being wrong.

- You want to get someone to do your bidding. This could happen when you assume they would be willing to do something for you and ask it in a way that makes it hard to correct your assumption. You need to get the clutter in your garage cleaned up. You assume your son doesn't want to do it, so you ask him a way that makes it hard for him to refuse you.

- You want to start a relationship in a positive way. This happens when you make an agreement and assume the other person will be honest or expect that a person will honor his commitment.

- You make assumptions guided by your anxiety that may or may not make sense to you or other people. This often results in arguments.

The problem in making assumptions is the likelihood you may be wrong.

Edward and Linda learned how this created stress in their relationship because they had difficulty in accepting each other's understanding of events. Sometimes you enter agreements with the assumption the other party would be cooperative in working out the details. Being wrong results in an argument. This is why it is essential that any agreement of importance should have all the terms and conditions spelled out in writing so there is no room for misunderstanding what was in the agreement.

Working with assumptions

1. Do not assume that another person is aware he is acting on an assumption. A person who is convinced his point of view is correct may discount the possibility of any other point of view. A handy rule of thumb is never assume that a given perspective is the only one without checking it out, even when it may seem obvious. The possibility of other perceptions should always be considered until determined otherwise.

2. Check out an assumption even if seems redundant and even if it might make you feel uncomfortable. It is the safest way to avoid misunderstandings. Edward and Linda would have avoided their struggle if they had checked out their assumptions about one another. Doing so is respectful to each other by ensuring each one was correctly understood. A good way to check out an assumption is to ask, " *Do I correctly understand that you X.*" This is preferable to "*What do you mean by X.*" The first approach puts the burden on the listener, whereas the second may come across as a challenge. The downside in not clarifying understanding is that it increases the possibility of masking an erroneous assumption rather than there being a true difference of opinion.

3. Meaningful communication starts with the assumption another person will relate in good faith with openness and honesty. Behaving in this manner is more likely to elicit the same behavior in return. At the same time, it is prudent to be alert to cues that suggest a person is being less than forthright.

4. Your behavior should never be based on assumptions about what another person thinks, feels, or intends by his action or behavior. No one takes kindly to this kind of intrusion. It should be your choice whether you will share your thoughts or feelings.

5. Don't assume you can read another person's mind or that they can read yours. This happens when you are so preoccupied with your own thoughts so that you don't track whether the listener is with you.

6. Don't assume you know what is meant by a nonverbal behavior: frown, body language, dirty look, silence or others. It is easy to do this when you know someone well. You are likely to be correct much more of the time than with people you don't know well. You will avoid problems when you check out your perceptions even with people you know well on important issues.

7. Be sensitive to cues that you and a person with whom you are speaking are not talking about the same subject. People often get into arguments when they think they are talking about the same subject only to find this isn't the case. When you are in a disagreement, make sure you are both talking about the same thing. It is not uncommon to find arguments are based on speaking about different topics than on the belief both people were talking about the same topic.

8. Recognize making assumptions is one way to avoid facing unpleasantness. Check out whether the pros and cons of doing so are worth doing it. You may want to avoid saying what's on your mind because you assume there will be an argument if you do speak up. Sometimes it may work, but oftentimes it leads to a bigger problem than if you had addressed it when you first became aware of it.

9. Recognize ambiguity invites assumptions. Avoid the problems that result by getting or giving enough information so it won't be necessary to make assumptions. Oftentimes, the problems that come from ambiguity are greater than those from speaking or behaving with clarity. Any resulting problems have a better chance of being resolved than if they are allowed to fester and become more difficult to resolve.

How We Know What Isn't So: The Fallibility of Human Reason in Everyday Life, Thomas Gilovich, Free Press, 1993, 224 pages. Paperback

Rational Choice in an Uncertain World: The Psychology of Judgement and Decision Making, Reid Hastie, Robyn M. Dawes, Sage Publications, 2001, 392 pages. Paperback

Judgment under Uncertainty: Heuristics and Biases, Daniel Kahneman (Editor), Paul Slovic (Editor), Amos Tversky Cambridge University Press, 1982, 544 pages Paperback

Inevitable Illusions: How Mistakes of Reason Rule Our Minds, Massimo Piattelli-Palmarini, Wiley, 1996, 256 pages. Paperback

Harvard Business Review on Managing Uncertainty, Hugh Courntney, Jane Kirlsnd, Patrick Viguerie, De Geus Arie P. Claton M. Christensen, Harvard Business School Press, 1999, 218 pages. Paperback

GIVING AND RECEIVING INFORMATION

Phoebe was manager of a Personnel Department in a hi-tech firm. She was nervous about her upcoming annual review. She felt very comfortable about her performance over the past year except for a few cliches. One had to do with two problem hires that didn't work out. The other difficulty involved complaints by some employees on how she handled questions regarding their benefits. Adding to her discomfort was her feeling uncomfortable in her standing with her boss.

She went into the review with sweaty palms, a twitching eye-lid and expected to hear harsh criticism. Much to her surprise she was greeted warmly. The meeting started with a review of her positive accomplishments. This relaxed her and put her in a more positive mind to hearing critical comments. All in all she came out of the review feeling energized. At some time she gave thought to why she left the meeting feeling good in spite of the critical comments. She felt that hearing the positive comments first left her less in need to defend herself. Instead, she was able to pay attention to hearing where she had erred and to the constructive suggestions made in how to better manage these situations in the future.

Satisfying and productive relationships, personal or business, depend on constructive and effective ways of giving and receiving information. Phoebe's self confidence enhanced her ability to pay attention to the merit of both the complimentary and critical statements that were given to her.

Characteristics of constructive ways of *giving* information:

- Give information in a positive conversational tone that is specific, devoid of anger, sarcasm or hostility.

- Indicate your level of knowledge on the presenting subject. This will help the listener know best to speak to you. Use familiar language free of jargon alien to the listener.

- Pay attention to the message in nonverbal cues: facial expression, tone of voice, eye contact and more.

- Check to see that you were understood as needed.

- Address any indications there is a problem in your message

- Provide an opportunity for questions or comments about your message

- Acknowledge any response you get to your message.

Sometimes it is necessary to give both positive and negative information as in a job evaluation and in many other situations. Give the positive information first. This will make it easier for the negative information that follows to be more readily heard. Doing this suggests fairness in paying attention to both positive and negative issues.

Constructive ways of *receiving* information include:

- Clarify any ambiguity in what you hear

- Inform the speaker of any difficulty you have in the way information is given to you or in the content of what is said. There is a mutual benefit in your doing this for both you and the speaker.

- Give the speaker your reactions to what you hear. This will give the speaker the opportunity to correct or clarify any ambiguities or misconceptions that occur from what he said.

- Eye contact and focused attention on the speaker will be in the best interest of both you and the speaker.

- Receiving negative information tends to arouse denial or other protective mechanisms. Start by acknowledging the information and check that the comments given were heard correctly. Consider whether there is merit to the criticism. Acknowledge whatever positive merit there may be and how it will be utilized. Acknowledge the part that doesn't have merit as a respectful difference of opinion. Unresolved differences are managed by agreement to disagree.

- Summarize what you have heard on matters where accurate understanding on information is of importance.

Simply Speaking: How to Communicate Your Ideas With Style, Substance, and Clarity, Peggy Noonan, ReganBooks, 1998. Paperback

Be Clear: How to Communicate Successfully, Christine Searancke, Stanley's Books Ltd, 2005, 200 pages.

How to Be a Great Communicator: In Person, on Paper, and on the Podium, Nido R. Qubein, Wiley, 1996, 272 pages. Paperback

The 5 Essential People Skills: How to Assert Yourself, Listen to Others, and Resolve Conflicts, Dale Carnegie Organization, Audiobook

NONVERBAL COMMUNICATION AND BEHAVIOR

Ann and Sue had been friends since childhood. Ann was very fond of Sue but her frequent unreliability in honoring her promises was very aggravating. She told Sue about her feelings because the friendship was important to her and she didn't know whether she could trust her follow through when she made commitments. Sue apologized and promised to be more mindful. Her good intentions waned over time. Ann wondered if there was a way to tell when Sue would follow through. To her surprise, she noticed over time that when Sue looked her straight in the eye when making a commitment, follow through was more likely to happen. This awareness helped Ann have a better idea when to know what she could expect from Sue.

Every conversation has two parts: what you say in words and what you communicate in your behavior. There is no difficulty when both forms of communicating give the same message. The message is clear when you do what you say you will do. If the two forms of message don't agree, your behavior will carry the message. When a person says he is not angry when his face is flushed and he is speaking in an angry voice, no one is going to pay any attention to his words. He obviously is very angry.

Most of the time the contradiction is more subtle as was the case with Ann and Sue. You may give a compliment but the way you do it can come across as insincere because your facial expression or your tone of voice gives a different message. When you say something that doesn't get the response you expect, consider that your nonverbal behavior may be giving a different message.

Part of the power in nonverbal behavior is the many forms it may take. This includes body language, manner of speaking, facial expression, eye contact, silence, tone of voice, and any behavior other than words. One of the problems with nonverbal behavior is that a given behavior may have more than one explanation. Silence can mean different things: disinterest, not knowing what to say, afraid to ask for clarification, fear of response, reluctance to show anger, and more. The person on the receiv-

Marvin Snider, Ph.D.

ing end of this behavior has no way to know which one of the possibilities is involved. He may not have much confidence that asking for clarification will be honest. It is very difficult to have a meaningful relationship when there is frequent disagreement between what one says and what one does.

Managing nonverbal behavior

1. Commit to following through on any promise you make. To do otherwise is to put your credibility at risk.

2. Let a person know when you experience that his nonverbal behavior contradicts what says in a constructive way. This will help minimize problems in understanding what is the real message. You might say, "I heard you said but the way you said it sounds like you mean something else."

3. Develop good nonverbal ways of communicating by:

   • Being an active listener: maintain eye contact, look interested, occasionally nod to show interest, ask thoughtful questions, give affirmations.

   • Keep in mind that tone of voice will carry the message when the words don't fit behavior.
   • Don't procrastinate, follow through on commitments
   • Be prompt in keeping appointments.

People often express in behavior what they can't say in words. You may feel obligated to agree to do something you don't want to do. Your true feelings may get expressed in procrastinating to do it. This may or may not be done with awareness.

Avoid silence when a response is indicated. If a period of silence in needed let the other person know why it is needed.

Be aware that sarcasm is an indirect way of expressing anger.

Teasing can also be an indirect way of expressing anger. The same can apply to making another person the butt of a joke.

Be aware that reneging on promises carries a rejecting message.

When confronted with bothersome nonverbal messages in other people, give feed back that the person is coming across unclear or that you are picking up a sense that something is troubling the person that isn't being expressed.

References:

The Power of Non-Verbal Communication: What You Do Is More Important Than What, Henry H. Calero, Silver Lake Publishing, 2005, 320 pages. Paperback.

The Definitive Book of Body Language, Barbara Pease & Allan Pease, Publisher: Bantam, 2006, 400 pages.

Nonverbal Communication in Human Interaction, Mark L. Knapp & Judith A. Hall, Wadsworth Publishing, 2005, 504 pages. Paperback

Nonverbal Behavior in Interpersonal Relations, Virginia P. Richmond & James C. Mc-Croskey, Allyn & Bacon, 2003, 368 pages. Paperback

EFFECTING CHANGE

ADJUSTING TO CHANGE

Janice was looking forward to her new job when she graduated beautician school. She couldn't wait to put the new learning into practice. Her thoughts were occupied with what she would wear, what it would be like to work with other people, and how it would be doing hair and nails for real. She visited her new job before starting so it wouldn't be overwhelming with too many new things all at once.

The day to start finally came. Janice found her preparations made getting started much easier. She was welcomed by other employees who helped her get started. Janice was pleased her clients liked the quality of her work. It didn't take long to get familiar and comfortable with her job.

After three years on the job she decided it was time to get some different work experiences. She would miss her co-workers and some of her clients. Janice felt confident there wouldn't be any problem in making the adjustment to a new setting.

Life doesn't stay the same. Adjusting to changes is part of normal daily living. Most of the time the changes are small and familiar: the weather, what you will wear, who you have to call and more. You make these adjustments without having to think about them. Adjusting to major changes is something else. Adjusting to a new job, moving to a new city, a divorce or illness is more challenging and will require much more attention.

These adjustment are much harder when you have to deal with an unexpected change. You don't have time to decide how to behave when you are driving your car and are about have an accident. The same thing happens with an unexpected visit from a relative, being fired, or any other event that will change your life in an significant way.

Fortunately, you often have time to prepare for a change you know is coming as was the case with Janice. She knew she was going to graduate on a certain date. This gave her time to plan for what she would do after graduation. When your youngest child is going to go to college and you have time to think about how you will adjust to not having any children at home. A man or woman knows when he/she will be discharged from the Army and has time to plan on what he/she will do when discharged.

Once the change has taken place you work on how to make it as comfortable as possible. This adjustment will be affected by whether the change is temporary or whether it is open-ended. You start a new job or relationship with idea of making it as productive as possible. You do whatever you can to make it a good experience.

The same applies in moving to a new house or new city. Making an adjustment to a chronic illness is more difficult.

Adjusting to temporary changes is much easier. You can put up with things you don't like because you know it won't last too long. This might be the case with a temporary job, having to deal with a visit from a family member you don't like, or having an unpleasant job assignment.

Another kind of adjustment is needed when an experience ends. The ending may be expected as in a graduation or it may be unexpected in being fired or in the death of a loved one. When things come to an you are faced with going from what was familiar to the unknown. Janice had to face this when she decided she needed to change her job. The transition would be easier for her because it was her choice. It would have been quite different if she got laid off or fired.

Being fired involves giving up all the familiarity of doing one's job, the satisfaction that went with it, and the lost work friendships. Death involves adjusting to loss of a loved one and the unknown of how you will adjust to it.

Anticipating an important event

1. Anticipate what and when important events are likely to happen.

2. Give thought to what you can do to prepare for the event happening

3. Make whatever preparations you can and have them in place when the event happens.

4. When possible rehearse these plans. For example, suppose you were going to have a job interview. Consider the kind of questions you might be asked and how you would answer them. Practice your answers enough times so that you will have the answers readily available if needed. This is the same process you would follow in rehearsing for a part in a play.

5. It is also a good idea to have a backup plan in case your intended outcome doesn't work out.

Adjusting to something you didn't expect

1. Give yourself time to pay attention to what you are feeling before you react to what has happened. Suppose you were feeling angry. It would be useful to consider how to handle expressing your anger so it doesn't interfere with what you want to accomplish. This will give you time to think about the best way to handle the situation.

2. Do whatever is necessary to meet the needs of the moment. In the case of something like an auto accident check for injuries to self or others. Get medical help as needed. Call the police.

3. Do whatever is necessary to meet physical needs of the situation. Exchange insurance information if another car is involved.

4. Give yourself a chance to get your emotions under control if you are upset. Don't make judgments about whether you should feel or what you are feeling. It will only make your adjustment more difficult.

Adjusting to a change that has happened

1. Assess what is needed to maintain the behavior expected in the new situation. In the case of an illness, develop a plan for how to manage it until you are well again.

2. Implement whatever is needed to make the ongoing situation work for as long as it will last. Arrange for medical care, medicines, nursing needs and whatever else is needed until recovery is accomplished.

3. Make provisions for managing any foreseeable problems that may come up. Provide the means for checking on medical progress and how to handle any emergency that might happen.

Adjusting to an experience that is going to end

1. If possible anticipate when the ending may come.

2. Make whatever preparation you can to cope with expected unhappiness or any problems that may come from the end of what you were experiencing.

3. Once the event has ended allow time to mourn any loss that follows.

4. Give thought to what you can do to adjust to the loss and search for ways that will help you to move on to a new situation. In the case of the loss of a close friend, look for new relationships. This won't take the place of your lost relationship but it will give you the opportunity for new relationships.

5. Put these plans into action as soon as you are able.

6. Don't make major decisions in the case of death of a spouse or other traumatic losses so that your coping with the aroused emotions don't unduly influence your judgment

Learning From an Experience That Has Ended.

Give some thought what you can learn from this experience and how it might be useful in the future. This will result in being better able to handle similar situations and reduce the likelihood you will repeat mistakes.

Managing Personal Change [AUDIOBOOK] Hyrum W. Smith, Audio Cassette

*Crisp: Managing Personal Change, Moving Through Personal Transition,*Crisp Learning, 2004, 88 pages. Paperback

Practical Stress Management: A Comprehensive Workbook for Managing Change and Promoting Health (4th Edition), John A. Romas & Manoj Sharma, Benjamin Cummings, 2006, 272 pages.

Managing Personal Change, Cynthia D. Scott & Dennis T. Jaffe, Crisp Fifty-Minute Series. Paperback

*The Prodigal Principle: The Essential Handbook for Managing Personal and Professional Change,*Worth Publishers,1995, 73 pages. Paperback

Managing Transitions: Making the Most Out of Change, William Bridges PhD, Nicholas Brealey Publishing, 1995, 140 pages. Paperback

Transitions: Making Sense of Life's Changes, William Bridges, Perseus Books Group, 1980, 170 pages.

GETTING WHERE YOU WANT TO BE

Debra wanted to be a nurse from the time she was eleven when she got captivated by a nurse in a movie about war. This motivated her to do well in school. She graduated in the upper twenty percent of her high school class which enabled her to get into a good bachelor of nursing program. She proudly became a registered nurse in a local hospital after graduation.

During the course of this work she met and married a medical student, Bob. He grew up in a family of lawyers: his father, grandfather, two uncles and an aunt. It was presumed by the family, as he also took for granted, that he would follow suit.

He grew up enjoying the saxophone. While in a pre-law college program he played in a small band. He found college increasingly tedious except for his music courses. He began to question whether the law is where he wanted to go. Music was his passion. Bob was often told he was very talented which helped him come to the decision it was time to do what he wanted not what was expected of him. He knew that this would come as a shock and disappointment to his family and especially his father. He was right. It was a shock that resulted in some very difficult times. His determination finally won out and was reluctantly accepted by his family.

Growing up involves deciding what goals to pursue in your life, the kind of person you want to be and the kind of life style you want to live. Setting goals focuses your energy on how best to achieve them. You start with what you want to get done in the next hours, days, weeks, or months. Then there are longer term goals that are measured in years. Planning for a career or retirement are two examples. Others may include trips you hope take, projects you plan to build and more. Success in achieving your long term goals depends on how well you manage short term goals that ultimately take you to achieving your long term ones. It would be too hard to stay focused without these short term goals.

You need to keep revisiting your goals because circumstances keep changing as does what you want to accomplish. You might start off wanting to be a doctor, athlete, lawyer, teacher or whatever as Bob did in thinking he wanted to be a lawyer. Each goal requires a different preparation. But interests and needs often change which may take you to different goals.

The same thing applies to the kind of person you want to be. Over time, you develop the values you want to guide your life. These are not static but change over time and with experience. You might grow up with one experience about religion and change how you feel about it and how you practice it as you get older. Or you might grow up being very self-centered and with maturity decide you need to pay more attention to consideration of other people's needs and feelings.

Once goals are defined, you will find value in reviewing them on a regular basis to see whether they are still relevant. This will depend on whether you have what will be needed in personal qualities, time, energy, interest, money and whatever else is required to accomplish these goals.

Setting goals

1. Consider goals long term that are at least a year away.

2. Work out the short goals which are the steps you need to take to get to the long term goal. Doing this helped Debra reach her goal of becoming a nurse.

3. Evaluate what will be needed to accomplish each of these steps.

4. Add consideration of the day-to-day goals that you have to do: work, shopping, child care, housework, entertainment.

5. See whether you have the time, energy, money, and the necessary skill to get all of the goals you want to achieve done. If this is not possible decide what combination of short and long term goals are possible.

6. Repeat this review on a regular schedule to make sure that what you planned still makes sense. You will be happier when you are able to keep up to date on your most important goals. The specific interval you set for evaluation will vary depending on the subject. It may range anywhere from once a month, once or twice a year, or another time period fits for you.

1. It is a good idea to take inventory of your strengths and limitations on a regular basis as well. It's the same idea used in businesses. They take inventory so they know what they have, what you might need, and how to get them. Also consider whether what you need is possible from time, energy, and money considerations. Start with once a month and then experiment with how often it is useful to do this. This might be learning to use a computer, master a new sport, play an instrument, and many more.

2. Make a self assessment when you are trying to solve a problem. It will help you decide if you have what you need. It will help you avoid wasting time and give you an idea of any help you might need to get.

3. Be realistic in deciding whether you can learn the new needed skills or whether it is better to get help from somebody who already has it.

4. Evaluate the qualities about yourself with which you are satisfied. Look at what you might be done to improve those qualities that need improvement. You might not like that you lose your temper too quickly. You might start by seeing if you can find a way to manage your anger better. Don't be reluctant to ask for help when you have gone as far as you can on your own.

5. Evaluate successful and unsuccessful experiences after they occur. This will give you more confidence in what you do well and will help you understand where you need improvement.

6. Getting information for how other people see you is helpful. You will have to sort out which things are relevant and which are not.

7. Make self assessments in all parts of your life: family, work, friendships and interests. You may find that a strength in area may be so in another one. Being assertive in work may be a strength but a weakness if you behave that way with family and friends.

8. Answers to the following questions are one approach

    - What qualities do I like about myself?

    - What qualities about myself would I like to change?

    - How can I go about making these changes.

    - What skills do I have that I want to keep?

    - What do I need to do to keep these skills sharp/

    - What new skills would I like to get?

    - How do I get them?

Is what I want to accomplish realistic in time, money, energy without interfering with responsibilities you already have.

References:

Goal Setting 101 : How to Set and Achieve a Goal!, Gary Ryan Blair, Blair Pub House, 2000, 58 pages. Paperback

What Are Your Goals: Powerful Questions to Discover What You Want Out of Life, Gary Ryan Blair, Blair Publishing House, 1999, 165 pages. Paperback

Motivation and Goal Setting: How to Set and Achieve Goals and Inspire Others, Jim Cairo, Career Press, 1998, 28 pages.

The Ten Commandments of Goal Setting, Gary Ryan Blair, The Goals Guy, 2005, 52 pages. Paperback

Planning And Goal Setting For Personal Success, Samuel Blankson, Lulu.com, 2005, 212 pages. Paperback

MONITORING FOR CHANGE

Alicia, 33, a sales representative for a children's clothing company, was experiencing difficulty in getting over a recently ended long term relationship. She tended to be outspoken and struggled to control her temper. This concern led her to seek therapy. After a good start, her interest and enthusiasm began to wain. She was becoming discouraged and questioned the benefit of therapy because change was so slow. I asked if she had been trying any of the new behaviors we discussed. She apologetically acknowledged that she had not and recognized her assumption that just talking about her problems would change things. I reminded her of our discussion about the importance of consistently practicing new behavior and how monitoring helps make this happen. She remembered that monitoring required checking to make sure the new behavior was practiced on a regular basis. Progress and optimism about the outcome of therapy returned once monitoring was again implemented.

People go for psychotherapy because they want something to change. They often come to my office expecting that I will "fix" the problem for them. We talk about what they need to do to overcome their problem and how understanding the nature of their problem can be helpful.

I give clients homework on how to change their behavior. Success in overcoming their problem is usually dependent on how well they have monitored their new behaviors. Sometimes they come back after a few sessions, as Alicia did, unhappy because not much has changed. When I enquire how they did with their home work, I get a variety of answers. The common bottom line is that they didn't get to do much

The main reason for their lack of progress was the absence of a way to make sure they did the home work. I have a five step process for making change happen. When clients follow the prescribed steps the rate of improvement improves dramatically.

This is not unusual. The major problem in achieving change is to interrupt the behavior you want to replace. Any behavior goes on automatic once you do it often enough. To bring about change you need to be able to interrupt the behavior you want to change and replace it with the new desired behavior.

Five steps to make change happen

1. Identify what behavior you want to change. General statements like wanting to be happier do not work because they are too general. You need to have a behavior you can see to make change happen. Examples include : Be a better listener, give recognition to other people when they do something you like, control your temper, and more.

2. Decide what new behavior you want to have happen, e.g. be better listener, better control of your temper, and others.

3. Determine what you need to do to make the change happen. This includes but is not limited to: knowledge, skill, energy, time, money, patience and more.

4. How much do you want the change to happen? The change will not happen if it isn't important enough to devote the needed time and energy to make it happen.

5. The key to changing behavior is a monitoring process. This involves a regular, usually daily, check to ensure that the new desired behaviors are happening This check should include looking at whatever positive accomplishments are made in part or whole. Also needed is to look at times you weren't successful so you can learn to do better the next time. You will gain confidence and encouragement as your success increases. Unsuccessful efforts should not be viewed as failures but as the need for additional learning. Failure occurs only when don't learn from experience.

The monitoring process requires you stop doing the behavior you want to change and to replace it with the new behavior. It is necessary to remind yourself everyday about the change you want to make and do it as often as possible. After you keep doing this long enough it will become automatic and you won't have to consciously think about the new behavior for it to happen. The length if time it takes will depend on how complicated the change is and how long you have been practicing. Change can often be seen in as little as two weeks of daily monitoring.

Marvin Snider, Ph.D.

A man consulted me about a problem he was having at work. He was getting a lot of criticism because he always needed to have the last word in a discussion. We went through the five step process for change.

Step 1: He decided that the behavior he needed to change was to stop having the last word in a discussion.

Step 2: He knew what change was needed. He needed to acknowledge other people's ideas and not need to have the last word.

Step 3: He knew what he needed to do to make this change happen.

Step 4: He was tired of all of the criticism he was getting. He didn't like the way people thought of him. He was very anxious to make the change. He was willing to do whatever it took.

Step 5: He agreed to spend time each evening reviewing how he did that day on his efforts to change his behavior. He was to look at those times he was successful and gain confidence that he could do what was needed, Then he was to look at those time he didn't make it. He was to see if he could understand why he had difficulty. Sometimes he would be able to talk to the people who were involved and correct his behavior. In his case it might mean giving the person acknowledgment he didn't give him the day before. If he hadn't been able to do this, he would have thought how he could do better in the future.

He gradually made increasing progress over a period of three weeks after he was able to keep up the monitoring in step 5.

References:

Learning from Change: Issues and Experiences in Participatory Monitoring and Evaluation, Marisol Estrella, Jutta Blauert,, Dindo Campilan, John Gaventa , Julian Gonsalves, Irene Guijt, Debra A. Johnson, Roger Ricafort, Editors, IDRC Books, 2000, 288 pages.

The Concise Time Management and Personal Development, John Adair, Thorogood, 2003, 200 pages. Paperback

Breaking Free: A Prescription for Personal and Organizational Change, David M. Noer, Jossey-Bass, 1996, 288 pages.

Crisp: Managing Personal Change,: Moving Through Personal Transition, Cynthia Scott, Crisp Learning, 2004, 88 pages. Paperback

Managing Personal Change, Hyrum W. Smith, Covey, 2001. Audio Cassette

EMOTIONS

ANGER MANAGEMENT

Casey tried o get along with his parents. He visited them when he could and would call regularly when he was too busy to visit. He would do things for them when possible. But it never seemed he could do enough. His mother would only talk about what he didn't do or didn't do right. She took for granted the positive things he did. She would add insult to injury by holding up his brother and sister as a model to follow. She approved of their life style and was critical of his occupation as a musician.

He' hit the wall' on one visit when his mother once again criticized him for not getting a more respectable occupation like his brother. He threw a glass against the wall, shattering it and swore at his mother for her lack of caring and refusal to respect for what mattered to him. He stormed out of the house slamming the door so hard the windows rattled.

He felt bad about his temper tantrum even though it was justified. He had never spoken to his mother that way or had become physical. After thinking about it, he realized that the problem was not in his anger but in the way he managed it. He kept it in too long to the point it overflowed which shifted the focus from the merit of his complaint to his emotional outburst which only gave her one more thing to criticize. "Now, now Casey, you'd better learn to manage your temper better." She would not see the part she played in what happened.

Anger can be constructive or destructive. It is constructive when expressed in a way that addresses the source of the anger. It is destructive when it inflicts emotional or physical pain on you or are another person. This happens when it is allowed to build to the point you lose control on how it will be expressed.

You can minimize getting into destructive anger when you anticipate situations you know are likely to get you going in ways you won't like. Casey would have avoided "hitting the wall" if he had let his anger be known when it first happened in a way that kept the issue on his mother's disrespect of him and not on his outburst. Casey might have reminded her that respect works both ways and that she isn't going to get it, if she isn't prepared to give it. This would have been a time to remind her that he isn't going to do things for her if the only response she gives is to criticize him. Holding her accountable is good for his self respect and lets him mother know what she needs to do if she expects to have a meaningful relationship with him.

Steps to managing anger

1. When there is the awareness that anger is building, take the time to consider why it is happening. If it gets to the point you sense you might lose control. Take a time out. Let other people involved know that you need to interrupt whatever you are doing because you don't want to say or do anything you would regret. Let them know you will return when you are in a better place.

2. You can expect to have a problem when you don't pay attention to your behavior that is inviting anger from others.

3. If you feel someone's angry at you, let them know how they are coming across. Invite discussion on addressing the source of the other person's anger and what might be done to reduce it.

4. Let them know what consequences may occur if he does not respond in a constructive manner. If you are not able to invoke any meaningful response, you have the option to leave the situation.

5. If you are not able to leave the situation, focus on how you can best protect yourself. Keep in mind that explosive anger shifts the attention away from what made you angry to the way you expressed your anger.

6. Do not ignore feelings of pent up anger. Find a constructive way to express it that will help you not lose control. Some form of physical exercise may help, venting your frustrations that are not aimed at a person, beating a pillow and other creative ways that do not add to your anger.

7. Avoid situations that you know will arouse your anger that do not permit constructive resolution.

References:

The Anger Trap: Free Yourself from the Frustrations that Sabotage Your Life, Les Carter, Jossey-Bass, 2004, 224 pages. Paperback

Taking Charge of Anger: How to Resolve Conflict, Sustain Relationships, and Express Yourself without Losing Control, W. Robert Nay, The Guilford Press, 2003, 246 pages. Paperback

Anger Management: 6 Critical Steps to a Calmer Life, Peter J. Favaro, New Page Books, 2005, 288 pages. Paperback

Anger Management For Dummies, W. Doyle, PhD, For Dummies, 2006, 384 pages. Paperback

Calming The Family Storm: Anger Management For Moms, Dads, And All The Kids, Gary D. McKay & Steven A. Maybell, Impact Publishers, 2004, 320 pages. Paperback

Melinda was a guidance counselor in a junior high school. She worked with a group of boys who were having difficulty in class because of their inability to do their work. She discovered they were struggling with fear of failing because they were getting poor grades.

She had other students who were in trouble because they exhibited too little interest in their studies. Academic work held little interest for them. This contributed to their becoming disruptive in the classroom. It became clear to her that too much anxiety or too little anxiety can become a problem. Both cases demonstrated the importance of helping children develop enough confidence in their abilities to engage their interest in academic work. She saw that too much anxiety about being able to do satisfactory academic work got expressed in fear of failing. Other children managed the same concern by developing an air of disinterest about their school. This protected them from facing their fears.

Anxiety is brought on by worry or tension from a real or imagined stress. It is your reaction to a perceived threat when your ability to cope with it is uncertain. Your choice is to hand wring about your fears and only get more anxious or put your energy to work to remove your need to worry.

Anxiety changes the physiology in your body. It increases your heart rate, there is greater blood flow to your large muscles such as the thighs and biceps, there is an increase in the speed and depth of your breathing, you sweat more, and there is decreased activity in your digestive system.

Chronic anxiety may eventually get expressed in physical symptoms. Doctors believe that chronic anxiety can contribute to major sicknesses like cancer, diabetes and ulcers among others. It is important to pay attention to anxieties that won't go away. When you have done all you can that doesn't work, get professional help.

Anxiety comes in three levels: too little, a productive amount, and too much. Too little anxiety leads to doing nothing because you seemingly aren't worrying about anything. Anxiety can bring out the best in you when something needs doing and you feel you can do it. Too much anxiety is overwhelming and can lead to becoming immobilized to do anything.

Coping with anxiety

1. Try to determine what is making you anxious.

2. Put the energy of your anxiety into efforts to eliminate what is causing it. Anticipate situations that might make you anxious. This will give you a chance to either avoid them or be better prepared to handle them.

3. Don't let other people's anxieties become yours. Sometimes this happens when you try to help a friend or family member with their problems. Be realistic about how much you can help somebody else.

4. Consult your doctor when you find you are not able to manage your anxiety on your own. Medication may help. It can be useful in helping to lower anxiety to a level that allows you to cope with it. Be careful not to use medication to avoid learning how to manage anxiety.

5. Consult with a mental health professional to help you understand and mange the source of your anxiety which may not always be obvious.

References:

Coping with Anxiety: 10 Simple Ways to Relieve Anxiety, Fear & Worry, Edmund J. Bourne & Lorna Garano, New Harbinger Publications, 2003, 150 pages. Paperback

Overcoming Anxiety for Dummies, Laura L. Smith & Charles H. Elliott, For Dummies, 2002, 360 pages. Paperback

Freeing Your Child from Anxiety: Powerful, Practical Solutions to Overcome Your Child's Fears, Worries, and Phobias, Tamar E. Chansky, Broadway, 2004, 320 pages. Paperback

The Shyness & Social Anxiety Workbook: Proven Techniques for Overcoming Your Fears, Martin M. Antony & Richard P. Swinson, 2000, New Harbinger Publications, 216 pages. Paperback

Easing Fear, Panic & Worry, Edmund J. Bourne, Arlen Brownstein, & Lorna Garano, New Harbinger Publications, 2004, 213 pages. Paperback

Transforming Anxiety: The Heartmath Solution to Overcoming Fear And Worry And Creating Serenity, Doc Childre, Deborah Rozman, & Doc Lew Childre, New Harbinger Publications, 2006, 157 pages. Paperback

EMPATHY/SYMPATHY

Ellen and Susan were good friends since elementary school. They were both married with children. Their husbands also became good friends and their families spent many pleasant times together. Tragedy struck one of Susan's son, Timmy, age nine, when he developed an aggressive cancer that had a poor prognosis for recovery. Ellen felt very sympathetic for all that Susan was going through. It hurt her deeply to watch the depth of pain her dear friend was enduring. She could image how she would feel if something like this happened to one of her children.

Empathy and sympathy give meaning to relationships. Empathy is the awareness and sharing of another's feelings. Sympathy is feeling bad for another person's suffering or bad experience . It is possible to be both empathic and sympathetic at the

what it feels like to have this happen. At the same time he can be sympathetic for the friend's unhappiness.

It is also possible for a person to be empathic but not sympathetic. A person can be empathic about a friend losing his job but not sympathetic because he behaved in a way that brought it about.

There is also the case where you could be sympathetic but not empathic. This could happen when you feel sympathetic about your friend losing his job but not be able to understand why he feels the way that he does since he brought it on himself.

You may also find there are some people who are not comfortable with accepting sympathy. They may see this as a sign of weakness. Other people may not believe that anyone could possibly know how they feel about something that happened to them. You can avoid getting into trouble if you watch for how a person reacts when you try to let them know you sympathize with their experience and can only guess how they feel. If they have a hard time accepting your feelings don't take it personally. Just accept that they can't handle it and move on to a different subject.

Receiving sympathy/empathy

1. Accept what is being offered at face value. If it does not seem genuine, accept as well intentioned. It may be hard to distinguish between an obligatory expression and discomfort about subject which prompts what is being offered as in the case of death or other painful event.

2. Some people view accepting sympathetic or empathic offering as a negative reflection on the person - a strong person shouldn't need it. This may be your presumption. Don't assume this is someone else's assumption.

3. There may be times when you are not receptive to receiving sympathy or empathy. Acknowledge what is being offered to be followed by assurances that you are doing well and attempt to change the subject. Doing this in a pleasant but not to abrupt manner will likely address what you need.

4. Don't dismiss someone's offering of empathy because you may feel that no one could possibly know how it is to experience your tragedy. To do so is disrespectful to someone trying to offer comfort and doesn't do much for the relationship. Accept such offerings graciously and harbor your own private thoughts abut how you feel.

Giving sympathy/empathy

1. Express your sympathy as appropriate to the given situation. It will be get the best reception when it fits the circumstances. Too much or too little diminish your intended effort.

Marvin Snider, Ph.D.

2. Some people are not comfortable receiving expressions of sympathy or empathy. They may feel they shouldn't need such acknowledgments.

3. Some people feel their experience is so intense that no one else could possibly appreciate how they feel. It is not helpful to either you or the person to whom you are making the offer to defend what you are saying. Accept the person needs to feel unique.

References:

Creating Harmonious Relationships: A Practical Guide to the Power of True Empathy, Andrew Lecompte, Atlantic Books, 2000, 256 pages. Paperback

Teaching Empathy: A Blueprint for Caring, Compassion, and Community, David Levine, Solution Tree, 2005, 218 pages.

Empowered by Empathy : 25 Ways to Fly in Spirit, Rose Rosetree, Women's Intuition Worldwide, 2000, 342 pages. Paperback

Empathy, Mark H. Davis,Westview Press, 2000, 272 pages. Paperback

The Power of Empathy : A Practical Guide to Creating Intimacy, Self-Understanding and Lasting Love, Arthur P. Ciaramicoli & Katherine Ketcham, Plume, 2001, 288 pages. Paperback

DEALING WITH LOSS

Ben and Sara had been married for forty-three years when he died suddenly of a massive heart attack. They had a good marriage in which their lives were closely intertwined on a day-to-day basis. Sara was his "rock" who supported him through his up and down career as a business man. Her day revolved around helping him out as needed, tending to their two children and managing their home.

The unexpected suddenness of his death was shocking. He was walking into the super-market when he had a heart attack. He was dead by the time the paramedics arrived. She will never forget her shock at the fateful phone call while preparing for dinner. There's not much that was remembered after that. Her first recollection was staring up at a paramedic and the tear stained eyes of her children.

Sara went through a roller-coaster range of feelings as she attempted to cope with the collapse of her world. She was in a fog through the funeral and burial. She heard voices and blurred images that seemed far off.

In her grief she was angry at Ben for leaving her. How could he do this to her! Then she would slip into guilt for what she should of done to prevent this from happening. She felt part of her died with Ben. What was going to happen to her now? She

lived each empty day on automatic drive. Eventually she began to get her bearings with the help of her children, friends and family. The first year was very difficult for her. Every holiday, birthday, anniversary or any other special time they had was a reminder of her loss. Eventually she resigned herself to work at finding a new life - one without Ben!

Losing something important hurts! Most difficult is losing a loved one or close friend. This may also apply in varying degrees to other things of importance to you depending on their level of importance to you: pets, prized possessions, loss of a relationship and more. Pay attention to your feelings in coping with a loss and the meaning it has for you. It is most upsetting when the loss is unexpected such as in a heart attack, as it was for Sara, or in an accident.

Dr. Kubler-Ross has described the stages that one usually experiences when this happens: shock, denial, anger, guilt, bargaining, and depression. Acceptance of a loss is easier when replacement of the loss seems possible.

A person in shock needs time and support to vent his feelings without being judged for expressing them. It is not helpful for anyone to attempt to discourage or shorten the time needed for this expression.

Getting mad at a person who died may seem odd to an onlooker. It isn't logic but heartfelt grieving at pain from the loss. An onlooker should focus on supporting the expression of feeling rather than the logic of what is being said. The same would apply to all other types of losses.

Your anger may give way to guilt in bereavement as it did for Sara. This may happen if you feel some responsibility for what happened because of what you did or didn't do. As a bystander to someone experiencing a loss, you might initially be sympathetic to hearing the feelings. This should be gradually followed by comments that help manage the guilt. Back off, if the bereaved person isn't able to pay attention to what you are saying. Try again when the person seems more able to talk about their guilt.

Sometimes you may try to bargain with God as a way to deal with the emotion of your loss. Once the emotion is vented the futility of the effort often gives way to depression and a sense of helplessness. During this time you gradually comes to terms with the reality of what has happened.

Bystanders can be helpful by being a patient witness to the expression of feelings. Making comforting comments may also be helpful. Do not take offense if the bereaved does not offer acknowledgment of your efforts. In some situations you may be the recipient of some of the anger that is vented at the loss. This should not be taken personally as the bereaved is not behaving out of logic but venting feelings at any available target.

Acceptance of the loss is gradually accomplished. This is likely to happen slowly. The time frame can be from the point of loss to months or even years. In some extreme situations it may never happen. People close to the bereaved can help by keeping in contact and encouraging the mourner to engage in activities that help the person redefine his life situation without the lost loved one. Finding replacements for the loss will help with this acceptance. Encourage a person who seems unable to make the adjustment to seek professional help.

Coming to grips with a loss is less complicated when it is a temporary one. This may be a job, a lost opportunity, a pet or a prized possession. The acceptance and availability of replacement makes coping with the loss easier. The bereaved needs to focus as much energy as possible on finding a replacement. Adjustment to a loss is also made easier when it can be anticipated. This gives time to prepare for the impact of the loss, planning for how to adjust to it and possibilities for replacement.

Coping is harder when replacement cannot be found as in the case of a man who lost his wife and felt she could never be replaced. Another relationship is not considered an option. He had to find other ways to meet his emotional needs.

Adjusting to a loss

1. A loss you know is going to happen gives an opportunity to prepare for it. This happens with someone who has a terminal illness. It could also happen in a marriage that has failed or a close friend who is moving to some distant place. Attempts to deny the loss will only make the adjustment more difficult.

2. There often is a tendency to focus on prayer and hope when someone is seriously ill. This can be helpful but should not be the only thing to do. You should also consider preparing for the loss. Being supportive to an ill person is both a help to that person and is satisfying to the person giving help.

3. Give yourself time, and space to do the grieving when you experience a loss This is the time to vent whatever feelings are present in a safe place both alone and with others as comfort and circumstances permit. This is not a time to 'keep a stiff upper lip".

4. There is no set length of time for mourning. Each person needs to follow his own needs. It is not a good idea to hide your own mourning to protect someone else. Those who are grieving need to find a workable way to manage it.

5. Developing some form of memorial for a lost relationship is a way to help bring closure to the loss and to keep the memory alive.

6. The loss of a marriage can have the same impact as the loss of a loved one. This is especially the case in a long standing marriage for the partner that didn't want the divorce. The challenge is to avoid focusing on blame which will only add the pain of the loss. It is better to deal with the mourning by focusing on what was right about the marriage, what can be learned from it that can help future relationships work better.

7. People who have been devoted to their pets may experience a similar mourning experience as the loss of a person.

References:

When There Are No Words: Finding Your Way to Cope With Loss and Grief, Charlie Walton, Pathfinder Publishing, 1996, 112 pages. Paperback

I Wasn't Ready to Say Goodbye: Surviving, Coping and Healing After the Death of a Loved One, Brook Noel, &b Pamela D Blair, Champion Press, 2000, 304 pages. Paperback

Living With Loss And Grief: Letting Go, Moving on (Overcoming Common Problems), Julia Tugendhat, Sheldon Press, 2006, 128 pages. Paperback

Helping Children Cope With the Loss of a Loved One: A Guide for Grownups, William C. Kroen, Pamela Espeland, Free Spirit Publishing, 1996, 101 pages.

When a Family Pet Dies: A Guide to Dealing With Children's Loss, Joann Tuzeo-jarolmen, Jessica Kingsley Publishers, 2006, 104 pages. Paperback

MANAGING EXPRESSION OF FEELINGS

Frank grew up in a family where expression of anger was considered a show of weakness. A person was supposed to 'bite the bullet' and show no emotion at all times. Frank and his wife Ann had three sons, Josh 22, Fred 19, and Charles 17. Josh had a hard time finding his place in life. He had been under psychiatric care for two years. The world came crashing in when Josh gave up and committed suicide. This devastated the family. However, Frank was at work the next day as though nothing had happened. He outwardly was stoic even though he suffered privately.

The way you express your feelings can help or interfere with what you are trying to do. Showing appreciation for an employees effort will encourage him to do a better job. Yelling at him will slow him down either out of anger or fear. Getting angry at your children will not make it easier for you to get their attention. Letting them know how pleased you are when they behave as expected will get better results.

Expressing happy or unhappy feelings in a constructive way helps build and maintain meaningful relationships. Withholding your feelings creates ambiguity and invites other people to assume what you are feeling which leads to stress in relationships. People will not appreciate having to guess what you are feeling, especially if they are wrong when they do. Frank's co-workers were uncomfortable with the way he handled his son's death. They heard what happened but he said nothing. They were in a dilemma. It did not seem right to avoid acknowledging his loss, yet he did not seem to want acknowledgment. Any mention of his son's death was met with a curt but civil response. They presumed he was suffering but respected his wish and no further mention was made of it.

Constructive expression of feelings

1. Be mindful that feelings are expressed in words and in behavior. When what you say and how you say it doesn't match, the way you say it will carry the message. Your anger will carry the message even though you tell somebody you aren't angry.

2. When you are angry and want to be heard, start by saying how you are feeling before you talk about what is making you angry. These feelings should be expressed in an "I" statement not a "you are" statement. I am angry at your behavior, instead of you made me angry. The "I" statement is about the person who is angry. The "you are" makes the other person responsible for your anger.

3. You do not control what you feel, but you are responsible for how you show what you feel.

4. Learn to pay attention to the 'music' of your body, these body signals tell you your feelings are in danger of getting out of control. It may be a twitching nose, your face begins to feel flushed, it is hard to keep eye contact, and many more. Be aware that ignoring these early warning signals will lead to a blow up. When this happens attention to what upset you will be overshadowed by the way you expressed your feelings. Your losing it gets all of the attention.

5. Manage the early warning signs that you getting upset by interrupting the conversation. Tell the other person(s) involved you need to stop talking because you are too upset to constructively continue the conversation. Say that you would like to come back to the conversation when you are in a better place and suggest when would be a better time.

6. Don't assume that what you feel is obvious to others. Nobody likes to be put in the position of mind reading or making assumptions that may not be accurate. Relationships are more meaningful and satisfying when there is trust and comfort in being able to express your feelings.

7. Pay as much attention to expressing positive as negative feelings. Giving positive feelings will help the other person be better able to pay attention to whatever negative feelings you have. Giving only negative feelings will make it harder to pay attention to what you have to say because the other person will be busy protecting himself.

References:

Interpreting the Personal: Expression and the Formation of Feelings, Sue Campbell, Cornell University Press, 1998, 232 pages. Paperback

Living with Feeling: The Art of Emotional Expression, Lucia Capacchione, Tarcher, 2001, 400 pages.

The in Zone: Feelings, Expressions, and Insights from Within, Aaron Dowdell, 2006, 83 pages. Paperback

Expressing Feelings: How to Improve Your Relationship Through Direct and Healthy Expression of Feelings, Matthew McKay & Patrick Fanning, New Harbinger Publications, 1994. Audio Cassette

Whose Life Is It Anyway: When to Stop Taking Care of Their Feelings and Start Taking Care of Your Own, Nina W. Brown, New Harbinger Publications, 2002, 172 pages. Paperback

GUILT/SHAME

Fred and Max had been friends and felt like brothers since they were in the first grade. They stayed in touch over the years. They were often helped each other out with loans, or when other kinds of help were needed. There was the shared expectation they would always be there for one another.

Max had agreed to cosign a loan for Fred because his house was badly in need of repair. Fred got very angry at Max for reneging on his promise at the last minute. Letting him down this way was an embarrassment. He told him how disappointed he was at being abandoned. He reminded him about the many times he had been there to help when he was in need.

Guilt and shame are judgments about your behavior. Guilt happens when you feel bad about something you did wrong or something you shouldn't have done. It might be telling a lie, not doing something you promised to do. It is often used to get another person do something they don't want to do as Fred was doing. It is also used to express anger by holding another person responsible for causing something bad to happen to you.

Shame is a judgment about your character and can reflect badly on your reputation You might feel shame when you have done something you feel is wrong that is about more than a particular behavior. It reflects on your sense of yourself as a person. Shame is often the expression of a frustrated parent or teacher that takes the form: "What's the matter with you?", "Who do you think you are?", "You should be ashamed of yourself?" and more.

Using Guilt

When you have guilty feelings

1. Sometimes you may find yourself in a situation when you feel guilty but are not sure why. Check out with other involved people whether your feelings are warranted. Don't live with ambiguity. This can be a source of unnecessary anxiety.

2. Take responsibility for whatever misdeeds are called to your attention. If they are legitimate take whatever corrective action is needed. If you decide they are not appropriate acknowledge a difference of opinion.

3. Be prepared to deal with guilty feelings when you behave in a way you don't feel is appropriate.

4. Don't hold other people responsible for your guilt feelings. Someone may try to arouse these feelings in you, but they will not succeed without your acceptance.

When guilt is put on you by other people

1. Decide on whether there is any legitimacy for the guilt. If there is do what you feel is appropriate. If not, indicate that you don't feel the expectation is appropriate. Show the other person why you feel that the guilt was misplaced. If you don't do this you will make it easy for this to happen again.

2. Distinguish between efforts to evoke your guilt when there is a legitimate basis from the desire to manipulate you to meet another person's need.

3. Following through on your commitments will remove opportunities for others to arouse guilt in you.

4. Don't allow other people to impose their expectations on you to arouse your guilt.

Addressing Shame

When you feel shame yourself

1. Try to understand what you did that made you feel ashamed.

2. Stay with the behavior that bothers you. Don't let it reflect on you outside of the specific behavior. If you did something you don't feel was right, focus on that behavior and not questioning your worth as a person.

3. See if you can figure out why you behaved badly and learn not to repeat it.

When shame is put on you by other people

1. Ask the accuser can tell you why he is upset with you.

2. Let the accuser know that you don't like the way he talked to you. Let him know that if wants your attention he should more respectful in how he speaks to you.

3. Do not accept any general statements of complaints about your behavior or character. Let whoever is making them know that you will only pay attention to specific complaints and not on global attacks on your personhood.

4. Don't let anybody get away with criticizing your behavior without letting them know how you feel about it. If they are right you do something to correct it. If they are wrong you make sure they understand why you believe this is so.

References:

Shame & Guilt: Masters of Disguise, Jane Middelton-Moz, HCI, 1990, 155 pages. Paperback

Shame and Guilt, June Price Tangney & Ronda L. Dearing, The Guilford Press, 2003, 272 pages. Paperback

Self-Conscious Emotions: The Psychology of Shame, Guilt, Embarrassment, and Pride, June Price Tangney & Kurt W. Fischer, Editors, The Guilford Press, 1995, 542 pages.

Shame and Guilt : Characteristics of the Dependency Cycle, Ernest Kurtz, hazelden, 1981, 57 pages. Paperback

Tragic Redemption: Healing the Guilt and Shame, Hiram Johnson, Langmarc Publishing, 2006, 184 pages. Paperback

PERSONAL QUALITIES

ACCOUNTABILITY TO SELF

Carol was having a hard time with her boss who was accusing her of being incompetent because he felt she did a poor job on an assignment. Carol's first reaction was to feel devastated. She felt guilty for the screwup and wondered what was wrong with her. After she got some distance from the discussion she re-examined what happened. She came to the conclusion that the only wrong thing she did was to let her boss tell her how she should feel about herself. However, he did say one thing which she needed to correct. She needed to pay more attention to details.

She had a good relationship with her boss and so she was able to give him some feedback about the way he came across to her. She let him know that the hostile way he criticized her made it hard for her to pay attention to the merit of what he had to say.

A compass is a must in finding your way through the woods when there isn't a marked path. Without it you could wander in the woods aimlessly. It is the same in finding your way through life. You can move in many directions and behave in many ways. What is needed is an internal compass that helps you to set goals and make choices that will lead to getting the life style you want. This internal compass is "accountability-to-self "(ATS) - a set of values and beliefs that guide your behavior.

When you get criticism from others about your behavior, you have three choices: accept it outright and behave accordingly, reject it as wrong, or reject part of it and accept part of it. How you make this decision is key. Accepting the criticism without question says that the person who criticized you knows better than you do. This gives that person permission to tell you how you should feel about yourself. This was the mistake that Carol made.

Rejecting the criticism out of hand is also a problem. You lose the opportunity for new learning if there is any validity to the criticism. You also run the risk of alienating the person who gave you the rejected information. The worst part of depending on how other people see you is the power you give them to tell you how to feel about yourself. This gets in the way of learning to trust your own judgment and self perception. Without this, the way you feel about yourself depends on who is giving you the information.

Ideally, you should think about the feedback you get to see if it fits. If it makes sense, accept it. That is why Carol was able to accept the comments about her need to pay more attention to details. If the criticism doesn't fit, respectfully indicate your disagreement and the basis for it. Another possibility is to accept the part that makes sense and the part with which you disagree. Your values guide your decision in how to consider what people tell you. In this way you gain confidence and trust in your judgement. When you made a mistake in judgment, you focus your attention on correcting it and learning from the experience instead of self criticism.

There are times you may be tempted to go against your preferred way of behaving. For example, if you make a mistake at work. You have a problem if you admit the mistake. You could be in trouble, maybe even lose your job. If you act on your value of honesty, you may face unpleasant consequences but would do so with your self respect intact.

If you value honesty and deny or lie about whether you made a mistake you are faced with guilt and a loss of self-respect. You are faced with the possible consequences of following your conscience or taking the safer route of denial. Which way you go will depend on your priority in the particular situation,

There are several benefits to being mindful of ATS. Over time it stimulates confidence and creativity in thinking and behavior. Thomas Edison would not have discovered the light bulb or the myriad of his other inventions had he not had confidence in his vision (ATS) when those around him said he was crazy. You cannot be creative if you are too involved in self-criticism for making a mistake. This undermines new learning. Mistakes should be thought of as an opportunity for new learning.

ATS also provides a model for others which is especially important as a parent or an employer. It has the added benefit of encouraging others to expect the same from you which helps to reinforce your own ATS.

How to use accountability

1. Decide what values you want as a guide for your behavior.

2. Take the time to enjoy the good feelings that come from behaving in ways you value.

3. Go over the times you behave in ways you don't like. See what you can learn to avoid repeating them. .

4. When someone makes complaints about the way you behave, think about whether you feel it is justified. If it is, change the behavior accordingly. If you don't agree, let them know this and that respect that they see things differently.

5. Don't let anyone tell you how you should feel about yourself.

References:

QBQ! The Question Behind the Question: Practicing Personal Accountability in Work and in Life, John G. Miller, Putnam Publishing Group, 2004, 128 pages

Marvin Snider, Ph.D.

How Full Is Your Bucket? Positive Strategies for Work and Life, Tom Rath & Donald O. Clifton, Gallup Press, 2004, 128 pages

Accountability, Rob LeBow & Randy Spitzer, Berrett-Koehler, 2002, 276 pages. Paperback

The Power Of Personal Accountability: Achieve What Matters To You, Mark Samuel & Sophie Chiche, Xephor Press, 2004, 133 pages. Paperback

Personal Accountability : Powerful and Practical Ideas for You and Your Organization, John Miller, Denver Press, 1999, 299 pages. Paperback

Accountability…A Noun or a Verb?, Richard L. Cassidy, BookSurge Publishing 2006, 42 pages. Paperback

*The messages in the business references are very applicable to personal life.

BENEFIT/COST BEHAVIOR

Harry was an electrician who worked on his own for twelve years. He decided he needed to get some help. He could hire an assistant or get a partner. He considered both. He concluded that he could make more money with an assistant even though it would take time to manage training and supervision. This didn't turn out to be the case. He found that the time he had to spend dealing with his assistant lowered his profit.

This left the alternative of finding a partner. He talked to a few of his fellow electricians whom he thought might be candidates. None of them worked out. He accidentally ran across an old friend, Larry, whom he hadn't seen in five years or more. It was a pleasant surprise to find that he was in the same place as Harry. They spent a good bit of time exploring the idea of becoming partners. They looked at how that would change the way they worked, what they expected of one another, and how well they got along. They also looked at the down side. After careful thought they decided it was worth a shot at being partners. This turned out to be a good decision. They worked well together, made more money, and managed to solve their infrequent differences without much difficulty.

All experiences are package deals - you can't have the good things without the baggage that comes with it. This applies to everything you do: relationships, purchases, making decisions, and others. The more that the benefits outweigh the baggage, the happier you will be in what you are doing. This was the case with Harry and Larry which resulted from thoughtful consideration of the risks and benefits of becoming a partnership.

How you feel may keep changing when the advantages and disadvantages are too close together depending on which is dominant at any given time. You will be unhappy when there is too much that is unpleasant for the benefits you get. This will lead you consider doing something else.

The excitement of a new job may distract you from noticing the parts of the job you don't like. You will stay with it as long as you get enough satisfaction to put up with the annoying and boring part of the job. The same applies to a couple who rush into marriage with the fantasy that love will conquer all. It is only after the glow of romance fades the couple becomes aware of what they don't like about one another. The success of the marriage will depend on their ability to make the positives more important than the negative ones.

Falling in love with a house and buying it may fuel the fantasy of a happier ever after life. That is, until realizing traffic problems, unexpected repairs, long commute to work and noisy neighbors come into sharp perspective. Life is not static. What works and what doesn't work changes as circumstances change. One needs to regularly ask, is what is good about a situation worth what it takes to stay with it?

A benefit can include any emotional or physical experience. This might be a compliment, promotion, getting power or prestige. It might be the good feeling that comes after a good work out. The same applies to material things like getting a raise, or a new car. It can include not having to do things you don't like to do such as long work hours, traveling, cutting your lawn or housework.

A cost is whatever it takes to gain a benefit. You know what you spend (psychologically or physically) on one thing will leave less for other things. Energy you put in one relationship will leave less for other relationships.

Who bears the cost for getting a benefit is not always clear. It may be the person who gets the benefit. You buy clothes and enjoy wearing them. It may also be that you pay for goodies other people to enjoy. Your child gets the benefit of a college education paid for by you. Often times you pay and both you and others benefit. You take your family out to dinner and everybody enjoys it.

The balance between benefits and costs fall into roughly three categories:

- The benefits are clearly worth the cost of getting them. The benefits of being married far outweigh the struggles that go with having it. This leads to a stable marriage or other partnerships. This was the case for Harry and Larry. Divorce occurs when this is not the case.

- The benefits and the costs that go with having them are too close to know whether getting the benefits are worth it. A rocky marriage that has as many serious problems as it has pleasurable times may periodically lead to question whether it makes sense to stay in the marriage. The result is an unstable marriage that chronically teeters on divorce.

- The benefits are clearly not worth the cost of getting them. A marriage that has many serious problems that doesn't have enough of what is valued will end in divorce.

How to make use of the benefit/cost balance

1. Approach the decision about whether to enter a new experience or stay with an existing one by looking at whether what is attractive about is worth what it takes to stay with it. Influencing this decision will depend on what other possibilities you have. Deciding on what job to take will depend on which offers the most benefits for the least disadvantages.

2. Periodically look at the things you are doing and see whether the good things are worth what it takes to get them.

3. When a good situation begins to lose its charm, look at what might be done to keep the good parts and how you can get rid of or at least reduce the parts that bother you. Martial problems would be easier to manage when attention is focused on how to improve the relationship rather than blaming one another. A job will be a happier place when a dissatisfied person pays more attention to what he can do to make the job better and changing the things that have been troublesome. This will yield far better results than complaining and wanting somebody else to make things better.

4. There are times when the benefits are clearly not worth the cost of getting them and there doesn't seem to be anything you can do to change it. This may signal it is time to move onto something else. If you stay, the situation is likely to only get worse and wind up having a more difficult time to leave it.

References:

Too Good to Leave, Too Bad to Stay: A Step-by-Step Guide to Help You Decide Whether to Stay In or Get Out of Your Relationship, Mira Kirshenbaum, Plume, 1997, 304 pages. Paperback

Making Choices: Practical Wisdom for Everyday Moral Decisions, Peter Kreeft, Servant Publications, 1990, 218 pages. Paperback

Making Choices, Alexandra Stoddard & Marc Romano, Collins 1995, 222 pages. Paperback

Hard Choices: Decision Making under Unresolved Conflict, Isaac Levi, Cambridge University Press, 2005, 262 pages. Paperback

Decisions, Decisions: The Art of Effective Decision Making, David A. Welch, Prometheus Books, 2001, 300 pages. Paperback

Smart Choices: A Practical Guide to Making Better Decisions, by John S. Hammond , Ralph L. Keeney, & Howard Raiffa, Broadway, 2002 256 pages. Paperback

CREATIVITY

Ellen was a law firm receptionist for five years. At first, her job was enjoyable because of the many interesting people she met. After awhile, the glitter wore off and the job settled into a familiar and increasingly boring routine. This inspired her to get creative. She challenged herself to find interesting ways to notify lawyers they had a call. Instead of just saying so and so was on the line, she would come up with some quip that was unique to the person calling. She found this challenging and entertaining. An unexpected benefit came in improved relationships with her boss and co-workers. They appreciated her creativity and were more respectful of her efforts. It was pleasing to see the model it set for others to follow. She applied the same creativity to changing the appearance of the reception area that was welcomed by staff and clients.

It's exciting to find you can express yourself in a way you never had before as Ellen found. This can happen in anything you do: the way you work, make a painting, compose music, write a poem, building something and countless more. Spending time doing something creative can be a refreshing break from your daily routine. It is an opportunity to express something you feel inside yourself. The satisfaction you get in doing something different can give you new energy to do the routine things. It is also a great way to help you feel better when you are feeling down. The nice thing about creative activities is you don't have to please anyone but yourself. It is a bonus if other people enjoy what you create. It is very important not to let other people's judgment take away your enjoyment or change what you do.

How to make the most of creativity

1. Make time on a regular basis to do things that you enjoy without needing to accomplish anything. It can be any kind of activity: writing, music, painting, crafts, gardening, woodworking, and many more.

2. You will never know what you are capable of doing if you don't try doing things that catch your fancy. It doesn't matter how well you do it, only that you enjoy trying. It is like taking a trip with a surprise ending.

3. Make the time to talk to people who enjoy their own form of creativity. Find out what they enjoy about what they do and how they got started. This may give some good ideas to try on your own.

4. Meet with people who have the same interests as you. Sharing experiences and supporting one another can add to your creativity and enjoyment.

5. Encourage your children to find and support their journey in discovering their own creativity. They will need your help in exploring new activities. Be careful to avoid the temptation to unduly influence them into things that you like. They need to fly free like a bird to discover where they want to land.

6. Treat time for creativity as a necessary part of your life that enhances your sense of well being. Having this outlet will make doing life's routine less tedious. Doing this helped Ellen turn a boring job into a rewarding one.

References:

Creativity: Flow and the Psychology of Discovery and Invention, Mihaly Csikszentmihalyi, Harper Perennial, 4 Tra edition, 1997, 464 pages. Paperback

Cracking Creativity: The Secrets of Creative Genius, Michael Michalko, Ten Speed Press, New Ed edition, 2001, 309 pages. Paperback

The Zen of Creativity: Cultivating Your Artistic Life, John Daido Loori, Ballantine Books, 2005, 272 pages. Paperback

The Creative Habit: Learn It and Use It for Life, Twyla Tharp, Simon & Schuster, 2005, 256 pages. Paperback

The Creative License: Giving Yourself Permission to be the Artist You Truly Are, Danny Gregory, Hyperion, 2006, 208 pages. Paperback

DECISION MAKING

Alfred and Clara were married for five years when they thought about buying their first home. At first, the idea of making this large purchase seemed daunting to them. They were also a little overwhelmed at all of the decisions they would have to make: where did they want to live, how big a house would they need, what could they afford, and more.

They talked to a few Realtors until they found one with whom they felt comfortable. It was possible to screen houses on the internet which saved them having to see every house that might fit their needs. It was also possible to get pre-qualified for a mortgage in case they found something. Three houses looked promising. Making a choice between them became difficult.

The Realtor helped them go over the benefits and limitations of each house. After a lot of deliberation and anxious moments they chose one. They felt comfortable with their decision because they carefully considered the merits of each house both for the present and foreseeable future needs. Their bid was accepted after a few days of nail biting negotiations. They were thrilled with the idea of finally having their own home.

A year after they moved in, the town changed the zoning laws from residential to limited commercial use on a nearby sizable parcel of land. This was very upsetting because they didn't want to be that close to commercial property and were concerned about how this would affect their quality of life and the value of their property. They worried they had made the wrong choice. After reviewing how they made their decision, they stood by it given the information they had at the time. There had been no indication that changes in the zoning laws were being considered.

It is not possible to avoid making decisions. Any behavior or lack of behavior is a decision. Be aware that behavior carries a message whether intended or not: what you wear, what you say, what you do, and even what you don't do. Consider possible results from any decision you are considering. This is often unclear. There are many times when the outcome of a decision may not be known for years as in the case of marriage, investments, and the house you buy among many others. Alfred and Clara became innocent victims to this happening.

Decisions come in all sizes - from life defining events to the routine of every day living. Big or little, decisions follow the same steps. You need to know what options you have in making a decision and what are the good and bad things that go with each one in making a wise choice. The process is the same for all decisions. The difference between major and minor decisions is its importance in the amount of time, energy, risk, and consequences that it takes to make a decision.

Usually, decisions are made out in the open-- "*I agree…I will do…*I won't…" But decisions are not always obvious. Less obvious ways of expressing a decision are postponing it, avoiding it, and being critical.

Decisions are usually made by going with what makes the most sense unless it is over-shadowed by emotion. Merit based decisions happen when people have the ability to carefully consider what is involved in a decision they need to make. Decisions can be time sensitive. Taking too long to make it can make the difference between success and failure. Be mindful that it is risky to make decisions when you are upset because your ability to make sound decisions will may be compromised by your emotions.

Timing can have as much to do with making a good decision as what the decision is about. Many decisions have to be made in a timely way – namely, paying bills, taking medication, meeting terms of a contract and more. A thoughtful decision made too soon or too late can become a problem rather than have the intended results.

An approach decision making

1. Recognize that whatever you do in word or deed is a decision that has an outcome. You need to decide when an outcome matters and when it doesn't. You decide to pay your bills because you don't like what will happen if you don't. You decide not to vote because you don't think it will matter.

2. Think about how your desires will be affected by the choice you make. You may want to remodel your kitchen. In order to do so you will have to make a lot of decisions: cost, architect, contractor, appliances, color, and more. The weight of having to go through this process may lead you to believe that staying with what you have isn't so bad.

3. Determine what information is needed to make the decision. The outcome of a decision can be no better than the quality of information on which it is based. Don't hesitate to get help in deciding what you need to know in making a decision. Then get as much information as you can on all the things that may affect your decision. Do this on your own or hire somebody to help you. There are many things to know when you are buying a house. Consult with a realtor, a bank, a home inspector and others to decide what are the important things you need to consider in making the purchase. Make sure you understand all of your information to provide the decision that best fits your needs.

4. There may be times you need to make a decision with too little information. Sometimes it is not possible to get all of the information you would like to have. Decide whether you have enough to warrant risking a decision. If not, you do better to pass on it. Buying a house may not afford the time you need to properly evaluate what you would like to know. You are faced with evaluating whether you have enough information to risk placing a bid.

5. Making decisions is easier to do then putting them into practice. A decision that makes sense may not work because unexpected problems prevented it from being implemented. Judging the wisdom of a decision should be based on two things: whether you had enough information on which to make the decision and were you able to make good use of it. If the answer to both questions is yes, the decision was a good one independent of the outcome. Don't berate yourself for a decision that didn't work out as was desired. You are likely to assume that the only reason for it not working out was because of your decision. What this doesn't take into account was that there may be other things out of your knowledge or control that affected the outcome. This is why you should separate out whether you feel you made a good decision from the outcome of it. Feel good about your decision and unhappy about the way it worked out.

6. A thoughtful decision requires careful attention to how it is put into practice. A good decision will not work out if it isn't put into practice with the same care that went into making the decision. Putting a lot of thought in how you want to remodel your kitchen will result in your being unhappy if you don't make sure the contractor does the work in the way he promised.

References:

Decisions, Decisions: The Art of Effective Decision Making, David A. Welch, Prometheus Books, 2001, 300 pages. Paperback

Smart Choices: A Practical Guide to Making Better Decisions, John S. Hammond, Ralph L. Keeney, & Howard Raiffa, Broadway; Reprint edition, 2002, 256 pages. Paperback

Primer on Decision Making: How Decisions Happen, James G. March, Free Press, 1994, 289 pages.

The Psychology of Judgment and Decision Making, Scott Plous, McGraw-Hill Humanities/Social Sciences/Languages, 1 edition, 1993 ,.352 pages. Paperback

Rational Choice in an Uncertain World: The Psychology of Judgement and Decision Making, Reid Hastie & Robyn M. Dawes, Sage Publications, Inc. 2001 392 pages. Paperback

Thinking and Deciding, Jonathan Baron, Cambridge University Press, 2000, 576 pages. Paperback

Value-Focused Thinking: A Path to Creative Decisionmaking, Ralph L. Keeney, Harvard University Press, 1996, 432 pages. Paperback

FEAR OF FAILURE

Eleanor was a top sales representative for a children's manufacturing company. She did very well with familiar products but had difficulty with new ones or in generating new customers. Fear of failure and the unknown inhibited her from moving into unfamiliar territory. The difficulty stems from viewing any missed sale or an appointment refusal as a reflection on her. She didn't take into account that she may not get a new customer for reasons other than about her. There may be a preference for a competing product, a commitment to another sales rep who happens to be a relative, or having a low priority for her clothing line. She overcame this difficulty once she was able to view losing a new customer in a different light. Getting satisfaction from feeling she did her best helped her gain a broader perspective when she didn't get an order.

You get into trouble when you view losing a job, not making a sale, not getting a promotion, or any other disappointment as a failure. This presumes that the only reason for this happening is some deficiency in you. It does not take into account that there could be other reasons for the same result. Your missed promotion may have nothing to do with merit and lot to do with the politics in a company. It is often the case that promotions are made more on having the right connections than on qualifications. To presume your loss is solely about you has the added problem of undermining your self confidence which runs the risk of affecting your future performance.

A more appropriate definition of failure is not learning from experience. This is something over which you have control. When things don't work out you have the choice of judging the outcome or making the most of what is possible. Judging involves blaming yourself, someone else, or something else as the reason for your

192 disappointment. These options only add to making an unhappy situation worse and distract you from productive efforts.

Making the most of a disappointing outcome involves evaluating what happened and figuring out what you can learn from the situation so you can do better in the future. This helps your self-confidence and improves the possibility you will be more successful in the future. This allows you to approach new experiences with enthusiasm for what might be gained rather than fear of failure.

Coping with fear of failure

1. You have the best chance of succeeding in whatever you attempt if you do your best to prepare for its happening: be it a test, job interview, sales call and more.

2. Focus on what you can learn from the experience if the outcome is disappointing. Focus on how to improve your performance in the future. Don't get into beating on yourself. It will only inhibit your learning to improve.

3. Take satisfaction in your performance if you feel you did your best. Don't let the positive aspect of what you accomplished get lost in your disappointment of a negative outcome. Consider whether there is anything you can do that will help achieve a more desirable outcome in the future.

References:

How to Overcome Your Secret Fear of Failure: Recognizing and Beating Your Achilles Syndrome, Petruska Clarkson, Vega, 2003, 224 pages. Paperback

Fear of Failure, James Marsh, all Galbraith, Benchmark Books, 1993, 176 pages.

Here's the Bright Side: Of Failure, Fear, Cancer, Divorce, and Other Bum Raps, Betty Rollin & Jules Feiffer, Random House , 2007, 128 pages.

Feel the Fear…and Beyond: Mastering the Techniques for Doing It Anyway, Susan Jeffers, Ballantine Books, 1998, 272 pages. Paperback

Failure Is Not an Option(TM): Six Principles That Guide Student Achievement in High-Performing Schools, Alan M. Blankstein, Corwin Press, 2005, 288 pages.

Fight Your Fear and Win: Seven Skills for Performing Your Best Under Pressure--At Work, In Sports, On Stage, Don Greene, Broadway, 2002, 240 pages. Paperback

Face Your Fear: Living With Courage in an Age of Caution, Shmuley Boteach, St. Martin's Griffin, 2005, 258 pages. Paperback

Fear and Other Uninvited Guests: Tackling the Anxiety, Fear, and Shame That Keep Us from Optimal Living and Loving, Harriet Lerner, HarperCollins, 2004, 256 pages.

Charles was a supervisor in a computer company. He always approached giving annual reviews with discomfort when he had to give more bad news than good news. Over the years he learned the importance of giving honest assessments. Giving false compliments only came back to bite him. The same applied to sugar coating criticism. He found that commending people for their accomplishments made it easier for his subordinates to pay attention to behaviors that needed improvement. He was always amazed when people responded to hearing criticism as it somehow made it his problem. If only he had done things differently they wouldn't have their problem. This was offset more often by other people who accepted critical feedback with thanks and a commitment to improve their performance.

Honesty is necessary to have meaningful relationships. Without it reality gets distorted whether you are the one being dishonest or whether some one is being that way with you. This leads to mistrust and problems in relationships. Honesty is possible for you when you feel good about yourself and feel confident in being able to handle reactions to your comments. You are likely to get a constructive hearing when complimentary or critical comments are made with sensitivity. The very same honest commentary made without sensitivity will bring very different results. Telling someone he/she is fat may be an honest appraisal but totally insensitive.

Hold other people to the same standard of honesty. You will get a clue it is being violated when what is said isn't consistent with the person's behavior. Let the person know when this happens in a non-judgmental manner. Allowing other people to practice dishonesty gives tacit permission that you will accept this behavior.

Honesty also includes following in behavior what you have said in words. This encourages the expectation for others to behave in a similar manner. Do not practice retaliating in kind when someone is dishonest with you. This is likely to allow the offending person to focus on your dishonesty to avoid focusing on his behavior.

Honesty does not include one person telling another what he should think, what he should feel, or what he should do. No one takes kindly to this kind of response. Respecting another's point of view doesn't mean you have to agree with it, but only to respect the difference. Do not let other people tell you how you should feel. Charles learned this from after years of experience.

It also includes taking responsibility for your behavior and expecting the same from others. You also need to be aware that honesty sometimes comes at a price. There are people who have difficulty being asked to be accountable for their behavior or being told things about their behavior they haven't wanted to face no matter how nicely you say it.

Practicing honesty

1. Speak the truth as you know it even when it works against you. This will work in you benefit in the long run.

2. You are being dishonest when you don't say what you know to be truth.

3. A white lie is dishonesty that is done to protect the feelings of another person. It stops being a white lie when you to do it for your own benefit.

4. Honesty is a problem when it is done without thinking about how it will feel to the to the person to whom you are speaking. Telling a person he/she is not very smart may be the truth but isn't paying attention to the other person's feelings. Adding to the insult is that no good purpose is served in making the judgment.

5. Recognize dishonesty in other people's behavior. They may look uncomfortable, find it hard to make eye contact, they are fidgety, they sweat when its not hot, and behave in ways that don't fit the situation. Their behavior may not follow what they say or they may sound different from the way they usually speak.

6. Let a person know when you feel he is being dishonest. It may be uncomfortable to do so, but to not do it gives the message that it is alright to lie. Doing it in an angry way makes the situation worse. Call the person who is lying on his behavior in a kindly way that is not judgmental. You might express being confused because what they said doesn't fit what happened. Another way is ask whether they were aware of what you know that doesn't fit what they said. These ways give the person a chance to correct their dishonesty in a way that isn't embarrassing. When subtle attempts do not work, there may not be any choice but to directly say why you feel what he did was dishonest. This has the best chance of being heard when you stick to what the person did and not treat him as though he lies about everything.

References:

Radical Honesty, How to Transform Your Life by Telling the Truth, Brad Blanton, SparrowHawk Publications, 2005, 277 pages. Paperback

Living the Truth: Transform Your Life Through the Power of Insight and Honesty Keith Ablow, Little, Brown and Company, 2007, 320 pages.

Emotional Honesty & Self-Acceptance, Ronald R. Brill, Xlibris Corporation, 2000, 328 pages. Paperback

Honesty Works! Real-World Solutions to Common Problems at Work & Home, Steven Gaffney, JMG Publishing, 2005, 167 pages.

Brutal Honesty, Leonard Chivers, Leonard Chivers, 2007, 164 pages. Paperback

MAKING COMMITMENTS

Henry grew up in a small Maine town. People made deals, gave credit and en-tered partnerships based on their word and a friendly handshake. That was sixty years ago. Over time informality gave way to the formality of written agreements shep-herded by lawyers. People also gradually shifted in the reliability of their commit-ments. Henry learned to take offering of promises with a grain of salt unless he knew the person well. Otherwise a commitment meant that a person would do what he said he would do unless something came up. He could understand this if the person gave him the courtesy of letting him know he couldn't honor his commitment.

He was very angry about a recent event. Henry was a lobster fisherman. He couldn't run his boat alone. His usual helper was ill. He asked his friend, Charlie, to help him out. Charlie said, "Oh sure!" Henry was up at his usual five a.m. getting his boat ready while he waited for Charlie to come, but he didn't show up. Henry was furious! This meant a lost day of work. Charlie was very apologetic when confronted . He said a friend came into town unexpectedly the night before. He assumed that Henry would have been able to find somebody else. That was the end of that friendship.

There was a time when making a promise was a serious matter. Men were proud to say that their word was their bond. Business deals, large and small, were made with a handshake. It was commonplace for promises to be made in personal relationships with the same trust.

In the present social climate promises are often made with the same good in-tention but they are subject to unilateral change as needed. This happens for various reasons. Trust in one's word is risky unless you know a person well. Henry found this out the hard way.

There may be times when you have to break a promise. Doing so may or may not be in your control. The way you handle it may be more important than having to break it. Ideally, take responsibility for not doing what was promised. Acknowledge your behavior and take responsibility for the consequences of doing so. Be account-able for changing your mind and do not blame somebody else for your behavior. Being forthright helps to build trust and invites the same in return, Do not assume a person is making a promise unless he is explicit in saying what he will do and when he will do it. Vague promises are very unreliable and are subject to misunderstanding resulting in strained relationships. Ask for clarification if you have any doubts. This will avoid problems of misunderstanding so both of you know what you can expect to happen. Following through on promises is key to building trust in relationships.

Things to consider in making promises

1. Make a promise only after you are sure you can honor it.

2. Think about the things that might happen to prevent your doing so.

3. When it looks likely that you can't do what you promised, let the people affected by it know as soon as possible.

4. Take responsibility for not following through on your promise even if it wasn't your fault.

5. Hold other people accountable for the promises they make to you.

6. Do not accept promises unless you know what you can expect and you have confidence it will happen. You both need to agree on what is supposed to happen. Otherwise you both can feel wronged.

References:

The Power of Commitment: A Guide to Active, Lifelong Love, Scott M. Stanley & Gary Smalley, Jossey-Bass, 2005, 288 pages. Paperback

The 10 Commitments: Parenting with Purpose, Chick Moorman & Thomas Haller, Personal Power Press, 2004, 157 pages.

Coaching for Commitment: Interpersonal Strategies for Obtaining Superior Performance, Dennis C. Kinlaw, Pfeiffer, 1999, 176 pages.

The Commitment Dialogues, Matthew McKay & Barbara Quick, McGraw-Hill, 2005, 304 pages.

Creating Commitment: How to Attract and Retain Talented Employees by Building Relationships That Last, Michael O'Malley, Wiley, 2001, 272 pages.

MANAGE A PROBLEM, DON'T JUDGE IT

Phil had an ongoing argument with his fourteen year old son, Carl. He was angry at him because he didn't clean the garage as promised. Phil criticized him for not honoring his commitment. Carl complained he did what he thought needed to be done. He said his father's expectations were unrealistic. The father recognized that if they continued the unpleasant exchange both would walk away being unhappy which will only set the stage for the next round.

Phil decided to use a different approach. He said to Carl, "It looks like you are having trouble with what I am expecting from you. Why do you think my expectations are unrealistic." A short conversation followed in which they exchanged their thoughts about what would be a reasonable standard for cleaning the garage. The conversation ended with an agreement. A few days later Carl cleaned the garage as promised in a timely manner. Two good things happened. Carl honored his agreement without having to be reminded and Phil was pleased he didn't have to remind Carl to follow through.

The relationship between father and son got stronger because both felt respected by the other. Carl felt good that his feelings and ideas affected what happened.

There are multiple choices to the resolution of any problem. You can be concerned about whose fault it is, ignore it, or work on how to make the best out of what is possible. When you focus on blaming, nothing useful is accomplished. The problem is not solved and there are bad feelings which only compounds the difficulty. So instead of having one problem, you now have two problems. Phil was wise to utilize a positive approach to his problem.

There may be a momentary sense of relief in blaming someone else, but this is short-lived. When blaming becomes a habit, it takes its toll on self-respect and invites unhappy relationships. This is what initially happened with Phil and Carl.

Ignoring the problem doesn't work either. Doing so only makes the problem worse and makes other people angry. The price for blaming or ignoring the problem takes energy away from solving the problem.

Making the most out of what is possible is a more useful approach. It recognizes the limitations in the problem. It also involves using your intellect to figure out what you will need to fix it. The solution can only work when it makes sense and feels right to you and anyone else that is affected by the problem. The solution not only solves the immediate difficulty but also helps to build trust in you by other people and gives you confidence in solving any future problems.

How to manage a problem

1. Resist the temptation to blame yourself or anyone else when faced with a problem.

2. Study the problem and decide what it would take to fix it.

3. Put the solution into practice.

4. Do the best you can if you don't have all you need to solve the problem.

5. If what happens is less than you would like, be satisfied you have done the most that was possible with what was available.

6. Keep your new learning for use in solving future problems.

References:

Don't Tick Off the Gators! Managing Problems Before Problems Manage You, an Irreverent Guide, Jim Grigsby, Highland City FL, 2006, 168 pages. Paperback

How to Manage Conflict: Turn All Conflicts into Win-Win Outcomes, Peg Pickering, Career Press, 1999,128 pages. Paperback

The Parent's Problem Solver: Smart Solutions for Everyday Discipline Dilemmas and

Behavioral Problems, Cathryn Tobin, Three Rivers Press, 2002, 368 pages. Paperback

Successful Problem Solving: A Workbook to Overcome the Four Core Beliefs That Keep You Stuck, Patrick Fanning & Matthew McKay, New Harbinger Publications, 2002, 128 pages. Paperback

Problem Solving, S. Robertson, Psychology Press, 2001, 288 pages. Paperback

POWER OF FAMILIARITY

Alex and Barbara were married for fifteen years. They were happy for the first five years. Over the following years it shifted into a love-hate relationship. There were times when they got along well and then there would be periods when they were at each other's throat. They periodically considered divorce. Things would get better and they would go through another cycle of good and difficult times. It became clear after awhile that it was easier to put up with what was familiar then it was to deal with the unknown that would follow divorce.

People like Alex and Barbara will often put up with unpleasant situations because dealing with the familiar is more comfortable than dealing with the unknown. Familiarity does not mean liking the situation. It does mean knowing what is required and having found a reasonable way to cope with it. Anxiety of the unknown comes from not knowing what to expect and uncertainty in your ability to deal with whatever it might be. Prejudice is a case in point. People are comfortable with what they know. People who are different either by race, religion, nationality or some other characteristic arouses the discomfort of unfamiliarity. This gets worse with the acceptance of stereotypes when you don't have first hand information. Research shows that people tend to judge with fear and judgment what they do not understand . Experience shows prejudice tends to diminish when people get to know each other.

Overcoming fear of the unknown

1. Try to understand why you are uncomfortable with having to make a change.

2. Look at the assumptions you make about a prospective change.

3. Check accuracy of assumptions to see if what bothers you is likely to happen.

4. See if you can try out the change before you have to make it. Test out new behaviors in small steps before giving up what is familiar. This will give you time to develop comfort in the new situation before having to totally give up what is familiar.

5. Checking out what bothers you will help you to learn more about what you

can and cannot manage. Without this you will stay stuck with your fears and miss changes that could improve your life.

References:

The Comfort Trap (or, What If You're Riding a Dead Horse?), Judith Sills, Viking Adult, 2004, 256 pages.

PSYCHIC ENERGY: MIX OF THINKING AND FEELING

Isabel, 30, was a court reporter for the past eight years. She liked her job but had a string of bad experiences working for court reporting agencies. Her last experience pushed her over the top. She decided to take the risk of going out on her own. She had anxiety about whether she would be successful and sought consultation for help in dealing with her anxiety which interfered with her usual ability for clear thinking. She learned that worrying didn't leave much energy for careful thought. She had to get her anxiety under control if she was going to succeed in getting the business started. The consultation enabled a refocus of her energy to working out a business plan that resulted in a brochure and a business card that was given to all of her contacts.

Psychic energy refers to the combination of a person's thought and feelings Everything you do involves some combination of both kinds of energy. The more energy that is devoted to one leaves less available to the other. A person who is very upset will have little energy available for thought. When you are totally absorbed in feelings you will not have much energy for appreciating how your behavior may affect you or someone else. Losing your temper doesn't leave much energy for realizing how you are hurting someone else or how you will be treated because you lost your cool. Ideally, try to find a balance between energy devoted to thinking and attention to what you are feeling.

Psychic energy does not exist by itself. Mind and body are connected. How you think and feel affects your physical energies. Being under great stress for too long will contribute to developing physical problems like ulcers, gut problems, heart problems among many others. Physical problems affect your ability to think and your mood. People who are sick get cranky, irritable and don't have much energy for rational thought. Managing the balance between your thoughts and feelings will make a difference in how productive your psychic energy will be.

In the normal course of daily life we are continually confronted with what mix of psychic energy is appropriate for any given situation. Work situations generally demand putting the bulk of effort in the thinking part of psychic energy. This works well until events happen that draw attention to the emotional part of psychic energy. This creates a competition between what you are feeling and thinking. This can give rise to deciding which part of your psychic energy, thinking or feeling, should be given dominance.

There are times when people make conscious choices in the mix of their psychic energies. Lawyers have a saying, "When the law is on your side, argue the law. When the facts are on your side, argue the facts. When you have neither, make a lot of noise."

Attempts to get a person who is very upset to consider rational thought will fail because most of their psychic energy is focused on what they are feeling. This leaves little or no energy left for logic. Occasionally you may hear someone say in the fit of anger, *"I don't care whether it makes sense, I just want it that way."* I had a situation occur at work one time. I was in a discussion with my boss. He wanted something done in a certain way. He rejected all my arguments about why what he wanted didn't make sense. When he finally ran out of counter arguments, he turned to me and said, *"I'm the boss and that is the way I want it."*

These situations can be avoided by paying attention to a person's feelings. Doing this will help restore a more productive balance between the thinking and feeling parts of psychic energy. Brief psychotherapy helped Isabel to be able to gain a better balance.

The reverse is also true. There are people who keep thinking about how to deal with their problems without leaving much room for attention to what they are feeling. They will have trouble being thoughtful because they will be blocked by their feelings that haven't been given needed attention. The goal in both cases is to get a useful mix of the psychic energies of thinking and feeling.

A man consulted me about a problem he was having with his wife. He went on and on with at detailed analysis of what happened and why it happened. It became clear that he was avoiding attention to feelings about what was happening. He kept insisting that this wasn't the problem. He was stuck on trying to figure out how to get his wife to see things his way. Eventually, he was able to see how his psychic energy was focused on what he was thinking and not enough to what he was feeling. Gradually, he was able to work out a better mix. This enabled him to see his contribution to the problem.

How to manage your psychic energy

1. Remember that your mind and body affect one another. Neglecting one will affect the other one.

2. It is a good idea to look at how you are doing with the mix of your thinking and feeling energies each day. This will help you keep a good balance.

3. The mix between what you think and feel will not be the same for everything you do. What fits in one situation may not fit in another one. You will need to decide the best combination for the different things you do.

4. Look at the mix between your thinking and feeling when you are stuck in solving a problem. An imbalance may get in your way of finding a solution.

5. It is a good idea to periodically look at an overview of whether you are

satisfied with the mix of your psychic energy in each aspect of your life. This may help you to spot early signs of heading for trouble that can be prevented from happening.

6. Avoid doing thinking tasks when you are upset. It will be hard for you to concentrate on what you are doing until you pay attention to your feelings.

References:

Psychic Energy: How to Change Desires into Realities, Joseph J. Weed , Prentice Hall Trade, 1989. Paperback

Psychic Protection: Creating Positive Energies For People And Places, William Bloom, Fireside, 1997, 176 pages. Paperback

Commentary on Psychic Energy, Torkom Saraydarian,TSG Publishing Foundation, 1989, 240 pages. Paperback

Positive Uses of Psychic Energy, Manly P. Hall, Philosophical Research Society, 1996, 32 pages. Paperback

The Power of Full Engagement: Managing Energy, Not Time, Is the Key to High Performance and Personal Renewal, Jim Loehr & Tony Schwartz, Free Press, 2004, 256 pages. Paperback

Leading Change, James O'Toole, Ballantine Books, 1996, 304 pages. Paperback

How People Change, Allen Wheelis, Harper Paperbacks, 1975, 128 pages. Paperback

The Change Function: Why Some Technologies Take Off and Others Crash and Burn, Pip Coburn, Portfolio Hardcover, 2006, 240 pages.

Mastering Change, Ichak, Adizes Ph., The Adizes Institute, 2006, 260 pages. Paperback

RESOURCES: WHAT IT TAKES TO MAKE THINGS WORK

Melanie was the mother of Amy 8, and Lisa 6. She was very unhappy with many of the mindless toys available. She had time on her hands once the girls were in school. She thought it would be neat to get into the toy business that featured toys that helped children's development. Her husband, Todd, was a lawyer and supportive of her interest. Together they thought through what would be needed to make this vision possible. She was bright, imaginative, and had experience managing a retail store before her marriage. They didn't think finances would be a problem. They had some money they could invest and thought they could get a loan if they needed more. She needed to define the kind of toys she had in mind. She thought that going through some of her favorite catalogues would be a good place to start. She remembered seeing a catalogue that featured the kind of toys she had in mind.

Success in life depends on knowing what you want to accomplish and being realistic about what you need to make it happen. A resource is anything you use to accomplish your goals. This may be something physical, a relationship, knowledge, finances, time, emotional capability, and more. Also necessary is the ability to get whatever you need that you don't have. Examples would be: education, experience, the ability to borrow money, get expert advice, have political connections, and more. Melanie and Todd made a good team in developing a plan for Melanie's project.

Getting what you need

1. Describe what you need to do to accomplish your goals and having a clear measure of knowing when you achieve them - to make a certain amount of money, to get a college degree, or to get a job. To be happy, popular or comfortable do not qualify unless they are tied to behaviors you can see or measure

2. Make a list of what you need to accomplish for each of your goals.

3. Check to see whether you have what you will need or whether you can get it.

4. Get the needed resources.

5. Decide how you will accomplish each of your goals.

6. Have backup plans for the important things you will need in case you run into unexpected plans. Otherwise you may not have the time to make corrections if things don't work out as you hoped.

7. Think about what you might need in the future and build a reserve as you are able to do so.

6. Check to see that pursing one goal will not interfere with accomplishing other needed goals. A man may want to start his own business but finds he can't do it without putting his family in financial jeopardy.

7. Redefine the goal to fit available resources.

References:

Handbook of Competence and Motivation, Andrew J. Elliot & Carol S. Dweck (Editors), The Guilford Press, 2005# 704 pages.

Mindset: The New Psychology of Success, Carol Dweck, Random House, 2006, 288 pages.

Why We Do What We Do: Understanding Self-Motivation, Edward L. Deci & Richard Flaste, Penguin, 1996, 240 pages. Paperback   203

Competence in Interpersonal Conflict, William R. Cupach & Daniel J. Canary, Waveland Pr Inc, , 279 pages. Paperback

The Development of Emotional Competence, Carolyn Saarni, The Guilford Press, 1999, 381 pages. Paperback

RITUALS

Frank, Tom and Sam became close friends and came to regard themselves as brothers during their years as college roommates. They made a commitment at graduation to keep in touch with one another. They weren't sure how to do this since they didn't know where their careers would take them. They came up with a plan. They would get together every year on the date of their graduation at some fun place to honor the memory of their college years separate from any other contact they may otherwise have.

A ritual is characterized by the presence of an established procedure or routine to acknowledge an important event. Sports events usually start with the national anthem and people stand with their hands over their heart. Sports teams that win a championship pour Gatorade over the coaches head and drink champagne. New year's eve would not be the same without singing "Auld Lang Syne.

Rituals are also useful in celebrating or honoring important events: weddings, funerals, graduations, and more. These rituals help in making the transition from one situation to another: going from being single to being married, from the coming to realize that a loved one will no longer be there, and from being a student to having a job.

Use of rituals

1. Any situation that involves a meaningful transition from one situation to another as graduation, marriage, loss of loved one, and others may benefit from having a ritual in making the adjustment.

2. The ritual should acknowledge the accomplishments prior to the change and what can be expected in the new situation. Rituals also help to make the change easier. Weddings, funerals, and graduations are familiar examples. Other rituals will require behaviors to fit the particular situation. Suppose you wanted to diet. You have tried different approaches that haven't worked. One approach to consider would be to write down the foods you will not eat. Then burn this list in front of family or friends. You then read a list of what will be your new diet. Making this public statement in front of others may help you to keep to your diet.

4. Engaging in a group ritual involves sharing common goals and has the added benefit of support from like minded people. The group may share a common goal of losing weight even though the details for each person may be different.

References:

Everyday Traditions: Simple Family Rituals for Connection and Comfort, Nava Atlas, Amberwood Press, 2005, 158 pages.

The Art of Ritual: Creating and Performing Ceremonies for Growth and Change; Renee Beck & Sydney Barbara Metrick, Celestial Arts, 2003, 144 pages. Paperback

Rites of Passage: Celebrating Life's Changes, Kathleen Wall & Gary Ferguson, Beyond Words Publishing, 1998, 202 pages

Ceremonies for Real Life, Carine Fabius, Wildcat Canyon Press, 2002, 194 pages. Paperback

Sacred Ceremony: How to Create Ceremonies for Healing, Transitions, and Celebrations, Steven Farmer, Hay House, 2002, 288 pages. Paperback

SELF ASSESSMENT

Margaret, 32, was an accountant with an established reputation in an accounting firm. She was getting tired of working for someone else and thought it would be a great idea to start her own firm. It was clear that doing this would require a range of new skills: marketing, administration, new people skills, and ability to manage other people. Help was needed in deciding whether acquiring these skills fit her personality and talents. She consulted a career counselor and was pleased to find that she had the potential to acquire what would be needed to go out on her own. She devoted two years of education and consultation to gain needed skills and confidence to start her business.

It gets easy to take your capabilities and limitations for granted. They don't stay the same. They change over time with experience and as your needs change. A pretty together person knows his strengths and weaknesses. An insecure person will tend to underestimate his capabilities and overly state his limitations. People are aware of the qualities they regularly use. You are likely to forget abilities you rarely use or ones you did not fully develop. Conducting periodic self assessments are a way to maintain a good current self-perception. Conduct this on two levels; personal qualities and capabilities in your occupation. Keep abreast of changes in your work and upgrade your skills as needed. Margaret's awareness that she did not have a comfortable sense of her capabilities led her to seek help from a career counselor to help her make the needed assessments.

1. Conduct an inventory of your strengths and limitations on a regular basis. It is the same idea used in business. They take inventory so they know what they have and what they need. Start with once a month and then experiment with how often it is useful to do this. Get professional consultation when you feel you are not able to do this on your own as Margaret did.

2. Make an assessment of what you will need to solve a problem. This will give you an idea of skills or information you will need and whether you will need help to accomplish your goals.

3. Be realistic in deciding whether you can learn the new needed skills or whether it is better to get help from somebody who already has them. Decide whether it realistic in needed ability, time and money to acquire them. This might be learning to use a computer, master a new sport, play an instrument, and others.

4. Give thought to the things about yourself about which you are not happy. Look at what you might do to improve these qualities. You might not like that you lose your temper too quickly. You might start by seeing if you can find a way to manage your anger better. If that doesn't work you could see somebody to help you do this.

5. Evaluate successful and unsuccessful experiences after they occur. This will give you further confidence in what you do well and help you to understand what didn't work so that you can do better in the future.

6. Getting information for how other people see you is helpful You will have to sort out which things are relevant and which are not.

7. Make self assessments in all parts of your life: family, work, friendships and interests. You may find that a strength in one area may not be helpful in a different one. Being assertive in work may be a strength but a weakness if you behave that way with family and friends. These efforts don't have to be laborious efforts. The idea is to be mindful in developing an ongoing self observation of what you need to achieve your desired goals and life style.

References:

Enhancing Learning Through Self-Assessment, David Boud, Routledge, 1995, 256 pages. Paperback

People Smarts - Behavioral Profiles , *Self-Assessment Pamphlet*, Tony Alessandra, Michael J. O'Connor, &, Janice Van Dyke, Pfeiffer, 1994, 4 pages.

Yale Assessment of Thinking: A Self-Assessment of Your Skill in the Areas of Reasoning, Insight, and Self-Knowledge, John Mangieri & Cathy Collins Block, # Jossey-Bass, 2003, 18 pages. Paperback

Career Management & Work-Life Integration: Using Self-Assessment to Navigate Contemporary Careers, Brad Harrington & Douglas T. Hall, Sage Publications, 2007, 248 pages.

Self-Determination: Instructional and Assessment Strategies, Michael L. Wehmeyer & Sharon L. Field, Corwin Press, 2007, 208 pages.

SETTING GOALS

Janice, Edward and their three children wanted to take a cross country trip to California on their vacation. They were casual in their planning and thought spontaneity would be fun. They stopped at sites that caught their attention that included the Baseball Hall of fame in Cooperstown, New York, Mammoth Cave in Kentucky, the French Quarter in New Orleans, the home of Mark Twain and a steamboat ride on the Mississippi River. They lost track of time and found they used all of their vacation without getting even half way across country. While they enjoyed what they did see, they were disappointed they hadn't accomplished more. They vowed to do a better job of planning in the future.

A map is very helpful when you need to find your way from one place to another. It is of little use when the you don't know where you want to go. The same is true in how you manage your life. Setting personal goals is the "map" that guides your life style. This works best when goals are specific and realistic. It is one thing to have a goal to be rich. This is an idea that is not measurable unless it includes a concrete goal such as making a specific amount of money. A goal is realistic when you have what it takes to get it in terms of time, information, skills, motivation, and money as needed.

Goals are made on two levels: short and long term. All other things being equal, the best chance of reaching a long term goal is to have a series of short term ones that lead to the long term objective. While a long term goal may require years to achieve, a short term one would be measured in days, weeks or months.

Long term goals will change as circumstances may dictate. Making them short term may lead you to question whether the long term ones still makes sense. The idea of becoming a medical doctor may seem very appealing until you realize what it takes to get there: bachelors degree, medical school, internship and the possibility of more beyond that.

Goals differ in the importance they play in your life. You have many goals with family, job, friends, entertainment, sports and involvement in the community. You also have to decide how important the goals are relative to one another because there won't be enough time, money or energy to work at all of them. You have to make choices on what comes first. After graduation there is the choice of whether to get a job or pursue more education. It might also involve deciding whether to marry or pursue a career.

You will be happier when you are able to keep up to date on your most important goals and that you are doing all you can to make them happen. Do this on a regular time table such as once a month, once or twice a year, or whatever time interval works for you.

Tracking goals

1. Decide your long term goals in money, education, marriage and other areas of importance

2. Assign priorities for these goals both in terms of their relative importance and in what order you want to accomplish them.

3. Goals that are long term should have short term goals to make sure you are on track for what you want to accomplish. Subgoals shouldn't take any longer than a few months. If you had the goal of becoming a doctor, it would be a good idea to set a number of short term goals. Your first subgoal would be to get a bachelor's degree. You might decide that four years is too long. You might find it helpful to take each year as a goal or even each semester. Doing this will help you keep focused. Each step along the way gives you a chance to decide if you are on the right track. At some point you might decide that a goal is more demanding than you thought and leads you to wonder whether achieving the goal is worth what it takes to get it.

4. Lack of clarity in goals often leads to disappointment in wasted time, resources and unfulfilled visions.

References:

Goal Setting 101: How to Set and Achieve a Goal!, Gary Ryan Blair, Blair Pub House, 2000, 58 pages. Paperback

What Are Your Goals: Powerful Questions to Discover What You Want Out of Life, Gary Ryan Blair, Blair Publishing House, 1999, 165 pages. Paperback

Motivation and Goal Setting: How to Set and Achieve Goals and Inspire Others, Jim Cairo, Career Press, 1998, 128 pages. Paperback

Make Success Measurable!: A Mindbook-Workbook for Setting Goals and Taking Action, Douglas K. Smith, Wiley, 1999, 256 pages.

Goal Analysis: How to Clarify Your Goals So You Can Actually Achieve Them, Robert F. Mager, CEP Press, 1997, 159 pages. Paperback

What Are Your Goals: Powerful Questions to Discover What You Want Out of Life; Gary Ryan Blair, Blair Publishing House, 1999, 165 pages.

Simpleology: The Simple Science of Getting What You Want, Mark Joyner, Wiley, 2007, 241 pages.

TIME MANAGEMENT

Carl was on the verge of burnout. He was always late and always had too much to do. Meals were often skipped to meet deadlines. There was little time for himself. He didn't understand why his life was so hectic when his colleagues seemed to have an easier time. He finally accepted his supervisor's recommendation to take a course in time management. He learned why he had a problem: he didn't pay enough attention to how long his assignments took, he took on new responsibilities without considering whether he had the time, and he did a poor job of managing interruptions. He was always allowing people to interrupt when he was busy. There also was the seduction of the unknown to answer the phone whenever it rang. These revelations were a real eye-opener to him. Once he changed these behaviors he was pleased to find that his life became more manageable and enjoyable.

Time and money have one thing in common. Both are available in limited amounts. People may differ in the amount of money available to them but everybody has the same amount of time: twenty-four hours a day. A person may be able to make more money but they can't get more time. They can only learn how to make better use of what they have. People often get into trouble because they are unrealistic about how long it takes to get things done. The result is often unnerving: missed deadlines, missed flights, burnout, angry people and on and on. It took a crisis for Carl to come to terms his difficulty in managing his time.

Putting time management into practice

1. Make your best guess in how long it will take to get what you want done. Doubling this estimate will give a better idea of when you will finish.

2. Set priorities on what has to be done. Setting a priority depends on: how important the activity is, when it needs to be done, how much time it will take, and whether it interferes with any other activity.

3. The time to do a particular activity is often underestimated because of the way it is measured. Measure the time from when you finish one activity until the time you start the next activity. Set up and shut times down are often not included in planning. These activities can take a lot of time and in some cases may take longer than the activity itself.

4. You may need to set up a schedule if you have a lot more to do than time available to do it. Start by entering into your calendar all the all the activities you have to do everyday: meals, travel, meetings, personal needs. Then assign a place in the calendar for each of these things or activities. After all available time is assigned any new activity that comes along has to pass the following test; Is the new activity important enough to bump an existing commitment or should you pass on it? Problems develop when you approach a new activity without thinking how this will affect your ability to meet other responsibilities. This can lead to feeling over burdened and upset when needed performance can't be done on time. The problem gets even worse when you will have to face major penalties for missed deadlines.

Time management gets easier when you are able to manage interruptions.

1. *Taking phone calls.* There is magic about the magnetic attraction of a ringing telephone. Curiosity about the unknown call can be compelling. It is also distracting. It is like the way a moth is attracted to light. Once interrupted, it takes time to get back to you were before the call. The pile up of too many interruptions can create a major problem in a tight schedule. One way to avoid this is to reserve one or more blocks of time each day for making or receiving phone calls.

2. *Interruptions.* A great deal of time can be lost when interruptions are permitted. This gives the message that what other people need is more important than what you are doing. This can only create tension, frustration and will likely result in conflict.

   A familiar example occurs when a mother is faced with many interruptions from children, neighbors, telephone, and others. It would be easy to becomes frazzled under these conditions let alone the toll it takes in accomplishing needed chores. You would have much less frustration if you set limits on when you can be interrupted. Phone calls are made and received at convenient times. Children are trained not to make interruptions except in emergencies and convenient times are negotiated with neighbors for visiting times.

3. *Learning to say no:* A desire to be helpful, a team player, or be liked can be a major distraction. Saying no to distractions is less the problem than how it is said. Being able to say no in a respectful and caring manner shows consideration for what a person is requesting. It also carries the message that you have more pressing priorities. Let the person making a request know when you can honor their request as it fits your mutual convenience.

References:

The 25 Best Time Management Tools & Techniques: How to Get More Done Without Driving Yourself Crazy , Doug Sundheim, Peak Performance Press, Inc.2005, 144 pages

Time Management from the Inside Out, second edition: The Foolproof System for Taking Control of Your Schedule--and Your Life, Julie Morgenstern, Owl Books, 2004, 304 pages. Paperback

Time Management for the Creative Person: Right-Brain Strategies for Stopping Procrastination, Getting Control of the Clock and Calendar, and Freeing Up Your Time and Your Life, Lee Silber, Three Rivers Press, 1998, 304 pages. Paperback

Time Management for Unmanageable People: The Guilt-Free Way to Organize, Energize, and Maximize Your Life, Anne Mcgee-Cooper, Bantam, 1994, 272 pages.

The Time Trap: The Classic Book on Time Management, Alec MacKenzie, MJF Books, 2002, 282 pages.

Manage Your Time, Tim Hindle, DK ADULT, 1999, 72 pages. Paperback

UNMET EXPECTATIONS

Eileen was a warm and engaging personality who was an accomplished business woman and wife and mother of three children. She set high standards for her own behavior and expected the same from others. Upset and disappointment would occur when people did not behave up to her expectations. She had difficulty accepting people as they were and judged their failings according to her expectations. Eileen would get frustrated, complain, and vent, failing to understand why people didn't behave as she thought appropriate.

It is satisfying and convenient to have people behave in ways that meet your needs and expectations. Difficulties arises when this is not the case as was often Eileen's experience. The resulting choice is between imposing your standards on other people or respecting that they have their own standards. The consequence is either in your disappointment in what they do or negotiating a standard acceptable to both. Discrepancies that are too great will lead you to look for relationships with values more compatible with yours.

You don't have the same luxury with family. If you are a parent you have the opportunity raise your children to behave as you feel appropriate. But even in the best of situations they will evolve their own standards which may not always please you. Your choice becomes learning to respect and negotiate differences, avoid one another, or precipitate an emotional disconnect at worst. This occurs when children develop life styles that leave little time or desire to spend time with you. Relationships that survive under these conditions are reduced to being obligatory, not very satisfactory for anyone.

Unmet expectations within a marriage that are not negotiable end in divorce. Marriages survive and even thrive when there is a commitment to respecting difference and being committed to finding consensus. This provides the opportunity for each of you to benefit from each other's uniqueness.

Coping with unmet expectations

1. Live by the adage of treating other people as you would like to be treated. Relationships are satisfying only when each of you feels respected by the other.

2. Do not impose your expectations on others. Let your desires be known in a manner that invites being heard in a caring and constructive manner.

3. When differences in expectations of one another occur in a relationship make it a priority to negotiate finding a consensus.

4. If you find it is not possible to negotiate a consensus, decide whether there is enough value in the relationship to tolerate what is displeasing. Continuing in relationship that is unpleasant will be a disservice to both of you and will likely lead to more unhappiness.

5. When you are obligated to stay in a relationship in which you are unhappy, let your feelings be known and work out how you will deal with them. This would involve informing the other person what they can expect from you. If you had a difficult relationship with a parent that resisted all attempts to improve it, you could let him/her know how you feel and that you would be relating solely out of obligation as needed and not out of desire.

References:

Necessary Losses: The Loves, Illusions, Dependencies, and Impossible Expectations That All of Us Have to Give Up in Order to Grow, Judith Viorst, Free Press, 1998, 448 pages. Paperback

Imperfect Control: Our Lifelong Struggles With Power and Surrender, Judith Viorst, Free Press, 1999, 448 pages. Paperback

Breaking the Power: Of Unmet Needs, Unhealed Hurts, Unresolved Issues in Your Life, Liberty Savard, Bridge-Logos Publishers, 1997, 253 pages. Paperback

Getting Together and Staying Together: Solving the Mystery of Marriage, William Glasser & Carleen Glasser, Harper Paperbacks, 2000, 160 pages. Paperback

Compelled to Control: Recovering Intimacy in Broken Relationships, J. Keith Miller, HCI, 1998, 250 pages. Paperback

Is It You or Is It Me?: Why Couples Play the Blame Game, Scott Wetzler & Diane Cole, Harper Perennial, 1999, 272 pages.

Busting Free: Beyond the Need To Control, Lazaris, Concept Synergy. (Audio Cassette)

VALUES AND BELIEFS

Simon worked for a large chain of supermarkets. He was responsible for managing the produce department. He had a disagreement with the store manager, Mark, about providing organic foods. Simon felt it was important to give this a high priority because of the growing customer interest in these foods. Mark, felt they should stay with what they knew. He believed that organic food was a passing fad. Simon tried to convince him otherwise with articles and statistics. They were at an impasse that strained their relationship. After a protracted struggle they worked out an agreement. Simon would limit purchase of organic produce to not exceed fifteen percent of purchases for the next year. They would then evaluate sales and see how to proceed from there.

Your values are a statement about the way you feel life should be. For example, you may feel a person should be honest, a child should respect his parents, people should drive safely, and more. Your values guide you in all parts of your life: how you behave with your family, friends, practice your religion, at work, about education and others. A belief is a statement about what you think actually happens. You may have the value that people should be honest and belief that this often doesn't happen.

A map helps you get to where you want to go. Values are like the map in helping you live your life in a way that is meaningful for you. Beliefs help you keep your perspective of what actually happens. When you run into a detour while traveling, you make an adjustment in the route to follow. When you hold a value you need to be able to adjust to experience that shows an adjustment is needed. You might value keeping a confidence. However, there may be a time when you feel trust should be violated if breaking the confidence protects someone's safety.

Some values are timeless like respect for other people. Many are not. What makes sense at one time in your life may not at another time. It is desirable to be sensitive to when a held value needs to be modified. Simon had a hard time getting Mark to recognize it was time to modify his value and belief about the sale of organic food.

Managing Values

Values are about deciding the kind of person you want to be. This is accomplished in the following ways

1. You decide on the way you want to behave

2. Observe values you appreciate in other and consider whether to add them to your values.

3. Try out new values to see how they fit.

4. Take on those that fit.

5. Be open to make changes in values as you learn from experience.

6. Periodically take a look at values to see if they continue to make sense.

7. Showing respect for other people's values invites the same in return. Respect acknowledges that everyone is entitled to his own point of view.

Working with beliefs

1. Beliefs are most useful when they are based on first hand experience.

2. Check out accuracy of a belief when it based on what someone says rather than from personal experience.

3. Respect that two people may have the same experience and walk away with different beliefs about it. This is not about right and wrong but differences in how people see things that comes from different histories. Past experiences influence how you understand what you see.

4. Don't assume that what was an accurate belief at one time will continue to be so. If significant time has passed since a belief was formed from personal experience, check to see that your belief still holds.

Managing When Values Conflict With Beliefs:

You are likely to get uncomfortable when things don't happen the way you think they should. The greater the difference on important issues, the greater will be your upset. This can be resolved in different ways. For example: Use the value that you should be honest.

1. Change the belief to fit the value: People are honest as they should be.

2. Change the value to fit the belief: People should be honest when they can be.

3. Deny that the difference between the value and its belief is accurate: there is no difference between people who value honesty and those who behave with dishonesty.

4. Accept the discrepancy: People aren't always able to act on their belief that one should be honest. It is something to aim at getting.

References:

The Power Of Living Your Values, Hyrum W. Smith, Ken Blanchard & Kenneth H. Blanchard, Simon & Schuster, 2000, 248 pages.

Values Clarification, Dr. Sidney B. Simon & Leland W Howe, Warner Books, 1995, 336 pages. Paperback

In Search of Values: 31 Strategies for Finding Out What Really Matters Most to You, Dr. Sidney B. Simon, Warner Books, 1993, 128 pages. Paperback

What Matters Most : The Power Of Living Your Values, Hyrum W. Smith, Ken Blanchard, & Kenneth H. Blanchard, Simon & Schuster, 2000, 248 pages.

Using Your Values to Raise Your Child to Be an Adult You Admire, Harriet Heath & Anna Dewdney, Parenting Press, 2000, 175 pages. Paperback

AVOIDING DISAGREEMENTS

Clara and Frank were married for twenty-five years. Their marriage had been comfortable as they raised their four children. They both took pride in proclaiming they never argued and hoped this would be a model for their children to follow. Unspoken by all, was the awareness that this didn't give an accurate view. Arguments made Clara very uncomfortable stemming from her childhood memory of parents engaged in perpetual arguing and yelling. She vowed this would never happen with her own family.

She would express her views to Frank. If he disagreed with her she would acquiesce. When an issue was important to her, she would find an indirect way to get Frank to do what she needed. This suited Frank because he also had difficulty with arguments. This worked for them because it left Frank with the unspoken fantasy he was the man of the house and it helped Clara avoid the unpleasantness of arguing.

Clara was aware their contrived absence of conflict came at the price of an intimate emotional relationship. She wished she and Frank had the trust that would enable them to openly talk about their feelings and work out their differences without getting into the ugly arguments of her childhood.

People are often reluctant to express their opinions to avoid the risk of unpleasant arguments. This inhibits having meaningful relationships and prevents benefitting from the exchange of different points of view. This reluctance feeds self doubt and undermines self confidence.

This reluctance stems from the underlying assumption that a disagreement means it will be necessarily become unpleasant. Absent is the awareness that a constructive argument can be enjoyable and informative. Speaking from knowledge rather than speculation contributes to productive conversations. People are more susceptible to unpleasant arguments when they are on the defensive and when they lack adequate information to support their views.

This heightens the possibility that a disagreement can become ugly and unpleasant. You can't always protect yourself from this happening but you can learn how to manage when they do occur. Confidence with this ability will free you to having challenging and informative conversations.

Coping with disagreements

1. Develop your coping skills to deal with disagreements. This ability will serve you well in achieving your goals. Knowing as much about the subject under

discussion as possible will enhance your confidence to have your point of view be heard.

2. Don't let other people decide how you should feel about yourself. You can do this by being the judge of your own behavior. You don't change how you feel unless you are given information that makes sense to you.

3. Consider that anger directed at you is about your behavior and not about you as a person. Sometimes people will express their anger by attacking to shift the responsibility for the disagreement. Remind them a disagreement is the product of the relationship. Try to get the other person to take ownership of his contribution.

4. Do not allow your feelings to get to the place you lose self control. When this happens the importance of what you are saying gets lost and becomes secondary to your emotional outburst. Take a break when this happens and return to the discussion when your feeling are in control. This helps to keep the focus on the subject and not your personality.

5. Comfort in being able to cope with angry disagreements makes it easier to avoid unpleasantness. People will be less likely to be angry when they know you aren't cowed by it.

6. Allowing an angry person to vent their feelings without reacting in kind puts the burden on the other person's behavior. This will hopefully invite the same behavior in return. Resolution of a disagreement has a better chance of success once people respect one another's feelings without judgment.

7. Confidence can be gained by practicing in safe relationships with family and friends.

8. Keep discussion focused on specific behavior. Attempts by the other person to generalize or distract by raising other issues will tell that he is not able to adequately defend his position. When this happens allow the person a face saving exit. Rubbing in one's victory does not accomplish anything useful.

9. The chance of getting into an unpleasant argument will be reduced when the goal to respect difference and not to have to win.

References:

Keep the Family Baggage Out of the Family Business: Avoiding the Seven Deadly Sins That Destroy Family Businesses, Quentin J Fleming, Fireside, 2000, 336 pages. Paperback

The 12 Bad Habits That Hold Good People Back: Overcoming the Behavior Patterns That Keep You From Getting Ahead,, y James Waldroop & Timothy Butler, Currency, 2001, 352 pages. Paperback

Why Marriages Succeed or Fail: And How You Can Make Yours Last, John Gottman,
Simon & Schuster, 1995, 240 pages. Paperback

BUILDING A RELATIONSHIP

*Kyle ran a successful furniture business that was getting too much for him. He
decided he needed a partner. A family friend introduced him to Frank, a possible candidate for a partnership. Frank recently sold his upholstery business and was looking
for new prospects.*

*They met over a drink to explore possible mutual interests. Their first impres-
sions of one another were unremarkable. They were about the same age. Kyle was
thirty-eight, with a broad build, dark hair and moderate height. Frank was blond, a
little taller than Kyle, thirty-five, and slender. Kyle was dressed casually, while Frank
had on a three piece business suit. This made Kyle wonder whether he was going to be
dealing with a stuffed shirt. It didn't take long to find out he was wrong.*

*They briefly exchanged personal histories and their business backgrounds. Kyle
wondered how transferable Frank's business experience would be in the furniture business. Kyle was concerned that Frank didn't know much about marketing. Frank had
some concern about Kyle's laid back manner. The met a few more times to explore their
respective views on running a business. They found they had their differences but were
able find agreement on major points. They also discussed how their partnership might
work. After further discussions they decided that they knew each other well enough
both on a personal and business level to consider entering a partnership.*

A relationship starts when two people come together out of a common interest.
This applies in family, friendships, work, and even in casual acquaintances. Relationships differ in degree of importance, commitment and length of involvement. The
underlying process is the same for forming any relationship. People come together
to see if they look like they may have a common interest. If they do, they explore
the possibility of a relationship in three categories: required behavior necessary to be
interested in pursuing the relationship. Acceptable behavior that doesn't matter one
way or the other. Unacceptable behavior that removes interest in pursuing the relationship. Examples of required behavior include acceptable appearance, speaking in
a respectful manner, having common interest, and appropriate language. Examples
of unacceptable behavior include: undesirable values, absence of common interests,
and an offensive personality. Permissible behaviors may move to either the required
or unacceptable category as either party finds necessary. Differences that are too great
will lead to ending the exploration of a relationship.

A relationship is not static. It changes over time as a relationship deepens and as needs and interests of both people merge. The survival of a relationship depends on both people putting their joint priority more on paying attention to what works for both of them than on trying to prevail over one another. Kyle and Frank were wise to cautiously approach entering a partnership.

Developing a relationship

1. The first step in a new relationship is surface compatibility: appearance, manners, manner and quality of speech. Check out your comfort level with each other's personality style and way of speaking.

2. See if you have values and interest in common.

3. Negotiate what is acceptable and unacceptable ways to communicate with one another. This happens gradually over a period of time.

4. There are disagreements in every relationship, even in the best of them. See if you are able to settle your differences in a way that feels OK for both of you.

5. See if you are comfortable with the way you both give and receive affirmation and criticism.

6. Relationships are like cars. Every so often they need a tuneup. It is helpful to periodically review how you both feel the relationship is progressing. This gives you a chance to clear up any problems that haven't been given enough attention. This should include reminding yourselves of the good things as well as any problems.

References:

Getting Together: Building Relationships As We Negotiate, Roger Fisher & Scott Brown, , 1989, 240 pages. Paperback

Building Relationships, Developing Skills for Life, by David H. Olson, John Defrain, & Amy K. Olson, Life Innovations, Incorporated, 1998, 258 pages. Paperback

Breakthrough Networking: Building Relationships That Last, Lillian D. Bjorseth, Duoforce Enterprises, 2003, 270 pages. Paperback

The Courage To Trust: A Guide To Building Deep And Lasting Relationships, Cynthia L. Wall, & Sue Patton Thoele, New Harbinger Publications, 2005, 160 pages. Paperback

Building Relationships, Steve Chandler, Quma Learning Systems, 1996. Audio Cassette

Being Happy Being Married: A Guide to Building a Better Relationship, Lee Schnebly, Da Capo, 2005, 240 pages. Paperback

DELEGATION

Don worked for a box manufacturing company. He had too much to do and felt he could get a lot more done if he had an assistant. He was able to hire Charles who was two years out of college. Things didn't work out quite the way he hoped. He found that having an assistant actually became an added responsibility rather than a help because of the time required for training and ongoing supervision. He concluded that the benefit gained from an assistant was not worth the time it took to have it.

Helen complained that she did not get enough help from her children in doing household chores. However, she found that getting this help had it's problems. She wasn't happy with the aggravation that came from getting them to do their jobs. Even then, it wasn't done to her standards. She had to decide whether getting this 'help' was worth what it took to get it. She wondered whether it might be worth just doing it herself.

It is often desirable or necessary to ask someone to do something for you. This happens in work as well as in the family. This will work out well for all concerned if adequate attention is paid to:

- Understand the goals of the delegation: Is it to save your time, make your job easier, teach someone how to do something, to avoid doing what you don't like to do, or get done what you don't know how to do.

- Recognize that supervising will take time

- Success will depend in part on the ability of the person to whom you are delegating and the training and supervision you give him.

Delegation is also useful when it will get things done faster or better. Nothing comes without a price. A mother who expects to save time by getting her children to do chores finds that it often takes more time and chores don't get done the way she would like. This means she has to spend more time getting it done than if she did it herself. The same applies in the work situation.

Delegation is useful when the investment in training and ongoing supervision provides benefits you wouldn't have without it. Delegation becomes a necessity when a skill is needed that you don't have. You call a plumber to fix your backed up sink because you are not able to do it yourself. Delegation can also be useful as training. You may delegate chores to children to teach them new skills or responsibility. In this case getting the chores done efficiently is a second priority.

Using delegation

1. Decide on whether you are interested in efficiency or training.

2. Decide whether you should do what is needed or whether you should get someone else to do it.

3. Is the person to whom you want to delegate receptive to the assignment? Does he have the needed skills to do what is required? Take into account the amount of time required to supervise or train the person if he doesn't have the needed skills.

4. Estimate the time the job should take.

5. Allow time needed for training.

6. Allow time for you to be interrupted to answer questions.

7. Allow enough time for supervision. If you don't do this, you will become irritated at the interruptions and undermine what you are trying to accomplish.

References:

Note: Business references provided involve principles of effective delegation transferable to other settings.

If You Want It Done Right, You Don't Have to Do It Yourself!: The Power of Effective Delegation, Donna M. Genett, Quill Driver Books, 2003, 112 pages

Making Delegation Happen: A Simple and Effective Guide to Implementing Successful Delegation, Robert Burns, Allen & Unwin Pty.Limited (Australia), 2002, 112 pages. Paperback

Effective Delegation, Chris Roebuck, AMACOM, 1999, 96 pages. Paperback

How to Delegate, Robert Heller, DK ADULT, 1997, 72 pages. Paperback

Empowering Employees Through Delegation, Robert B. Nelson, McGraw-Hill, 1993, 175 pages.

LEADERSHIP

Margaret and Pam were friends since Junior High School. They enjoyed fantasizing about their respective visions of what they would do after they finished graduate school. Margaret wanted to start a school for gifted children after gaining enough experience teaching. During her training she learned that gifted children did not get what they needed in large school programs. She had a charismatic personality along with good people skills. She developed business plan with the help of her father. She was able to recruit five teachers to work with her in putting her vision into practice. It was a rough go for awhile, but her inspired leadership and support of her colleagues paid off. They had the program up and running after five years of struggle.

Pam was not as fortunate. She hoped to start her own design studio after working in one for five years. She had an excellent eye for design and color. She did well as

a solo practitioner. However, she didn't have the needed skills in attracting and mo-tivating other people to work with her. After three attempts to develop her own studio she gave up and decided she would be happier working on her own.

A leader has two major qualities. You have a vision of what you want to accomplish and the personality that motivates others to want to work with you to make it happen. People will be more interested in helping you when it also fits what matters to them. You need to be a good listener, let people know when they have something good to say or performed well, and can offer constructive criticism that guides them to improve their performance. A leader is a role model for motivating people to behave as needed.

Being a leader

1. Be able to explain your vision in a language that makes clear in observable terms just what you want to get done.

2. Decide whether you have the necessary qualities to motivate others to join you. Consider whether you are able to improve or acquire skills in which you are deficient.

3. Select people to work with you who have the skills needed to accomplish your vision.

4. Let people know when they are doing a good job and help them learn how to improve when they make mistakes.

5. Encourage your workers' suggestions in how to improve their performance and help in achieving your vision. Let them know you appreciate and welcome their effort and suggestions.

6. Let people know what is happening that may affect their work. This helps them to feel valued and respected more than just a pair of hands.

7. Encourage and give recognition to people for being able to work together. Help them to respect differences and place a high priority on skills in achieving consensus.

8. Give adequate acknowledgment of the contributions that were made to fit the value of what was accomplished.

References:

Note: The principles described in these business books are applicable in other settings as well.

Great Motivation Secrets of Great Leaders, John Baldoni, McGraw-Hill, 2004, 220 pages.

The 21 Indispensable Qualities of a Leader: Becoming the Person Others Will Want to Follow , John C. Maxwell, Thomas Nelson, 1999, 160 pages.

Developing the Leader Within You, John C. Maxwell, Thomas Nelson, 2005, 224 pages. Paperback

Leadership and Self Deception: Getting Out of the Box, Arbinger Institute, Berrett-Koehler Publishers, 2002, 192 pages. Paperback

Primal Leadership: Learning to Lead with Emotional Intelligence, (Paperback)

by Daniel Goleman, Richard E. Boyatzis, & Annie McKee, Harvard Business School Press, 2004, 336 pages.

Leadership: Theory and Practice, Peter G. Northouse, Sage Publications, Inc., 2006, 416 pages. Paperback

Leadership Jazz, Max Depree, Dell, 1993, 240 pages. Paperback

MANAGING CONFLICT

Alfred and Mary disagreed on how to handle discipline of their eleven year old son, Ben. Alfred was angry at Ben's disrespectful way he talked to his mother and wanted to discipline him. Mary dismissed it as transient behavior that would change as he got older. Alfred strongly disagreed. He felt that allowing Ben to behave way gave tacit permission it was ok. He felt the longer they let this happen the harder it would be to change it. They started out believing they could reach consensus. After struggling for a couple of months there was recognition nothing was getting accomplished. Neither one of them was prepared to agree to the other's point of view.

They decided they would have to shift to a new approach. Alfred accepted he may have been too harsh. Mary accepted that she was probably coming on too easy. A plan was made on which both could agree. They would start by jointly telling Ben they were unhappy with his behavior and the consequences he wouldn't like if he didn't change his behavior. Alfred and Mary privately agreed that he would be given two chances. If it came to a third time they would impose consequences that would have meaning for him. Mary agreed that she would back Alfred up.

As would be predicted. Ben didn't take his parents seriously. He thought they woul complain and do nothing. To his surprise and disappointment he was grounded for a weekend after his next misbehavior. That got his attention until he reminded himself it was easy to get his mother to come around. He found that was not to be. He knew he had lost when his mother did not succumb to his usual effort to charm her. After his parents stood their ground on two more occasions, he decided he better take them more seriously.

When does disagreement become a conflict? Disagreement happens when you and another person believe it is possible to reach an agreement on how you see things differently. It becomes a conflict when you are not able to settle your differences in a way that works for both of you. Conflicts that don't get solved do not go away. They often hang around, get looked at every so often, and again get pushed aside because you can't find a solution. This leads to increasing tension and ultimately an argument and at worst a blowup;. If left unchecked, this unpleasantness will spill over onto other issues. It makes good sense to do what you can to avoid chronic conflicts. This may mean having to give up something so it either gets resolved or is no longer relevant.

Conflict management

1. Each person states his feeling on the subject of the conflict.

2. Each person explains how he feels. It is helpful if the person listening tells the person speaking what he heard without making a judgment about it. Doing so helps to make sure that each person knows he got his point across in the way he wanted.

3. Each person tries to get the other person to agree to the way he thinks. This doesn't usually work but it should be tried.

4. When it is clear neither person is willing to agree with the other's point of view. You both need to shift from each one trying to win his point to thinking about a solution that pays attention to what they both want. This will lead to exchanging ideas until they can find enough of what they each need to reach an agreement. Both people walk away feeling they didn't get all they wanted, but they got enough of what each one needed to make an agreement possible.

References:

Anger and Conflict Management: Personal Handbook, Gerry Dunne, Personhood Press, 2003, 96 pages. Paperback

The Eight Essential Steps to Conflict Resolution, Dudley Weeks, Tarcher, 1994, 304 pages. Paperback

Conflict Management: A Practical Guide to Developing Negotiation Strategies, Barbara A. Budjac Corvette, Prentice Hall, 2006, 336 pages. Paperback

Conflict Management: A Communication Skills Approach, Deborah Borisoff & David A. Victor, Allyn & Bacon, 1997, 247 pages. Paperback

Conflict Management: The Courage to Confront, Richard J. Mayer, Battelle Press, 1995, 176 pages.

Marvin Snider, Ph.D.

The Dynamics of Conflict Resolution: A Practitioner's Guide, Bernard Mayer & Bernard S. Mayer, Jossey-Bass, 2000, 263 pages.

Coward's Guide to Conflict: Empowering Solutions for Those Who Would Rather Run Than Fight, Tim Ursiny, Sourcebooks, 2003, 288 pages. Paperback

MANAGING POWER

Helen was promoted to manager of a data processing department in a large bank. She was having difficulty getting her staff of nine people to perform their jobs as was needed. They continued to function by the standards of their former manager. Her first goal was to implement their transition to having a new boss. Helen started by meeting with each employee to establish her credentials and authority. This included demonstrating her expertise in the work of their department. She also let them know what was expected of them and what they could expect from her. Helen encouraged any ideas they had in how to improve the work situation. She gained their loyalty and respect after a few months of experiencing her follow through on her promises.

Power has common usage in everyday language. You hear statements like, he has a lot of power, he is power hungry, all he wants is power, and more. Control is often used to have the same meaning. Power is about one person being able to get other people to think or behave as he would like. Power is a statement about a relationship. You give power to another person when you let them influence how you think or behave. People become powerful (are able to influence other people) because they have something other people want or need. This happens in one or more of the following ways.

- By the job you hold: policeman, doctor, parent, mayor, teacher and any other position of authority because of the special knowledge or authority you have: doctor as lawyer, teacher, plumber.

- When you expect something from another person who wants to please you: children behave to please their parents, you do what is important to your spouse because you want his/her approval.

- You want what somebody can give you. You try to please your boss so you will get a raise or a promotion. A child behaves so the parent will buy what he wants.

- You behave in a certain way to avoid being hurt. You do your job so you won't get fired. You do what your parents want so you won't get punished.

- You show strong feelings to get what you want. You do what your parents want so they won't be angry at you. You give enthusiastic compliments so you will be liked.

- You use guilt to get people to do what you want. A mother says to her child, "How could you behave that way after all I have sacrificed for you." Another person says, "You promised you would help me,"

- You shame people to get them to do what you want. "How could you behave that way." A parent says to a child, " Who do you think you are?"

- You feel indebted to another person for having done you a favor. This concept is a commonly used tool in politics, *"You scratch my back, and I'll scratch yours."* The same happens in work.

There also are indirect ways of influencing behavior. They can be helpful or harmful.

- You can help somebody to learn by not giving them answers to their questions but helping them discover answers for themselves. A child will benefit far more from a parent helping him think through how to solve a problem than giving him answers.

- Admiring a person's behavior may help another person behave the same way. A parent who praises another child's behavior may encourage his own child to behave the same way.

Destructive methods of influence take different forms.

- Silence can be a powerful way to influence behavior because it can mean different things: the message wasn't heard, a person doesn't answer because he is angry, the message was not understood, and lack of interest in what was said. This leaves it up to the person speaking to guess what the silence meant. This usually creates problems if the guess is wrong.

- Indifference is a protection against showing true feelings or interests. It is one way to discourage teasing or other annoying behavior. It is also a way to express anger by not seeming to care about what was said or by expressing hostility in not valuing what somebody else cares about.

- Incompetence is a way to get out of doing something you don't want to do. The person trying to get you to do something gets impatient and decides do it himself.

- Doing things that interfere with what is happening is a way to keep some thing you don't like from happening. Anti-abortionists picket clinics to prevent them from giving abortions.

- Distraction is a way to avoid or delay doing what you don't want to do. A child who doesn't want to go to bed will try different way to keep a parent busy.

Use of power

1. Decide on what influence you would like to have on another person's behavior.

2. Find out what is important to the person's behavior you would like to influence with regard to what you want to change

3. Decide on which of the above options would likely bring about the desired change using them separately or in combination.

4. Be alert to changes that may occur in what will influence a person. A person may at first be influenced by his boss's authority. Once you get to know him/her you may be more influenced by his expertise and wanting his/her approval.

5. Deal with destructive efforts of influence by confronting the behavior in a constructive way. If someone is using distraction to avoid doing what is being asked to do, acknowledge that the task is one the person may not want to do. Then use one of the other approaches to convince the person why it would be in his best interest to do it.

An example of how these principles apply in a family situation occurred when two parents, George and Margaret, were trying to get their children to clean their rooms once a week. They would agree and then express their opposition by not following through in behavior.

George and Margaret were faced with what to do about the insurrection. They considered what might motivate them to change their ways: reminding them to respect their parents wishes, desire to please you, gain your approval, reward for performance, taking things away that matter to them, get angry at failure to perform, make them feel guilty, out of obligation for what was done for them, and shame them for doing less than their friends do.

After a period of trial and error, they found that different combinations of these possibilities worked for different chores. Success depended on following through on whatever they said they would do.

References:

The 48 Laws of Power, Robert Greene, Penguin, 2000, 480 pages. Paperback

Influence: The Psychology of Persuasion, Robert B. Cialdini, Collins, 2006, 336 pages. Paperback

How to Win Friends & Influence People, Dale Carnegie, Pocket, 1998, 288 pages. Paperback

The Science of Influence: How to Get Anyone to Say "Yes" in 8 Minutes or Less! Kevin
Hogan, Wiley, 2004, 256 pages.

PROFESSIONAL SERVICES

*Ellen was doing well in her catering business. She had two problems that needed
resolution. She had a client who was challenging the terms of their contract. Three attempts to work out their differences did not work. She decided it was time to consult an
attorney. Colleagues gave her referrals that yielded several possibilities of lawyers with
the desired experience. Ellen interviewed three attorneys and decided on the one who
had the best background for what was needed and with whom she felt comfortable.*

*The other problem concerned trouble with her aching back. Her doctor thought
she might need surgery. She decided to get two other opinions before making any decision. One recommendation came from her doctor and two from friends who had good
results with a similar problem. After getting these consultations she decided that there
were other solutions to explore before considering surgery.*

Everyone needs help from professionals (doctors, lawyers, accountants, financial
planners, and many more) with varying frequency. It is wise to use care in selecting
with whom to work. Guide your choice by the person's competence, experience, and
chemistry between you and the professional from whom you are seeking consultation.
People frequently have the tendency to defer to the professional on matters they don't
understand. This is done at risk that your interests may not be well served. Assertive-
ness is needed to get the professional to explain options and the consequences in lay
terms that go with each one. He does not live with the consequences and so should
not be the one to make the final decision. His responsibility is to help you understand
your options and the choices that go with each one. A professional who finds this bur-
densome should be discarded for one who will be more accommodating. Be especially
careful with professionals who may be operating in potential in a conflict of interest.
This occurs when they have a financial or other stake in the advice they give. This
may occur with lawyers, financial planners, insurance brokers and others.

Working with professional providers

1. Take the time to interview at least two and preferably three prospective ser-
    vice providers. Base your choice on competence, experience and chemistry
    between you and the provider. Also put a priority on the provider having
    considerable experience in your area of need. This might be the doctor who
    done many procedures under consideration, the lawyer who specializes in
    the area of interest, and others.

Marvin Snider, Ph.D.

2. Look for the provider's willingness to take the time to educate you on options and consequences and his willingness to be available for questions.

3. Determine who will actually be doing the proposed work. Senior people often do the initial evaluation and then have associates actually do the work. Decide for yourself whether this is acceptable. A subordinate may be acceptable if you are satisfied his work is being supervised by the senior person you have employed.

4. Always keep in mind that the professional is working for you. Be skeptical of a professional who answers questions with "leave it to me "or "trust me". This implies that the professional knows best and you are not capable of understanding what is involved. He is not in a position to decide what is right for you because he is not the one who has to live with the consequences.

5. Do not to hesitate to fire a professional who becomes unavailable or who procrastinates in providing his service in a timely fashion. Tolerating mistreatment gives tacit approval to continuing the behavior. Do not give full payment until the service has been satisfactorily completed.

6. Negotiate what you can expect from the professional and what the professional expects of you.

7. Determine the professional's availability for phone calls and the importance that is placed on being responsive.

References:

Seeking Wise Counsel: How to Find Help for Your Problems, David A. Stoop, Vine Books, 2002, 143 pages. Paperback

How to Go to Therapy: Making the Most of Professional Help, Carl Sherman, Random House, 2003, 192 pages. Paperback

How to Get the Most Out of the Legal System Without Spending a Fortune, Claudia Gasparrini, Space Eagle Pub. Co., , 71 pages. Paperback

Your Body, Your Health: How to Ask Questions, Find Answers, and Work With Your Doctor, Rowena Sobczyk, Neil B. Shulman, & Jane Fond, Prometheus Books, 2002, 300 pages, Paperback

How to find the right accountant: seven ways to avoid making a costly choice, William J. Lynott An article from: Black Enterprise [HTML] (Digital)

How to Find an Expert: Tips and Tactics for Finding an Expert, from an Accountant to a Writer, Marc Bockmon,Summit Publishing Group, 1994, 338 pages. Paperback

Harold had a successful furniture business for three years. Prior to this he had another furniture business which failed. After recovering from this failure he decided never to repeat the same mistakes again. Before considering another venture he carefully reviewed what went wrong. He did this with the help of his friend Sam who was very successful in running his appliance businesses. Harold learned from this analysis that his major mistake was not paying attention to receivables that were getting too high or to customer complaints about poor service, and inadequate supervision of his sales staff.

This new perspective gave Harold the incentive to try his own business again. He vowed to learn from these mistakes by setting up a regular review of the major parts of his business every month to make sure things were going as they should. He was committed to paying close attention to correcting any problems as soon as they surfaced.

Attention to early signs of budding problems in relationships will help to minimize or resolve them before they are allowed to fester and become much harder to solve. There is a natural tendency to avoid doing this in hopes that they will self correct. An understandable tendency but all too often costly. Signs of budding problems take different forms: Examples include

- Sometimes it is what people say or don't say. A person may give a compliment that doesn't seem genuine.

- A person says he is not angry when his behavior says otherwise.

- A person who is fidgety or has trouble with eye contact when this is not his usual behavior.

- Changes in mood. A person who is usually cheery and chatty becomes quiet and sad.

- Someone who is usually prompt comes late for or forgets appointments or commitments.

- A person who loses interest in activities that used to be of interest.

- Deterioration in physical appearance and personal hygiene.

- A person who is usually conciliatory become argumentative.

These events become of importance when they persist over time or occur in combination with others. Becoming aware of these signs is the easy part. How to relate to them can be more difficult. People who are the causing the problem may not be very receptive to being called on their behavior. The way to respond will depend on the relationship in which it occurs. A casual relationship will have less leverage than an intimate one as a marriage or close relationship as with a parent or sibling.

Attention to signs of trouble in others

1. When an event occurs that seems out of a person's usual behavior, make note of it. Put it aside if appears to be a passing event. Repetition of these events that occur over time should be addressed. Early intervention in a developing problem can avoid dealing with a full blown problem.

2. Give thought to what might be signs of problems developing in major parts of your life. This would include health, financial security, job security, children's behavior, stress in the marriage. Also included would be other significant relationships or activities of special interest.

3. There is a limited amount one can do when a friend shows signs of having a problem. Call the persons attention by indicating they seem unhappy and not his usual cheery self. The way a person responds will indicate whether they invite further discussion by giving information or they do not wish go any further.

4. There are more options in an intimate relationship as with a spouse, parent of child. One can press further than with a friendship. If the concern is denied or rejected, you can suggest that their reluctance to discuss your concerns has impact on your relationship. If the problem becomes chronic and not open to discussion, help from a third party may be needed.

Signs of trouble brewing in you

1. Be aware of changes in your mood. This may be warning of an impending problem that hasn't yet surfaced. Review what is going on in your life for any clues about things that are bothering you.

2. You are not feeling well without any real physical symptoms. Consider whether there is something bothering you that you haven't addressed.

3. You are feeling anxious without being sure what is its source. Review possible sources.

4. Pay attention to changes in enthusiasm in your usual behavior, lowering standards in your behavior, diminished interest in things that are usually important to you, and more.

5. Pay attention to other people's report you seem troubled or not like your usual self. Get them to tell you what they notice that is different. Review is going on in your life that they are picking up that you have not noticed.

References:

How can we banish bad behavior? Watch for these five signs of trouble--and take action accordingly, An article from: Association Management [HTML] (Digital)

Warning Signs: A Guidebook for Parents : How to Read the Early Signals of Low Self-Esteem, Addiction, and Hidden Violence in Your Kids, John Kelly & Brian J. Karem, LifeLine Press, 2002, 250 pages.

Violence Proof Your Kids Now: How to Recognize the 8 Warning Signs and What to Do About Them, For Parents, Teachers, and other Concerned Caregivers, Erika V. Shearin Karres & Diane Loomans, Conari Press, 2000, 192 pages. Paperback

Dangerous Relationships: How to Identify and Respond to the Seven Warning Signs of a Troubled Relationship, Noelle Nelson, Perseus Publishing, 2001, 334 pages. Paperback

Turning a Business Around: How to Spot the Warning Signs and Ensure a Business Stays Healthy, Mark Blayney, How to Books, 2006, 205 pages. Paperback

TWO-TIME RULE

Helen and John have agreed that they need a new couch for their living room. Helen had been the initiator, repeatedly asking John to plan a shopping trip. He agreed but couldn't commit to a time. She asked again with the same response. At that point, she told him she would buy a new couch on her own if he didn't follow through on his word. True to her word, she followed through and made the purchase without the aggravation of being ignored.

Patricia, mother of Shawn, an active ten year old, is continually frustrated by her son's ignoring her request to hang up his coat when he came home. After feeling totally frustrated, helpless, and angry at Shawn, Patricia concluded that continuing reminders make it easy for him to see her as a nag and shift the problem to her behavior. She decides that if a third reminder is needed, something very different will happen. The next time he didn't hang up his coat she didn't say a word to him. She took him by the arm when he was watching a favorite program and marched him over to pick up his coat and hang it up. It didn't take to long for Shawn to recognize that it was better to follow through on his agreements.

These are two examples of applying the *Two Time Rule*. Sometimes repeated efforts to end objectionable behavior are not successful. The more the unsuccessful efforts continue, the greater the problem becomes. In time the person who is feeling offended is viewed as a nagger, and the offending person gets tacit permission to continue the behavior.

The *two-time rule* can be used to avoid this problem. This rule states that if an effort to correct an offending person's behavior fails after two attempts, it should not be repeated a third time. The third attempt should be something qualitatively different. Patricia applied this when she stopped repeating herself and acted in a way that got Shawn's attention. Doing this keeps the issue focused on the objectionable behavior and not on the request. It carries a message of accountability

Applying the two-time rule

1. Don't repeat a request for someone to stop an offending behavior more than twice. If a third time is necessary, take an action that keeps the focus on the objectionable behavior and not on you.

2. It may take the application of the two-time rule a few times for the message to get across that it is better to do what is needed at the expected time rather than to be inconvenienced.

3. This is a simple and effect tool that is useful in any relationship at any age and in any situation.

References:

Setting Limits: How to Raise Responsible, Independent Children by Providing Clear Boundaries, Three Rivers Press, 1998, 384 pages. Paperback

Family Rules: Helping Stepfamilies and Single Parents Build Happy Homes, Jeannette Lofas, K Trade Paper, 1998, 128 pages.

Learning the Rules: Anatomy of Children's Relationships, by Brian J. Bigelow, Geoffrey Tesson, & John H. Lewko, The Guilford Press, 1996, 255 pages.

Creating Perfect Relationships ~ wisdom on creating and affirming the relationships you desire, Paula T. Webb, Spiritual Network Publishing Company, 2006, 196 pages.

People Styles at Work: Making Bad Relationships Good and Good Relationships Better, Robert Bolton & Dorothy Grover Bolton, AMACOM/American Management Association, 1996, 194 pages. Paperback